KU-338-538

Are Genes Us?

The Social Consequences of the New Genetics

EDITED BY
CARL F. CRANOR

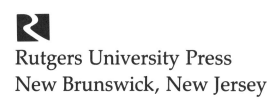

Rutgers University Press
New Brunswick, New Jersey

Library of Congress Cataloging-in-Publication Data

Are genes us? : the social consequences of the new genetics / Carl F.
 Cranor, editor.
    p.   cm.
   Includes bibliographical references and index.
   ISBN 0-8135-2123-8 (cloth)—ISBN 0-8135-2124-6 (pbk.)
    1. Human Genome Project.   2. Human gene mapping—Moral
 and ethical aspects.   3. Human gene mapping—Social aspects.   I.
 Cranor, Carl
 F.
 QH445.2.A74   1994
 174′.9574—dc20   94-14617
                                                                   CIP

British Cataloging-in-Publication information available

This collection copyright © 1994 by Rutgers, The State University
Individual chapters copyright © 1994 in the names of their authors
All rights reserved
Manufactured in the United States of America

Are Genes Us?

Contents

Acknowledgments   vii

CARL F. CRANOR,
Introduction   1

1   LARRY L. DEAVEN
Mapping and Sequencing the Human Genome   12

2   CHARLES WEINER
Anticipating the Consequences of Genetic Engineering
Past, Present, and Future   31

3   RICHARD DOYLE
Vital Language   52

4   JAMES R. GRIESEMER
Tools for Talking
*Human Nature, Weismannism, and the Interpretation of Genetic
Information*   69

5   EVELYN FOX KELLER
Master Molecules   89

6   ELISABETH A. LLOYD
Normality and Variation
The Human Genome Project and the Ideal Human Type   99

7   CAMILLE LIMOGES
Errare Humanum Est
Do Genetic Errors Have a Future?   113

8   CARL F. CRANOR
Genetic Causation   125

9   DIANE B. PAUL
Eugenic Anxieties, Social Realities, and Political
Choices   142

10   GREGORY S. KAVKA
Upside Risks
Social Consequences of Beneficial Biotechnology   155

11   WILLIAM C. THOMPSON
When Science Enters the Courtroom
The DNA-Typing Controversy   180

Notes   203

MICHAEL S. YESLEY
A Selective Bibliography on Ethical, Legal, and Social
Implications of the Human Genome Project   239

About the Authors   255

Index   259

Acknowledgments

Several individuals and institutions have made this volume possible. Murray Krieger, the first director of the University of California Humanities Research Institute (UCHRI), invited me to convene an interdisciplinary faculty research seminar on biomedical ethics which became a seminar on the Human Genome Project. Continued support and encouragement from Mark Rose, the second director of UCHRI, facilitated the seminar, a follow-up conference, and publication of this book. Funding from UCHRI and from the University of California's Biotechnology Research and Teaching Program made possible both the seminar and conference from which the essays in this volume resulted.

One essay in this volume appeared in a journal before the anthology was completed: Diane Paul's "Eugenic Anxieties, Social Realities, and Political Choices" appeared in *Social Research* 59.3 (1992): 663–683.

I owe debts of gratitude to several individuals whose work on this volume has been enormously valuable. Most important, of course, were my co-contributors; we learned much from one another in our seminar and from our papers. Cindi Smith typed many versions of my own essay and of the introduction. John Fowler provided much-needed detective work in the library during copyediting. Without the generous and professional assistance of Kerrin McMahan, an advanced graduate student in philosophy, this book would not have been published on time. Her outstanding work relieved me of many tasks and much anxiety I could ill afford given my administrative and other duties as the book moved toward publication. I am deeply grateful to her and the others who have contributed to this volume.

Finally, I met Crystal at the beginning of this project; she and our son Christopher make all this worthwhile.

Are Genes Us?

Introduction

CARL F. CRANOR

Advocates of current research in molecular genetics point to a future with marvelous pest-resistant crops, wonderful new therapies for cancer and other diseases, and nearly infallible methods of identifying criminals. Almost weekly, new research is reported linking one or more genes to diseases or even to behavior that we would like to control. Scientists have claimed linkages between various genes and diseases such as cystic fibrosis, Tay-Sachs disease, sickle-cell anemia, Alzheimer's disease, and various forms of cancer. Some reports have claimed that genes may predispose people to behavioral traits such as alcoholism, schizophrenia, depression, and even "aggression." Whether these reported connections between genes and diseases or undesirable behavior will be verified depends upon further research, but these and other genetic inquiries hold enormous promise for the future.

Moreover, many of these benefits will come sooner, we are told, as a consequence of the Human Genome Project (HGP), the $3 billion federal project that has as its goal the mapping and sequencing of the entire structure of human DNA. But, not everyone is so sanguine about the promises of molecular genetics or the benefits of the Human Genome Project. Critics' fears range from anxieties about eugenics to concerns about the improper use of genetic information to how such changes might affect the field of biology and our conceptions of ourselves. Still, supporters and critics of the collection of activities gathered under the name of the Human Genome Project are agreed upon the magnitude of the transformation in our thinking about ourselves and our place in the universe that molecular genetics is producing.

The papers in this volume, the products of a research group that was in residence at the University of California Humanities Research Institute at Irvine in 1991, attempt to address some of the social, political, and philosophical issues associated with current research in molecular genetics. Typically, discussions of ethical issues related to new developments in genetics—discussions of, for example, ways in which the use of genetic information might lead to stigmatization or unjust discrimination against bearers of genes deemed undesirable—are applications of ways of thinking that derive from traditional biomedical ethics. Such discussions tend to accept the science as presented and then to address the resulting questions of bioethics. The papers in this volume, however, written by sociologists, lawyers, political scientists, historians of science, and rhetoricians, as well as biologists and philosophers, pursue a different set of issues, and focus on questions that might not be readily addressable in the normal discourse of bioethics and that might not accept the science as presented.

What effects might the emphasis of genetics in biological processes have on the science and its development and on our understanding of our humanity? How might such developments affect our institutions and our social practices? The authors of the papers that follow share the view that words and concepts shape how we think about what we are doing and who we are, and that therefore the description and conceptualization of a field are important to understanding both the science and the significance of the moral and social issues that might arise as a consequence. Some authors are concerned about various metaphors—notions of "genes as master molecules," "genetic error," "genetic normality," and "genetic causation," for instance—that could mislead scientists as well as laypeople about what might be achieved by genetics and about how we should conceive our social institutions and practices. Others address more straightforward ethical issues—the nature of eugenics, the collective consequences of individual genetic decisions, the use of DNA typing in the law. All share the view, however, that at this moment when the field of molecular genetics is undergoing rapid and dynamic development, it is critical to address its presuppositions, concepts, and self-descriptions in order to attempt to identify and understand the science and some of its implications for social practice. In this way important ethical, legal, and social issues that otherwise might be hidden or ignored can be subjected to scrutiny. Finally, all have the view that even if the HGP is wildly successful in achieving its goals, the problems identified below will remain until we rethink our concepts and our language for describing the contributions of genetics to biology and their effects on our lives.

I

The first group of papers is concerned roughly with the science of genetics, the Human Genome Initiative, and the characterization of work in these areas. Larry L. Deaven's "Mapping and Sequencing the Human Genome" describes the Human Genome Project, its scope, and some of its hoped-for products. There are advantages to having a coordinated national effort to map the human genome, Deaven argues, especially in providing cost-effective discoveries of disease-related genes. Moreover, because the project will fund research into simple as well as more complicated nonhuman genomes for comparison, it will illuminate the relationship between species and provide insights into the nature of evolution. Deaven describes the projects that are under way at Los Alamos National Laboratory and elsewhere and explains the "library" of the human genome that is being constructed. Since individual human beings differ from one another significantly in their genetic makeup, what, then, constitutes "the human genome"? Does this imply a paradigm (ideal) human? Deaven holds that the project's goal of constructing a composite genome drawn from many individuals does not pose serious difficulties at this stage of research, since the essential elements of genetic structure are identical from one person to another and individuals are similar enough for present purposes.

But are the presuppositions and goals of the Human Genome Project plausible and desirable? Charles Weiner's "Anticipating the Consequences of Genetic Engineering: Past, Present, and Future" puts the development of the Human Genome Project under critical historical scrutiny. Although the effort to geneticize many biological and behavioral issues, a practice that leads to thinking about problems in terms of seeking to correct genetic "deviants," is a concern Weiner shares with other authors, he focuses on the response of biologists to the ethical issues and possible negative consequences of their work. Weiner's concern is that scientists have advertised the ethical issues that genetic research involves—and have thereby projected an image of sensitivity that can be used to sell the overall endeavor—while at the same time they have trivialized matters by presenting the issues raised by genetics as fundamentally no different from those raised by other biomedical advances in the past. Finally, by consigning consideration of the legal, ethical, and social issues to special agencies, they have compartmentalized the problems so that their research can proceed without distraction. The "technical sweetness" of their research was so attractive that they did not want consideration of ethical issues to interfere with it. A much better approach, he says, would have been to address some of the ethical, legal, and social issues before the project started and before many of the issues were bypassed by market-driven forces and scientific research. Ethical and scientific inquiry should have influenced each other's development. Now we risk the genie of geneticization being out of the bottle and our not being able to address in a timely and adequate way the requisite ethical issues. These decisions about scientific research and their accompanying ethical consequences are a product of scientific culture we would do well to examine.

Assessment of that scientific culture and descriptions of the research and some of the ethical implications that result are the focus of the next five essays. These address how significant normative questions, both about the science and about moral issues, are raised by certain descriptions of the science. Typically such issues are posed inadvertently as a result of the use of particular words and concepts that characterize the science. Richard Doyle's essay raises a general issue about some classic papers in the history of genetics; the remaining four papers analyze particular concepts and ideas used in describing genetic advances.

Richard Doyle's "Vital Language" takes seriously the language used by scientists and focuses on the metaphors and characterizations in historically important documents in genetics and DNA research that led to the idea that DNA contains the "book of life." What, he asks, has been the import of characterizing the material of chromosomes as a "code-script" and thus coming to speak of the human genome as the "book" of life? Might the field of molecular genetics have developed or been understood differently had its subject been represented differently? Doyle reminds us of the power of metaphors to shape our comprehension of a field of knowledge even in such seemingly "objective" fields of study as biology. The practice of science, he argues, is that "stories we tell about and with 'nature' are not simply scientific; they are bound up with other historical, political, and theological narratives that are deeply ingrained in our cultural practices." As a result, they are shot through with language and linguistic choices that both "make possible the moments of invention" and "make plausible different scientific regimes and researches."

In "Tools for Talking: Human Nature, Weismannism, and the Interpretation of Genetic Information," James R. Griesemer briefly explores some of the history of genetic explanations in biology, how this has influenced the field, and how it could be distorting our scientific, moral, and social views at present. "Weismannism," a long-standing doctrine about the continuity of the germ cells and the discontinuity of the body cells from person to person, has served, Griesemer argues, as a guiding metaphor in the development of biological discourse, one that has contributed to the establishment of genes as the central players in biological theory. But in fact, he urges, a historical understanding of this influence "suggests a gradual impoverishment" since the nineteenth century "of the conceptual tools available" for presenting the complexity of biological causality and the field of biology. Griesemer is concerned about the intellectual and social consequences of de-emphasizing the contributions of ecology and population genetics (which emphasize the differences between individuals) to our understanding of biology, while elevating the authority of molecular biology (which emphasizes the similarities between people) in both scientific and social thinking. A "significant social danger of the [Human Genome Project] is that it may slight further the role of organismal and population biology in interpreting molecular mechanisms whose control offers hope with respect to problems of human health." A further negative consequence of this emphasis is the elevation of geneticists as ethical or social authorities. However, reform of the guiding metaphor might allow us "to envision different roles for the public, scientists, and other would-be users of biological information, genetic or otherwise."

Evelyn Fox Keller examines a particular manifestation of the emphasis on genetics in biology: the idea of genes as "master molecules" that control the structure, behavior, and development of living organisms. This notion is misleading as a matter of empirical experiment, she argues, because a section of DNA

that constitutes a gene must function as part of a biological system capable of identifying and translating it into a protein.
Moreover, recent research indicates that far from genes controlling cellular form and function, organisms possess biological
mechanisms that most of the time control their genes by regulating transcription. Are genes, then, really the masters? But the
idea of genes as master molecules can have a life of its own that
may have subtle, but substantial, scientific and social consequences. For instance, the idea of reducing a great many diseases to genes may lead to a radical depersonalization of
medicine and a shift in responsibility for the detection of disease
from patients and physicians to DNA-sequencing technicians
and biological database managers. And one of the more insidious consequences of the geneticization of disease, Keller argues, may be a tendency to promote "biologically and socially
unrealistic standards of normality," a "eugenics of normalcy."
Thus, we should be wary of such tempting metaphors and think
more carefully and seriously about the "social and individual
bodies on which the very meaning of health and disease, normal
and abnormal, depends."

At present, if an organ or organism is functioning sufficiently abnormally in the judgment of a patient or a doctor, it
may be regarded as diseased. However, we now have the idea
of the mutant (abnormal?) gene that codes for a particular disease such as sickle-cell anemia. These ideas of normality and
disease are analyzed in Elisabeth A. Lloyd's "Normality and
Variation: The Human Genome Project and the Ideal Human
Type." Some genetic variations, she notes, are merely statistical
and have nothing to do with disease. Genetic variation alone,
then, cannot constitute the definition of disease or abnormality.
The problem, she argues, is that fine-grained genetic information may or may not be physiologically significant for our
coarse-grained concepts of health and disease. What is abnormal according to a biochemical model is not necessarily abnormal according to a medical model. And yet, geneticists routinely
slip from the use of "abnormal" in reference to a molecular level
of description to the same term at the medical level. Thus, Lloyd
argues, we must understand that conceptions of disease are social issues which cannot simply be reduced to molecular descriptions and that they must be addressed accordingly.

A fourth, related concept that may undergo evolution in the

genetics revolution and that also has substantial normative implications is the idea of genetic "error" or "mistake." It may be related to the model of "one gene, one enzyme," Camille Limoges suggests. However, as he argues in *"Errare Humanum Est:* Do Genetic Errors Have a Future?" a better understanding of biology tells us that genetic influences are not so simple as this model would suggest. In many cases genetic variations that might be considered "errors" may be compensated for by other genes, other biological processes, or the wider environment. Thus, Limoges urges, simply to label genetic diversity as an error or mistake begs some moral and social questions. Moreover, as the example of genetic error suggests, biological research is not necessarily prior to and distinct from the consideration of the social and ethical issues such research raises. In fact, some of the most decisive and significant of those issues "are already being given form and substance in the very process of doing science." Agreeing with Weiner and others, Limoges argues that key normative questions ought to be raised "while and where the science is being done, in the scientific process itself: before the technologies and procedures have been packaged and black-boxed."

The essays of Griesemer, Keller, Lloyd, and Limoges discuss various ways in which characterization of scientific issues or the use of metaphors in science might beg or inadvertently influence ethical issues or introduce ethical or normative terms into the debates, thus precluding clearer and less question-begging discussion of the issues. They also implicitly raise questions about the causal influence of genes. My own contribution, "Genetic Causation," addresses this idea directly. Reports have claimed causal linkages with diseases such as cystic fibrosis or sickle-cell anemia or with behavior such as alcoholism, depression, or aggression. Most such claims will require much more research to establish their truth or falsehood. Yet critics and advocates alike tend to use causal claims to argue for their preferred research or therapeutic strategies. Some authorities tend to exaggerate the causal role of genes in order to argue for the value of investment in such ventures as the Human Genome Project. Others, concerned that the success of such projects and resulting genetic therapies may have unpredictable negative consequences, tend to underemphasize the causal role of genes. Both succumb to a temptation to use conceptual arguments to make normative points, and both, therefore, are misleading as to the complexity of moral and social issues that are raised as a consequence. Freeing ourselves from the use of conceptual arguments to promote normative points will permit better discussion of the normative issues, put the argumentative burdens where they belong, and, perhaps, foster clearer discussion of the important normative issues.

II

While most of the first seven essays suggest implicit connections between scientific characterizations and moral issues, the last three essays focus directly on explicit social and legal issues raised by new genetic technologies. These essays accept both the descriptions of genetics and its success, but proceed to evaluate some of its social and political implications. There is, for example, general agreement that "eugenics" is a bad thing, but as Diane B. Paul indicates in "Eugenic Anxieties, Social Realities, and Political Choices," there is no single conception of what eugenics is because the word has been variously used. Sometimes, for example, eugenics has been defined in terms of intentions—the "improvement" of the gene pool—and sometimes it has been defined in terms of effects. Governmental or community programs designed to affect the gene pool are generally considered bad because they infringe upon personal autonomy. As Paul points out, though, private, autonomous reproductive decisions also can have undesirable social consequences, and in a market system "the privatization of those decisions will result in their commoditization." Are these results of less concern?

Moreover, not only may individual reproductive decisions based on genetic information have undesirable collective consequences, but their solutions are not always obvious. In "Upside Risks: Social Consequences of Beneficial Biotechnology," Gregory S. Kavka explores some of these issues and their possible solutions. For instance, if each couple can ensure that its first or only child is male, there will be an imbalance in the sex distribution of the population. Yet, seemingly obvious private solutions to this problem may not work. Similarly, if the benefits of genetic technology are scarce and expensive, and therefore available only to privileged members of the population, existing patterns of social inequality may be exacerbated. And "if our capacity to manipulate genes develops so that we determine the identity of our offspring in a biological as well as a social sense, this may influence—in ways that are not benign—our *collective consciousness*, including our conception of who we are and what our place is in the overall scheme of things." Despite the obviousness of the problems, modifications of private behavior may not rectify them, and collective solutions can pose problems of their own.

One of the most significant benefits of current DNA research is the promise it holds for uniquely identifying people, members of families, or even criminals—so-called DNA fingerprinting. Yet even this potentially important social benefit is not without difficulties. In "When Science Enters the Courtroom: The DNA-Typing Controversy," William C. Thompson provides a short history of the use of DNA typing in criminal law and identifies some of its problems. Some of these result from a faulty understanding of the science, while others are traceable to poor data and laboratory procedures in DNA-typing laboratories that lack the kind of controls that would be present in a research environment. One significant scientific problem is that genetic typing frequently gives insufficient attention to genetic variation between subpopulations (another oversimplification) which can result in the production of misleading evidence and may very well lead to the conviction of innocent persons. A richer conception of the genetics would be more accurate and would lead to less social stress. Even if these problems are adequately addressed, however, and even if sound scientific procedures are followed by forensic laboratories, DNA-typing problems remain that may result in the conviction of innocent people. Part of the difficulty has been a clash between science and law. The legal debate about the use of DNA fingerprinting created perverse incentives for "behavior contrary to the ideal norms and values of science," but the adversarial debates ensured that the new scientific techniques were critically assessed and explored. Echoing Weiner's chapter, Thompson argues that perhaps some of these problems would have been reduced if the scientific techniques had received "broader scrutiny" and discussion before they were implemented socially.

III

The essays in this volume address various topics, but as a group they suggest, among other things, that the manner in which issues in genetics have been characterized has helped to determine both how the science has developed and which ethical and social problems appear to be important. Moreover, these problems remain, or may even worsen, even if the HGP is wildly successful. Indeed, it may become difficult to ferret out some of the social implications because of its success. To extend this point a bit further, let us consider some issues concerning "individualism"—in several senses of the term—some of which have not been explicitly explored in these essays but are suggested by developments in genetics and by concerns expressed in the papers that follow. We can note, for example, that the privileging of molecular genetics with its emphasis on the DNA as the "master molecule" of life leads to an emphasis on the individual organism rather than on, say, the interaction of the organism with its environment (ecology) or rather than on the organism as an outcome of a particular historical process (evolution). Is this shift of emphasis desirable for the development of biology and for the resulting social policies?

Furthermore, the advances in medicine promised by the genetic revolution are promises of advancement in the diagnosis and treatment of individuals. Will the emphasis on curing diseased individuals lead to a de-emphasis of communal preventive efforts? For instance, if geneticists and physicians discover that they can treat lung cancer by introducing a tumor suppressor gene into a patient, will the communal resolve to prevent lung cancer through environmental efforts be affected?

When we turn to the question of who should make decisions regarding the use of genetic techniques, should we legitimate individual parental autonomy in genetic counseling—which can have collective bad consequences, as both Paul and Kavka note? Is it possible or desirable to try to regulate, influence, or control parental decisions in order to try to avoid collective bad consequences?

Deeper questions of individualism are posed as well. For example, will people who learn they have a genetic "defect" come to think of themselves as defective individuals? Will people who have a genetic component to their diseases take less individual responsibility for them? Or will a collective concern for genetic characteristics go too far in the other direction and suggest collective ownership of the genetic pool, echoing earlier societies that exercised too much coercive force over individuals?

These questions, clustered loosely around the idea of individualism, do not all raise the same issues or even the same notion of individualism from case to case. Answers to different questions push us in different directions—some toward one kind of individualism, some toward other kinds, and some away from individual concerns. My aim is not to settle these discussions, but to suggest how particular emphases and uses of genetics and its application through technology can have substantial social consequences and can beg or reinforce various moral, social, and political practices and institutions. We cannot appreciate some of these issues and consequences unless we are clear about the subtle conceptual influences in the science and in the social issues and how these affect the characterization of the resulting moral and social problems.

The authors of the papers in this volume tend to share the view that we should not acquiesce in processes that appear to be inevitable but are not. Just as genetic information will empower us in various ways, so too will conceptual scrutiny of the science in the light of moral and social insight. To be informed is to be empowered. Our studies try to suggest some of the ways we should inform ourselves so that we can more consciously shape and influence our futures rather than being the pawns of forces we do not understand.

Chapter 1

Mapping and Sequencing the Human Genome

LARRY L. DEAVEN

The Human Genome Initiative is a worldwide research effort that ultimately will lead to an understanding of the structure and function of the genetic information contained in each human cell.[1] This project is expected to have a substantial impact on medical science and the practice of medicine. More than four thousand genetic diseases afflict humans, and work done within the project is expected to lead to an understanding of the precise nature of the changes in genetic material that are associated with these diseases. In many cases, this information will lead to new methods of treatment. The project is also expected to yield definitive information on the role of genetics in the predisposition to certain diseases. In the course of this work, new technologies will be developed that will permit accurate and precise assessments of environmental effects on genetic material. In addition to these health-related issues, the project is expected to benefit our level of understanding in such areas of basic science as evolution and developmental biology and to add new technologies that will benefit agriculture and other fields.

The Congress of the United States launched the Human Genome Project in 1988, appropriating funds to two federal agencies: the Department of Energy and the National Institutes of Health. The current scope of the project includes work in seven areas: (1) mapping and sequencing the human genome; (2) mapping and sequencing the DNA of model organisms; (3) informatics: data collection, analysis, and distribution; (4) ethical, legal, and social considerations; (5) research training; (6) technology development; and (7) technology transfer. Most of the chapters in this book are addressed to considerations of the ethical, legal, and social issues associated with the Human Genome Initiative. The primary aims of the present chapter are to discuss the experimental and technical approaches used in genome mapping and to describe the expected products of this work, especially as they relate to ethical, legal, and social issues.

A genome is one complete copy of the genetic material of a particular organism. The human genome consists of approximately 100,000 genes localized on 46 chromosomes. Each human chromosome contains a molecule of the chemical compound that carries genetic information, deoxyribonucleic acid (DNA). In human cells, DNA usually exists as two linear strands wrapped around each other as a double helix. Each strand of DNA is composed of units of three smaller chemical compounds: a base containing nitrogen, a phosphate molecule, and a sugar molecule. When combined, these three compounds are called nucleotides, and the basic building blocks of DNA are four nucleotides, each of which is formed from a different nitrogenous base; the four nucleotides are adenine (A), guanine (G), cytosine (C), and thymine (T). The two strands of a DNA molecule are held together by hydrogen bonds, and the bonds between the nucleotides in each strand are specific: A binds only to T, and G binds only to C. Each pair of bases, AT, TA, GC, or CG, is called a base pair. The size of a genome is often given as the number of base pairs in that genome. Genetic information is contained in a code based on the sequences of nucleotides. A gene may be as small as 2,000 base pairs or as large as 2 million base pairs. Between genes are long stretches of DNA that are not involved in protein synthesis and contain large numbers of repeated-sequence units. These repeated sequences account for more than 90 percent of the 3 billion base pairs of DNA in the human genome.

The goals of the Human Genome Project include the completion of two kinds of maps: genetic and physical. A genetic map is constructed by determining the chromosomal location of genes or other identifiable fragments of DNA called DNA markers. The relative distances along the length of a chromosome from one gene or DNA marker to another are also determined by the process of genetic mapping. A completed genetic map for a chromosome would contain all of the genes on that chromosome in their correct linear order and estimates of the relative distances between them. The distances between genes or other sites on a physical map are measured in units of physical length, such as single base pairs, thousands of bases (kilobases), or millions of bases (megabases). These maps may have low resolution, such as microscopically visible landmarks on chromosomes, or high resolution, such as an ordered set of small fragments of DNA (clones) that covers all or part of the DNA in a chromosome. The resolution of a microscopically visible map, such as two stained areas of a chromosome, is on the order of 10 megabases (Mb). An ordered clone map may have a resolution of at least 100 kilobases (kb). The highest-resolution physical map is the base-by-base sequence of the DNA in a chromosome.

In order to find the location of 100,000 genes and to determine the sequence of 3 billion base pairs of DNA, it is useful to subdivide the human genome into smaller, less complex units. Such a subdivision is possible owing to a series of technical advances that preceded the formalization of the Human Genome Project. A description of some of these methods will be helpful in defining the characteristics of the first human genome map and sequence.

Methods for Genome Analysis

Separating Chromosomes

The human genome is subdivided in each cell into 22 pairs of chromosomes called autosomes and an additional pair of sex chromosomes, either XX (female) or XY (male). These 24 chromosomal types provide a natural subdivision of the genome that has been exploited for genetic studies by several approaches. One of these is called somatic-cell hybridization. In using this technique, cultured cells from two different species are fused together, resulting in a hybrid cell that initially contains a complete set of chromosomes from each parental cell. Common fusions include Chinese hamster × human and mouse × human. When a rodent/human hybrid cell begins to divide, it also begins to lose some of its human chromosome complement. Some of the hybrid cell lines lose all of their human chromosomes, while others retain one or a few of them for various lengths of time. Single cells can be isolated from a population of hybrid cells, grown as a cloned culture, and analyzed for the specific human chromosomes they contain. Through the use of these techniques, we have available a series of cell lines that contain only one to three human chromosomes in a background of mouse or

Chinese hamster chromosomes. In some cases, only a portion of one human chromosome remains in the hybrid. These cell lines have been useful in mapping small fragments of DNA (DNA probes) of unknown chromosomal location to the proper chromosome. They have also been used to produce collections of cloned DNA fragments (DNA libraries) for physical map constructions for single human chromosomes or parts of human chromosomes.

A second method that has been used to isolate single human chromosomes is to sort them physically from other chromosomes, using flow cytometer instruments. These instruments can be used to identify and sort cells and subcellular particles according to size or DNA content (Fig. 1.1). Single human chromosomes can be sorted from normal human cells; however, any contaminating DNA will be of human origin, and it is difficult to distinguish this from the DNA in the chromosomes being sorted. In addition, with the exception of the sex chromosomes, all human chromosomes occur in pairs. If chromosome 22 is sorted from normal human cells, half of the sorted chromosomes will be of maternal origin and half of paternal origin. The subtle differences in DNA sequence between these two types of chromosomes would complicate their use in physical map construction. For these reasons as well as others, hybrid cell lines are the best source of chromosomes for sorting purposes. Any DNA that contaminates the human chromosomes sorted from hybrids will be of rodent origin, which is relatively easy to distinguish from human DNA. Because hybrids contain only one human chromosome, all the chromosomes sorted from hybrid cells will be either of maternal or of paternal origin and not a mixture of both types.

DNA Library Construction

The ability to isolate single human chromosomes from the total DNA in human cells facilitates certain types of map construction; however, the most important technical advance necessary to map and sequence the human genome was the development of recombinant-DNA technology in the early 1970s. Using recombinant-DNA methods, it is possible to take a single fragment of DNA and make or clone many identical copies of it. Molecular cloning of a gene requires three ingredients: one copy

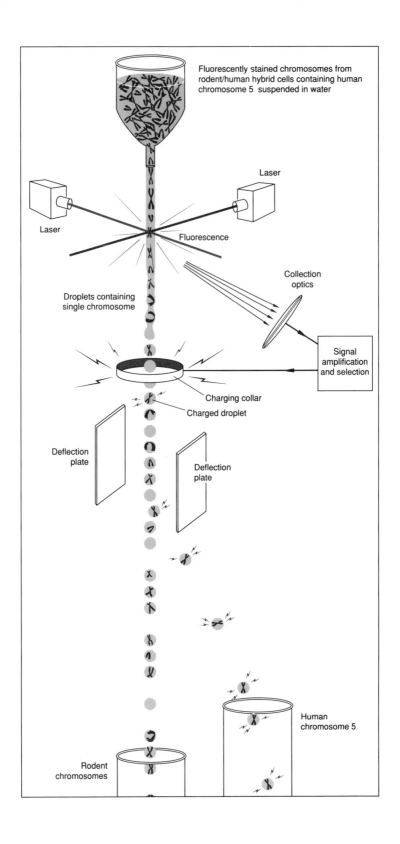

or a few copies of the gene to be cloned, a biological cloning vector, and a host cell. Cloning vectors are small molecules of DNA, often circular, that can be replicated within a host cell. Host cells are usually single-celled organisms such as bacteria and yeast. The first step of the cloning process is to combine the DNA fragment containing the gene sequence with the DNA of the cloning vector. If the vector DNA is circular, the circle is cut, and the gene to be cloned is joined to each end of the opened circle. The new, somewhat larger circle of DNA is called a re-combinant molecule, as is any molecule formed from a cloning vector and an inserted DNA fragment. The recombinant molecule can now be allowed to enter a host cell, where it is duplicated by the replication mechanism of the host cell. Each time the recombinant molecule is replicated, a new copy of the gene it contains is produced. Furthermore, each of the two daughter cells formed by the division of the original host cell receives copies of the recombinant molecule. When the host cell has grown into a colony, it is referred to as a recombinant clone, and the DNA fragment contained within each cell of the colony is said to have been cloned.

Figure 1.1. Purifying Human Chromosomes through Flow Sorting. Flow sorting provides a way of separating chromosomes of one type from a mixture. The example in this illustration is the separation of human chromosome 5 from the rodent chromosomes found in a rodent/human hybrid cell line. A liquid suspension of chromosomes is carried through the flow sorter in a narrow stream. The chromosomes have been stained with two fluorescent dyes: Hoechst 33258, which binds preferentially to AT-rich DNA, and chromomycin A^3, which binds preferentially to GC-rich DNA. The stained chromosomes pass through a point on which two laser beams are focused, one beam to excite the fluorescence of each dye. Each chromosomal type has characteristic numbers of AT and GC base pairs, so individual chromosomes can be identified by the intensities of the fluorescence emissions from the two dyes. If the fluorescence intensities indicate that the chromosome illuminated by the lasers is the one desired, the charging collar puts an electric charge on the stream shortly before it breaks into droplets. When droplets containing the desired chromosome pass between charged deflection plates, they are deflected into a collection vessel. Uncharged droplets lacking the desired chromosome go into a waste-collection vessel.

During the recombinant-DNA revolution of the 1970s, molecular cloning was also applied to the study of entire genomes with even more dramatic results. In that application, instead of cloning one gene at a time, all of the DNA in a genome is cut into small fragments, and each of those fragments is cloned. The resulting collection of cloned fragments is called a DNA library. The word "library" was chosen because collectively those cloned fragments contain all the genetic information in an organism. Like a library of reference books, a library of cloned human DNA, for example, represents a collection of reference material for studying the genetic information in human beings. However, whereas conventional libraries are ordered collections of information, DNA libraries are unordered and uncharacterized collections of recombinant clones. These collections provide the starting materials for almost all the current techniques used to decipher the instructions contained in DNA.

Continued progress since the 1970s has made it possible to construct many kinds of recombinant-DNA libraries. Libraries differ in the way the DNA to be cloned is prepared, in the choice of the host strain, and in the design of the cloning vector. Each variation produces a library that has advantages for specific applications. The most significant characteristics of a library are usually determined by the choice of the cloning vector. Four different vector systems are in common use today: plasmids, bacteriophages, cosmids, and yeast artificial chromosomes (YACs).

By selecting the appropriate cloning vector, a library can be made that contains inserts of different average sizes. Plasmids or some of the bacteriophage vectors can be used to construct libraries with inserts ranging from 1 to 9 kb; other bacteriophage vectors have acceptance ranges of 10–25 kb; cosmids carry inserts of 15–40 kb; and YAC vectors typically carry inserts ranging from 50 to 1,000 kb. Although insert size is an important library characteristic, there are other strengths and weaknesses for each vector system. Some vectors have distinct advantages over others with regard to the quantity of starting material or target DNA required to make a library; some have features that facilitate the recovery of the inserted DNA fragments; and some are better than others at retaining the inserted DNA without deleting or rearranging it.

While it is possible to make many different types of DNA libraries, with some types more useful than others for a given application, subdividing the DNA of an entire genome before library construction is almost always advantageous. The resulting set of libraries covers all the genomic DNA, but each library is less complex than a single library containing all of the cellular DNA. By combining flow sorting with recombinant-DNA techniques, libraries can be constructed that represent individual chromosomes. To include all of the nuclear DNA in human cells, 24 different libraries are necessary (22 autosomes plus the X and Y chromosomes). The libraries will vary in size, with the largest (for chromosome 1) being five times the size of the smallest (for chromosome 21).

Hundreds of different types of libraries are in use today. They have been constructed from the DNA of many different individuals or from the DNA in single chromosomes from a large number of hybrid cell lines. In order to draw together mapping information from the various libraries used in different laboratories throughout the world, a system has been devised that will result in the establishment of a set of universal markers found in all human genomes. These markers consist of short segments of sequenced DNA spaced at approximately 100,000 base pair intervals. Because these regions are unique-sequence DNA common to all human genomes, they will enable one map to be compared with another and will permit work done in different laboratories to be merged. The segments of DNA that make up this set of markers are called sequence-tagged sites (STSs). The STS system has some additional advantages. Once these markers are identified, the sequence information for each site can be stored in an electronic database available to the public. If someone wants to recover a specific region of DNA from a new library, the database information (sequence) for the STS in the desired region can be used to identify it. Once a complete set of STSs is identified, cloned fragments of DNA will not have to be stored because they will be recoverable from any good DNA library.

Genetic Map Construction

Genetic maps are constructed by determining how often identifiable sites on a chromosome are inherited together. During the formation of reproductive cells (meiosis), there is an exchange of DNA between each pair of chromosomes. The relative distance between two genes on a chromosome can be measured by the frequency with which they are exchanged during meiosis. For example, a portion of, say, the maternal chromosome may exchange position with an identical portion of the paternal chromosome. If an exchange occurred at a position one-third of the way from the top of these chromosomes, the new gene arrangements would be upper one-third maternal and lower two-thirds paternal in one chromosome and upper one-third paternal and lower two-thirds maternal in the other. All genes on the upper third of the new chromosomes would be exchanged with respect to the genes on the lower two-thirds of each chromosome. Because these exchanges occur at random, genes located far apart on a chromosome will be exchanged more often than if they are close to each other. If two genes exchange 1 percent of the time, they are said to be 1 map unit or 1 centimorgan (cM) apart. This distance can be related to physical maps because a centimorgan is approximately 1 million base pairs in length. In the classical period of genetics research, genetic maps were constructed for *Drosophila* (fruit fly) and corn genomes. In each of these experimental organisms, it was possible to study large numbers of offspring from controlled matings. Because this approach cannot be applied to the construction of genetic maps in humans, a useful genetic map of the human genome had to await the development of somatic-cell hybridization and recombinant-DNA technology.

Somatic-cell hybrids were used to find the chromosomal location of genes by looking for a specific protein produced by a gene of interest and then correlating the presence of the protein with a particular human chromosome in the hybrid cells. Later, when genes could be isolated by DNA-cloning methods, a panel of somatic-cell hybrids could be used to identify the chromosomal location of the cloned gene. In some cases, panels containing only parts of a chromosome could be used to identify the region of a chromosome that contained sequences of DNA that were complementary to a cloned gene.

A dramatic improvement in human genetic mapping came with the discovery that fragments of DNA in close proximity to a gene of interest could be used to identify the gene. This method, based on the existence of particular base-sequence changes that are commonly found between individual genomes, involves the

use of "restriction enzymes," or class II restriction endonucleases. These are found in bacteria, where they help to protect the bacterium from foreign DNA. They perform this
function by recognizing certain specific sequences in DNA and
cleaving the DNA molecule at or near these recognition sites.
The discovery in 1970 of these restriction enzymes meant that
large molecules of DNA could be cut into fragments of repro-
ducible size.[2] If the DNA from two different genomes is cut with
a restriction enzyme and the resulting fragments are separated
according to size, the size patterns will not be identical. Differences result from the loss of some restriction sites owing to base
changes at the site and the consequent inability of the restriction
enzyme to recognize the site and cleave it. Because these base
changes are relatively common in populations, they are called
DNA polymorphisms, and because the changes are detected by
differences in the length of DNA fragments generated by restriction enzymes, they are called restriction fragment-length polymorphisms (RFLPs).[3] In order to use the RFLP approach to
locate genes associated with disease, DNA is collected both from
normal and from afflicted family members. This DNA is cut with
a restriction enzyme, and the resulting fragments are separated
according to size. The size distributions are then hybridized to
DNA probes selected from a library. A useful probe will identify
a polymorphism that corresponds with the pattern of disease
inheritance. It will differentiate family members who have the
disease from those who do not have it. The best probes identify
a polymorphism so close to the gene that it is extremely unlikely
for the gene and the polymorphism to be separated by a meiotic
chromosomal exchange. Libraries constructed from sorted chromosomes are a valuable resource in the search for informative
probes for RFLP analysis. Once the chromosome that carries a
disease gene has been identified, a chromosome-specific library
helps to overcome the "needle in the haystack" dilemma of selecting probes from a total genomic library. Even with chromosome-specific libraries, however, it can be difficult to locate
informative polymorphisms.

The five-year goal of the Human Genome Project is to produce a human genetic map with 600 to 1,500 informative
markers on it. This would provide a resolution of 2–5 cM. Each
marker is to be identified with an STS. In order to achieve a

resolution of 1 cM, approximately 3,000 markers will be needed. This is the long-term goal of the project.

Physical Map Construction

Low-resolution physical maps have been under construction since the 1950s, when improved techniques provided the first clear pictures of human chromosomes. The human set of chromosomes, or karyotype, was organized into a standard arrangement in the 1960s, and in 1971 this was refined on the basis of newly discovered banding technology.[4] Chromosomal banding patterns are a series of light and dark staining bands along the length of each chromosome. These permit each human chromosome to be identifiable and to be subdivided into chromosomal regions. More recently, methods have been developed for hybridizing DNA probes directly to the DNA in chromosomes visualized on microscope slides. By combining banding analysis with in situ hybridization, it is now possible to localize genes within the limits of chromosomal band resolution (10 million base pairs). These low-resolution maps are very useful for the rapid mapping of genes and also as a means of establishing landmarks on chromosomes for orienting sections of high-resolution physical maps.

There are many different protocols for constructing high-resolution physical maps, and an attempt to describe even the major ones would be beyond the scope of this chapter. Still, the basic approach needs to be considered because the construction of a high-resolution physical map is a fundamental goal of the Human Genome Project. A high-resolution physical map consists of an orderly arrangement of DNA fragments that begins at one end of a chromosome and continues to the other end. One way to assemble fragments is to select a clone from a library, cut it with a restriction enzyme, and isolate a DNA fragment from the end of the clone. The end fragment is then used to probe the library for complementary inserts. With luck, a newly selected clone will partially overlap the original clone but will also extend beyond it. The end fragment of the second clone is then used to reprobe the library, and another overlapping clone is isolated. This process is repeated until the desired region of a chromosome is covered by overlapping clones called contigs. The procedure is called chromosome walking (Fig. 1.2). If a segment of DNA is missing from the library used in the walk, a second library must be used to locate the fragment needed to complete the contig.

The process of chromosome walking would be far too slow to complete a genome map in a reasonable period of time, and a number of more rapid approaches have been suggested and utilized. For example, personnel in the Human Genome Center at Los Alamos have been using a process that simultaneously identifies overlapping clones or contigs over the span of an entire chromosome. By using this approach, 553 contigs containing about 60 percent of the chromosomal 16 DNA were assembled in approximately two years. In order to complete this map, the gaps between the 553 contigs will need to be closed. Because the size of the average gap is estimated to be 65 kb, a chromosome walk from each of the contig ends should bring this map close to completion.

The insert size of libraries plays an important role in both genetic and physical map construction. Small-insert libraries are useful in genetic mapping because they have a high probability of having inserts with unique-sequence or single-copy probes that hybridize to only one site in the genome. Repeat sequences are not useful as probes because they occur as many as 300,000 times per genome. Repeat sequences are dispersed throughout the genome, and the larger the insert size of a library, the more likely it is to contain a repeat sequence. On the other hand, for physical mapping, libraries with larger inserts have a distinct advantage. A library with an average insert size of 4,000 base pairs would require the ordering of 750,000 clones to cover the genome. A library with large inserts on the order of 200,000–400,000 base pairs could cover the genome with only 10,000 clones. Completed physical maps will include inserts from many types of DNA libraries and will provide coverage of each human chromosome at many levels of resolution (Fig. 1.3).

The five-year goals of the Human Genome Project include completion of an STS map for the entire genome, with markers spaced at approximately 100,000 base-pair intervals. In addition, overlapping sets of cloned DNA, spanning lengths of 2 million base pairs, are to be generated for large parts of the human genome. Major efforts are now under way to map parts or all of chromosomes 3, 4, 5, 11, 16, 17, 18, 19, 21, 22, and X.

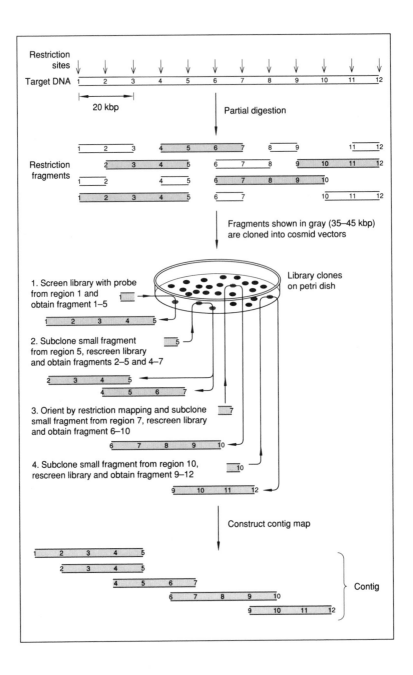

Sequencing

Sequencing is the determination of the order of base pairs in a stretch of DNA. Although the Human Genome Project is often described as "the plan to sequence the entire human genome," the current goals of the project do not include a commitment to sequence 3 billion nucleotides of DNA. The cost and inefficiency of currently available sequencing technologies make such a commitment unreasonable at the present time. Current cost projections for large-scale sequencing run between $1 and $2 per nucleotide. In order to complete a sequence of the human genome (and enough comparative sequencing of model organisms to make the human sequence useful) approximately $6 billion would have to be expended. This would require 60,000 person-years of work at very uninteresting sequencing factories. Although a long-term goal of the project continues to be a complete reference sequence, the current five-year goal is more modest. Attempts are being made to improve existing technology or to develop new technology that will permit large-scale sequencing at a cost of no more than 50 cents per base pair. At the same time, research support is being provided in order to sequence genome regions of known biological interest in the size range of 200,000 to 1 million base pairs. The largest region that has been sequenced to date is the 150,000 nucleotides encoding the gene for human growth hormone. At the end of the first five-year

---

Figure 1.2. Chromosome Walking. The aim is to recover fragments of cloned DNA that span a gene or any chromosomal region of interest. A DNA library constructed from partially digested DNA provides a source of overlapping cloned fragments of the entire genome. A DNA probe know to be close to the gene of interest is used to screen the library for fragments that contain sequences complementary to that of the probe. In this illustration (kbp = kilobase pairs), the original probe comes from region 1; the screening shows that fragment 1–5 contains that region. Now a small single-copy portion of the DNA in region 5 is used as a probe to identify other clones in the library that contain DNA from region 5. This second screening identifies two fragments: 2–5 and 4–7. A third screening, using a probe from region 7, identifies the fragment 6–10. The process is repeated until a set of clones containing the entire region of interest has been identified. The organized set of DNA fragments is called a contig.

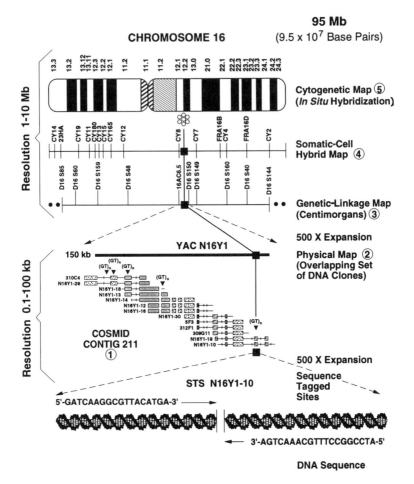

95 Mb
CHROMOSOME 16   (9.5 x 10^7 Base Pairs)

Figure 1.3. Levels of Resolution in a Physical Map for Human Chromosome 16. This diagram illustrates how a cloned DNA fragment can be related to the cytogenetic map and how sequence-tagged site (STS) markers (a short segment of sequenced DNA) can aid in integrating the genetic and physical maps. The location of an STS (STS N16Y1-10) is shown from the bottom up in (1) an ordered set of cosmid clones (cosmid contig 211); (2) a 150 kb yeast artificial chromosome (YAC) insert (YAC N16Y1); (3) a genetic-linkage map of chromosome 16 between two genetic markers (16AC6.5 and D16S150); (4) a somatic-cell hybrid map between two markers (CY8 and Cy7); and (5) a chromosomal band or cytogenetic map between 16q12.1 and 16q12.2, as determined by in situ hybridization.

period, new recommendations will be made to sponsoring agencies regarding the initiation of large sequencing projects.

The interdependence of physical mapping and sequencing becomes apparent in cost considerations. Much of the time required in sequencing is devoted to preparing cloned DNA for the actual sequence analysis. Yeast artificial chromosome inserts are too large to be used in sequencing procedures. They must first be subcloned into cosmid vectors—a difficult and time-consuming procedure. Therefore, if the most expedient and least expensive method is used for physical mapping (YAC contig assembly), the costs for sequencing are considerably more than they would be if physical maps were based on cosmid contigs.

Products and Benefits of the Human Genome Project

The preceding outline of aims, procedures, and materials to be applied to the analysis of the human genome makes it apparent that the Human Genome Project is an orderly outgrowth of progress in molecular genetics research. Just as the discovery of restriction enzymes led to the construction of DNA libraries, so the existence of libraries will lead to the construction of physical maps and the sequencing of clones in those maps. A major change brought about by establishing and funding the project is the acceleration in output that can now be expected for the coming ten to fifteen years. The new, consolidated approach to genome mapping should prove to be cost-effective. The search for disease-related genes has been under way for many years, and it would continue with or without the establishment of the Human Genome Project. These piecemeal searches are like discovering a needle in a haystack and then returning to look for a second needle. With today's techniques, a complete map of chromosome 4 could probably be assembled in the same number of person-years already devoted to finding the location of the gene causing Huntington's disease, a very small region of chromosome 4. A complete map of chromosome 4 with publicly available STS markers could be used by anyone interested in finding other genes on that chromosome.

In addition to the human genome map and sequence, the project will also provide increased levels of support for mapping and sequencing the genomes of model organisms. Included in this work will be studies of the genomes of bacteria, yeast, fruit flies, nematode worms, and mice. The data obtained from this comparative work should provide new insights into our understanding of the process of genome evolution, especially the evolution of genome size. In bacteria, genome size is closely correlated with genetic activity and organismic complexity. Nearly all of the DNA in bacteria is utilized for encoding genes; in more complex organisms, however, a large proportion of the nuclear DNA is not used in protein coding. Indeed, the percentage of genomic DNA not involved in protein coding varies considerably from one species to another, and in spite of much scientific attention and speculation, the proper function of non-protein-coding DNA is not understood. Comparative genomic analyses should clarify this issue.

Because the amount of human DNA involved in protein coding is estimated to be 5 percent or less, criticisms have been made about the goals of the project with regard to sequencing the entire genome. The concern centers on the unknown function of noncoding DNA and the large effort necessary to sequence DNA of no apparent significance. Comparative genome sequencing is likely to reveal evolutionarily conserved sequences that have important functions involved in gene regulation and nuclear organization. The current state of sequencing technology would not permit the completion of these useful studies in a reasonable or cost-effective manner; however, the developmental support of sequencing technology should lead to rapid, inexpensive methods for sequencing large regions of cloned DNA. Until these new methods are in common use, genome sequencing efforts will be directed primarily at sequencing clones of DNA that are known to contain genes (complementary or cDNA clones).

Questions are often raised about whose genome is to be mapped and sequenced and about the value of devoting so much effort and money into sequencing one genome. Those questions are prompted, at least in part, by the known extent of human genetic diversity and the resulting concern that one genome sequence would have limited value because each individual has a DNA sequence that differs from all others. I have tried to describe the available tools and techniques in enough detail to show that, with currently available methods, it would be impossible to sequence the DNA from a single individual. In order to do this, much of the basic work (construction of somatic-cell hybrids, sorting of chromosomes, library construction) would have to be repeated, and this would be an overwhelming endeavor. Thus, for example, somatic-cell hybrids were first constructed more than twenty years ago, yet a set of hybrids containing only one human chromosome and including the entire human complement was only recently assembled. Gene libraries from sorted chromosomes were first constructed in the early 1980s, yet a complete set of libraries suitable for physical mapping purposes is not yet available.

It is not important that the first genome map and sequence come from a single person. Studying the genome is similar to the study of human anatomy. Although there is substantial physical diversity in human populations, we are also very similar. Our livers and hearts may differ slightly in size and structure, but they are located in the same positions, and they function in a very similar manner. In the genome, genes are located in the same positions, and the essential elements of structure are identical from one genome to another. The small differences between two people are believed to be limited to somewhere between 2 million and 10 million nucleotides, less than 1 percent of the total.

It is important that comparative work among many genomes be initiated in parallel with the Human Genome Project and that it continue after the reference sequence has been completed. The reference genome will be organized by specific STSs that define small regions of the entire sequence. Therefore, it will be possible to isolate and analyze the same subsets of DNA from many individuals. This will enable new levels of understanding of the extent and the nature of human genetic diversity. A comparative study of the genomes in aboriginal populations from different parts of the world should yield new insights into our current understanding of human evolution. One of the chief aims of the present genome initiative is to identify genes that are defective and that cause human genetic diseases. Comparative studies across genomes may provide new insights into the relationships between normal genetic variation and extreme variation that result in physical and mental disorders. Such data are essential if we are to determine the limits of the genetic component of disease and will help define proper applications of the genetic information derived from the Human Genome Project. Finally, genetic variation plays an important role in medicine. Current treatments and dietary regimens do not reflect the range of variation in response owing to genetic variability. Increased levels of understanding of the subtle genetic effects on metabolism should result in a more individualized therapeutics.

One common misconception is that the human genome will be understood by the time the project is completed. Although our knowledge will certainly expand in the course of this work, the most important contributions of the project are the development of new technologies for genome analysis and the establishment of a reference tool for future studies. The full impact of the project will only be realized when this reference genome can be used to compare and contrast many individual genomes.

Chapter 2

Anticipating the Consequences of Genetic Engineering
Past, Present, and Future

CHARLES WEINER

Scientists in the Human Genome Project are engaged in a multi-billion-dollar, government-funded biological crash program to "decode the Book of Life."[1] Their emphasis is on the alphabetical code GATC, representing the four nucleotide bases—guanine, adenine, thymine, and cytosine—whose myriad combinations metaphorically spell out the "words" that control our genetic "destinies." James Watson, the initial head of the Project, claims that "we used to think our fate is in our stars. Now we know, in large measure, our fate is in our genes."[2]

The project is clearly an important event in the history of science, whether measured by the resources allocated to it or the extraordinary claims made for it. Yet even the project's organizers acknowledge the public concern about the ethical implications of the enterprise, and attention to such issues has been built in from the start.

Why and how are the ethical issues included? Is "the ethics thing" just tacked on like the tail of the donkey in the traditional children's game, or is it a serious effort integrated into the research itself? It is clear that the ethical issues were not raised initially by the scientists who originally conceived of the project, nor did these issues figure in the debates with other leading biologists who opposed the enterprise on technical grounds and challenged its priority for research funding.[3]

What is the message embedded in the seemingly obligatory brief section on ethical issues that appears in the proliferation of popular magazine articles, books, and television shows about the impending genetic revolution? How is it related to the likewise obligatory paragraph on relevance to cancer, or some other life-threatening disease, in molecular biology research grant proposals?

I will provide historical perspectives on these questions in the hope that they will contribute to better understanding and better answers. First I will focus on the responses of biologists to the ethical issues raised by their work in recent decades, exploring patterns relevant to the present. Then I will give my interpretation of how the ethical, legal, and social issues generated by the Human Genome Project are being approached in the present.

My purpose is to focus attention on several major obstacles impeding efforts to anticipate and prevent negative consequences of the project. The obstacles include ways of thinking as well as professional and institutional cultures that discourage scientists from seriously considering and acting on the ethical, social, and political dimensions of their work. Scientific leaders call for educating the public in order to achieve "scientific literacy," but little attention is given to the need for scientists to achieve "public literacy." One of the major problems is that the decision to map, sequence, and interpret the entire human genome is treated as a "done deal," separated from the uses or abuses of the information it generates. In this compartmentalization, providing early warning to ensure only beneficial uses is separated from the "inevitable" creation of the knowledge itself. A striking example from an earlier period illustrates the lure of technology and its relation to how scientific cultures set their priorities.

It took place at the U.S. Atomic Energy Commission (AEC) in 1954. J. Robert Oppenheimer, who had led the Los Alamos scientists in the development of the first atomic bombs, was being interrogated by the AEC personnel security board to determine why the scientific advisory committee he headed in the postwar period had initially opposed the launching of a crash program to develop a hydrogen bomb, and then later endorsed it. Of special interest to Oppenheimer's interrogators was that the advisory committee also had expressed moral qualms about the weapon when they first considered it, but made no mention of them later.

> *Question:* Your deep concern about the use of the hydrogen bomb, if it were developed, and therefore your own views at the same

time as to whether we should proceed in a crash program to develop it . . . became greater, did it not, as the practicabilities became more clear? Is that an unfair statement?

The Witness [Oppenheimer]: I think it is the opposite of true. Let us
not say about use. But my feeling about development became quite
different when the practicabilities became clear. When I saw how
to do it, it was clear to me that one had to at least make the thing.
Then the only problem was what would one do about them when
one had them. The program we had in 1949 was a tortured thing
that you could well argue did not make a great deal of technical
sense. It was therefore possible to argue also that you did not want
it even if you could have it. The program in 1951 was technically so
sweet that you could not argue about that. It was purely the military, the political and the humane problem of what you were going
to do about it once you had it.[4]

This separation of technical questions from ethical questions
and from discussions of the appropriate time and place for exploring the possible undesired consequences of research choices
was of great interest to many biologists in the 1960s when the
"technical sweetness" of genetics research was steadily emerging.

Anticipatory Concerns in the Sixties

When and where to draw the line in the applications of human
genetic engineering was an important subject of discussion in
the l960s. This was before the fact, before recombinant DNA and
related genetic-manipulation techniques were available. Discussion of the prospects for human genetic intervention overflowed
from scientific meetings to the news media and to Congress,
and some biologists began to worry about losing control of the
conversation. They feared that public "overreaction" would interfere with their research interests and their funding, and they
tried to reassure the public that the work would be beneficial or
that it was too early to worry about negative effects. Others argued that the ethical consequences of genetic engineering
should be anticipated and discussed in advance, before it was
too late as in the case of the atomic bomb.

Let us look at some examples from the period. In 1963, the
New York Times made an editorial comment on the Eleventh International Congress of Genetics, which had just concluded in Europe:

Geneticists are on the threshold of a historic breakthrough in their efforts to probe the secrets of heredity. The prospect is that in the next few years humanity will understand—and be able to control at least in part—the fabulously intricate mechanism through which each species of living organism transmits its essential properties to the next generation. . . . Is mankind ready for such powers? The moral, economic and political implications of these possibilities are staggering, yet they have received little . . . organized public consideration. The danger exists that the scientists will make some of these God-like powers available to us in the next few years well before society—on present evidence—is likely to be even remotely prepared for the ethical and other dilemmas with which we shall be faced.[5]

Again in 1963, at a scientific conference on the "control of human heredity and evolution" the distinguished biologist Salvador Luria was questioned during the discussion period by another participant, who asked: "In your visions of the possibilities of engineering on man based on knowledge of viruses and bacteria, haven't you ducked the moral and ethical aspects?" Luria replied:

Yes. I think that in the matter of responsibility and the kind of obligation that this places on biologists, many of the things that have been said may sound a little callous. However, our task was to discuss only the technicalities of the work that could conceivably be done. Actually we have already overstepped our assignment quite a bit by all of our warnings. I expect that the ethical and moral issues will be the topics of much discussion later."[6]

"Technical sweetness" and the appropriate time and place for discussing ethical consequences was also an issue at a small private meeting of biologists at Rockefeller University on October 1, 1966, including Ernst Caspari, Rollin Hotchkiss, James Watson, Salvador Luria, Edward Tatum, Seymour Cohen, and Norton Zinder among others. The invitation to the meeting reviewed work being carried out in several laboratories that seemed promising for human genetic engineering, noting that "the problem is obviously immense and almost fantastic in implication. Unless a massive frontal assault is made, it will be many years before something that could be accomplished in the foreseeable future will be achieved." The intention was to set up a committee "to discuss and program what could and should be done and after deciding this and its cost to get support and hire the proper scientists."[7] The minutes of the meeting, prepared by Zinder, reveal the participants' views on the advent of genetic engineering and their reluctance to discuss it publicly.

> The meeting was called to discuss informally the prospects for genetic intervention in humans based on the understandings and insights that have been obtained in molecular biology. . . .
> A series of questions was then raised. How do we build genetic material? How do we test it? Do we use it? They were answered more or less as follows:
> 1) Organic chemists know how to do most anything. They just have to be made aware of the problem so a certain amount of proselytizing is in order. . . . 2) Testing is also a technical problem. . . . 3) Such reagents, if made, will be used whether we like it or not. What can be done, is done, and what can be used, is used. The main variable is the rate of development and application. Proper use depends on active supervision by interested persons who are involved in the original accomplishment.[8]

Then they discussed whether they should stimulate anything of this kind:

> Is any step an escalation? The general conclusion seemed to be that if it is not done by us, others will do it and they won't do it as well. Can we really discuss the feasibility of such endeavors without discussing the desirability? Some feel yes, others no. Caspari pointed out that eugenic potential has been available for many years and has not been used. Hotchkiss points out, however, that eugenic measures generally have negative elements which involve large social structures and are therefore resisted while genetic intervention is mostly positive and on an individual basis and as such has qualities analogous to those which sell soap.[9]

The minutes conclude: "What to do about this meeting itself. It is generally agreed that there be no publication of the discussion nor an official report. Primarily, there is too little in the way of hard materials, and secondly, this area is so highly charged that no matter how carefully anything is said, it gets overplayed and over-interpreted."[10] The decision by these scientists to control the information and keep it from the public was paternalistic and unrealistic, since the research was publicly funded and the possible applications to human genetic engineering were clearly of public concern. Here again, "technical sweetness" took precedence, and public discussion of the ethical dimension was deferred.

Moreover, the question would not long remain private. It was soon public, and it would continue to be. Eight months later, in an editorial in *Science* magazine, Marshall Nirenberg, the biologist who had contributed one of the important steps to the new genetic revolution and who was to win a Nobel Prize in 1968, took a different position:

> Man may be able to program his own cells with synthetic information long before he'll be able to assess adequately the long-term consequences of such alterations, long before he'll be able to formulate goals and long before he can resolve the ethical and moral problems which will be raised. When man becomes capable of instructing his own cells, he must refrain from doing so until he has sufficient wisdom to use this knowledge for the benefit of mankind. I state this problem well in advance of the need to resolve it because decisions concerning the application of this knowledge must ultimately be made by society and only an informed society can make such decisions wisely.[11]

The new developments in genetics were also discussed publicly by the geneticist Joshua Lederberg in a series of columns in the *Washington Post*. This Nobel laureate's reassuring views were challenged by Leon Kass, a young biologist at the National Institutes of Health, who responded in a letter to the *Post* on November 3, 1967:

> The possibility of genetic manipulation in man raises fundamental and enormous questions, theological, moral, political. These questions must be carefully stated, the issues clearly articulated and the alternative policies fully and soberly considered. . . . The development of science and technology, once begun, often proceeds without deliberated and considered decisions. Considerations of desirability rarely govern the transition from "it can be done" to "it has been done." Biologists today are under strong obligation to raise just such questions publicly so that we may deliberate *before* the new biomedical technology is an accomplished fact, a technology whose consequences will probably dwarf those which resulted from the development of the atomic bomb.[12]

These issues were highlighted in a 1970 London conference on "the social impact of modern biology." The speakers included leading biologists, and many nonscientists were in the audience of more than eight hundred. In one discussion, a geneticist argued:

> We are just deluding ourselves if we think that human genetic engineering is so in the realm of science fiction that we don't need to start thinking about it. My worry is that the advances will be extremely slow and minor to begin with. For instance, I would estimate that within four or five years it will be possible to cure, to a very minor, limited extent, by genetic engineering, certain genetic deficiencies. Nobody will object to that. And so we will go on to the next step, and the next step, and so on. If we don't start discussing these matters now we shall get to the state as we did with the atom bomb, when nobody knows what is going on.[13]

These biologists were emphasizing that prior discussion provided time to think about the issues, before technological momentum builds up and applications are imminent, before vested interests take over. The symbol of the mushroom cloud was becoming intertwined with the symbol of the double helix.

Congressional Interest

The concerns of the period emerged within the political process in 1968, when a series of hearings was initiated in the U.S. Senate to consider the need for a national commission on health, science, and society. The purpose: to *anticipate,* to *examine in advance,* and to *report on* the *legal, ethical, and social implications* of biomedical research, including genetic engineering. It was meant to be a study commission, without any intention of interfering with research. The focus was on nascent medical technologies such as the artificial heart, organ transplants, new reproductive technologies, and also genetic engineering, which was not possible at the time but was on the horizon. Senator Walter Mondale explained:

> This society is in a constant race to keep up with advancing technologies, understand them, and see that they are put to constructive use. We have been too late, too secret, and too superficial in

too many cases. . . . In this case, we have an opportunity for previous, public, and penetrating examination of the implications of
the developing technology in health science. These new developments are as dramatic as the dawning of the nuclear age. And
some of them, like genetic manipulation and behavior control, are
potentially as dangerous. Their potential benefits to human physical and mental health are tremendous, of course. But our experience with the atom teaches us that we must look closely at the
implications of what we do.[14]

The biologists' participation in the hearings illustrates a cu-
rious mix of motivations: genuine concern about the issues
raised; a fear that their funding might be cut off or severely cur-
tailed; defensiveness about the nature and usefulness of their
work; and worry about what they perceived as public intervention in the scientific process, resulting in a loss of control. Several of them tried to reassure the public by arguing that concerns
about human genetic intervention were premature and that it
was too early to deal with them. Some pointed to several immediate, visible problems arising from new medical interventions,
maintaining that they were more worthy of concern than "the
more lurid speculations" about future applications of genetics.
Although the proposed advisory commission was intended only
to study the issues and not to regulate, they argued that government intervention would stop progress and delay cures for
dread diseases. They talked about needing more funds in order
to proceed with beneficial research.

The *New York Times* headline concerning Arthur Kornberg's
March 1968 testimony gives an indication of this effort to deflect
concern about possible negative effects: "Scientist Doubts Genetic Abuse, Calls Research the Best Defense."[15] During that
hearing the Nobel laureate acknowledged that the goals and objectives of the resolution were laudable, "but with respect to the
work that I am involved in, research on gene structure, I do not
see any immediate legal, moral, or ethical problems." Senator
Mondale pointed out that Kornberg focused on the need for
more funds for the research but was reluctant to review "the
social problems that might flow from the research." He suggested that the biologists' public image and funding problems
would be improved if scientists took more of an interest in the
societal implications of their research. Kornberg replied: "Sena-

tor Mondale, you must know the kind of creature you are dealing with in the scientific community. He is not congenitally
reluctant to communicate. He is immobilized only when he
steps into the social and political arena. . . . The biochemist who
deals with molecules cannot afford any time away from them."
Kornberg wanted assurance that the proposed commission
"would immediately dispense with unnecessary extrapolations,
and focus quickly on what a great opportunity we have now to
expand our basic knowledge to make it of greater service to
man."[16]

Deferring Action

The congressional attempt to establish an early-warning system
did not succeed. No action was taken in 1968 on the bill to establish a National Advisory Commission on Health, Science, and
Society. It was referred in 1969 to a Senate committee. Two years
later, Mondale revived the resolution; similar measures were
considered in the House. The Senate bill was taken up by the
Subcommittee on Health at a day of hearings in 1971, together
with the issue of the rights of human subjects in biomedical experimentation. The bill was amended and passed by the Senate
in December 1971 but was not subsequently acted on by the
House. In 1973 it was submerged in a series of hearings and
resolutions by the Senate Subcommittee on Health in response
to increasing public concern over the specific issue of the role of
human experimentation in biomedical research.

Congress created the National Commission for the Protection of Human Subjects of Biomedical and Behavioral Research
in 1974. Included in the tasks assigned to the commission was a
"special study" to analyze and evaluate the ethical, social, and
legal implications of past, present, and projected advances in
biomedical and behavioral research and technology. But the
study did not enjoy high priority within the commission, which
focused on more immediate problems, including the formulation of guidelines for protecting human subjects in current research.

The special study was of limited scope and duration, and it
did not consider human genetic intervention. The small group
who conducted it made a number of useful recommendations

and observations, including the need to establish the kind of commission proposed by Mondale and others during the period 1968–1973. They pointed out that "the ethical, social, legal and public policy problems connected with biobehavioral technology have arisen, and will continue to arise, in largely *unpredictable* ways" and therefore had "to be kept under continuing scrutiny and review." They hoped that Congress would act to provide such continuing education because the task of evaluation would "have to be tackled afresh, repeatedly and in new contexts, in the light of future technological innovations whose nature and social implications cannot at present be foreseen; and also with an eye to future changes in the broader economic and social, political and cultural situations."[17]

Congress did not act on the recommendation, revealing once again the reluctance of government to anticipate and attempt to prevent or control the possible negative consequences of scientific research and its applications. Policymakers reacted to immediate problems causing harm to specific groups, in this case human subjects of biomedical and behavioral research, whose plight was articulated in the political arena with considerable public support. It was also more expedient politically to enlist in "the war on cancer," that ever-popular cause which loomed so large in government hearings and funding during the early 1970s.

An important exception was the establishment of the Congressional Office of Technology Assessment (OTA) in 1972, after six years of hearings and proposals. In 1969 the National Academy of Sciences (NAS) issued a technology assessment report commissioned by Congress. The report urged that efforts to reduce uncertainties should precede or accompany decisions on the development of new technological projects and that the reversibility of an action should be counted as a major benefit and its irreversibility a major cost. Moreover, it said, limits should be set "on the extent to which *any* major technology is allowed to proliferate (or conversely, to stagnate) without the gathering of fairly definite evidence, either by the developers themselves or by some public agency, as to the character and extent of possible harmful effects." The NAS committee also warned that "society simply cannot afford to assume that the harmful consequences of prevalent technological trends will be negligible or will prove readily correctable when they appear."[18] The OTA began operations in 1974, but it responded to more immediate congressional interests, and the prospects and problems of human genetic engineering were not a priority.[19]

Despite the failure of the congressional attempt to establish a commission to anticipate and study possible negative consequences of biomedical technologies and genetic engineering, the growing concern about these issues motivated several institutional efforts. Within the National Science Foundation (NSF), biologist Herman Lewis urged the establishment of an NSF office to deal with "the social and moral implications of scientific and technological progress." In a 1971 paper circulated within NSF, Lewis spoke of the "growing concern for the ethical, social and legal problems that arise from biomedical advances . . . which make possible the prolongation of life, the manipulation of embryos and the manipulation of nucleic acids, the genetic material itself. . . . After World War II physicists, stimulated by their concerns with the political use of atomic energy, brought these concerns to the public attention. More recently, biologists have expressed their concern particularly about the ethical implications of genetic engineering."[20] In 1973 a program on ethics and values in science and technology was announced by NSF, and a related program was launched by the National Endowment for the Humanities.

Other efforts during the period included a National Research Council project on assessing biomedical technologies, completed in 1973, in which Leon Kass played a pivotal role. In 1969 the Salk Institute's short-lived Council for Biology in Human Affairs was initiated. The Institute of Society, Ethics, and the Life Sciences (Hastings Center) was founded in 1969 and still plays a major role in education and research on ethical issues in medicine and the life sciences.

The Future Arrives

While congressional action to anticipate and study the ethical, legal, and social implications of genetic engineering faded in the early 1970s, the new recombinant-DNA techniques were being invented.[21] At the Gordon Conference on Nucleic Acids in July

1973, scientists revealed research results that had enormous potential for manipulating genes. They did express concern about the possible implications of the work, but that concern was limited to the possibility of immediate laboratory safety hazards associated with the research being launched.

In November 1974, during the six-month period when a temporary moratorium was invoked by the scientists in the field on those particular experiments thought to be potentially hazardous, two university biologists applied for a patent on the recombinant-DNA technique. Thus, the age of genetic engineering was under way with the commercial applications protected and discussion of the ethical implications postponed.

Biologists' original concern about recombinant-DNA laboratory safety was influenced by their prior sensitization to issues of social responsibility, a product of the discussions during the 1960s regarding medical technologies and genetic engineering. These scientists were also motivated by the possibility of what they regarded as public intrusion in their research unless they acted to reassure the public that they would anticipate and reduce risks.

The February 1975 Asilomar Conference brought together scientists in the field to consider the hazards of recombinant-DNA research and to find ways of reducing them. In his opening remarks at the conference, David Baltimore expressed the views of the organizers:

> Although I think it's obvious that this technology is possibly the most potent potential technology in biological warfare, this meeting is not designed to deal with that question. The issue that does bring us here is that a new technique of molecular biology appears to have allowed us to outdo the standard events of evolution by making combinations of genes which could be immediate natural history. These pose special potential hazards while they offer enormous benefits. We are here in a sense to balance the benefits and hazards right now and to design a strategy which will maximize the benefits and minimize the hazards for the future.[22]

The scientists' concerns were narrowed to the immediate technical problems of laboratory safety, and they developed technical solutions to these problems. During the political controversy in the mid-1970s about whether these "tech fixes" were adequate, leading scientists in the field argued that the imminent practical benefits of the research and the absence of demonstrated risk meant that it was imperative that the research proceed as rapidly as possible. Public expectations of valued benefits were raised while possible hazards were played down. Ethical issues related to the potential applications of the new research tools and techniques were largely ignored.[23]

One major concern of the recombinant-DNA scientists was that their own early caution with respect to laboratory safety had initiated public scrutiny of the new research. This was emphasized by local hearings and inquiries in Ann Arbor, Cambridge, San Diego, New Haven, Princeton, and many other communities, followed by the introduction of sixteen separate bills in Congress to regulate recombinant-DNA safety standards. Research universities and scientific organizations were worried about public "overreaction" and about losing control of the decisions regarding laboratory safety procedures. A slogan among some biologists at MIT in 1976 was "Shut up or be shut down." Who was overreacting?

The desire for greater public participation in decisions regarding science was emphasized by Senator Edward Kennedy in an address to scientists at the Harvard Medical School in May 1975, just a few months after the Asilomar Conference:

> When science develops techniques that have the potential to fundamentally change society, society has the right to determine how the technique is to be used, whether it should be developed in the first place, and if so, under what constraints. A decision to pursue the kind of research discussed at Asilomar requires the informed consent of the society—which, after all—is called upon to fund it.
>
> I am not raising the specter of having laymen pass judgement on scientific protocols. I am suggesting that there is a role for the public in the setting of research priorities; there certainly is a role for the public in the evaluation of research at the frontier of medicine. So too must the public be involved in decisions regarding the application of new knowledge.
>
> With society's informed consent, scientists can devote their creative talent to the scientific problems at hand; without it their energies will be diluted by the need to fend off challenges from a hostile society. There can be no turning back to the days when scientists were left totally on their own to chart their own course. . . . The public will immerse itself in the affairs of science. Whether it does so constructively will depend on the willingness of scientists to welcome public participation.[24]

Scientists involved in recombinant-DNA research vigorously resisted local and national legislation that would have made mandatory the National Institutes of Health (NIH) guidelines for laboratory safety. Congressional representatives and staff were subjected to intensive lobbying by leading scientists, professional societies, and research universities. Four of the universities formed a lobbying group that they called the "Friends of DNA." Testimony by researchers at congressional hearings heralded imminent new medical applications made possible by recombinant-DNA techniques, before these preliminary results had been submitted for publication in scientific journals. Several prominent biologists who had shared the early concern about possible safety hazards of the research recanted publicly, saying that they had overstated the risks and now could provide reassurance that the work was safe. In the end no legislation was passed by Congress, and in 1979 those who had linked arms to resist it declared victory in what Norton Zinder has called "the recombinant DNA war." By that time, the NIH recombinant-DNA guidelines had been made far more permissive than the original 1976 version. More than 90 percent of U.S. research in the field was either no longer covered by the guidelines or was subject to only minimal controls equivalent to standard laboratory practice. Despite the calls for increased public participation in the mid-1970s, research in molecular genetics has largely been self-regulated during the past two decades.[25]

New Tools, New Roles

Recombinant-DNA techniques have had an enormous scientific and social impact. They have made possible new basic research on the structure and function of genes, opened up new fields of inquiry, and led to a variety of applications in industry, agriculture, and medicine. Biology has been transformed and *so have the biologists.* Starting very rapidly in the early 1980s, academic biologists never before involved with industry became consultants, advisers, founders, equity holders, and contractees of new biotechnology firms or new divisions of multinational corporations. Current disputes over patents on DNA sequences, human cells, tissues and body parts, and experimental processes and products are prominent in the scientific and public media. New companies are continuing to form around the developing technologies of gene sequencing, DNA identification, and human gene therapy.

The rapid, large-scale commercialization of academic biology has created conflicts of interest that may seriously erode public trust. Now more than ever biologists' expert advice is urgently needed on questions of public policy. The issues include the following: deciding priorities in the public funding of biology research and in the application of genetic engineering and biotechnology; assessment of the possible environmental and health hazards of biological research products and processes; and the ethical, political, and legal implications of forensic DNA identification, expanded genetic screening, and human gene therapy. These questions must be decided with full public participation, and biologists can provide expert information needed in the deliberations. But the commercial roles and possible conflicts of interest of many biologists and their institutions have influenced their perceptions and their willingness to speak out, and have thus limited their effectiveness as credible public advisers.[26]

A New Code?

The recent history of biologists' responses to the ethical dimensions of their work may help us to think about the potential value of the Ethical, Legal, and Social Implications (ELSI) program component of the Human Genome Project. Continuing themes from the past are clearly evident, including scientists' efforts to obtain massive public funding by linking their projects to public health and cures for disease (while resisting public "intrusion" in their work) and defusing public skepticism and worry about possible negative consequences by acknowledging these concerns (while separating them from the doing of the science). The pattern in the 1960s discussions of the prospects for genetic engineering was to separate the technical from the ethical questions, focusing resources and intellectual effort on developing the science and deferring serious consideration of the ethical consequences until "the future." When the technical means for genetic engineering became available just a few years later, in the early 1970s, biologists did call attention to potential negative consequences of the new research but restricted that concern to laboratory health hazards, ignoring or deferring the ethical issues once again. Their aim was to provide reassurance that the public was not at risk so that the recombinant-DNA experiments could proceed, self-regulated by the researchers, their universities, and NIH, which funded and promoted the work.

Now that the DNA molecule is manipulable and salable, the life letters GATC can be interpreted anew to characterize how genetic knowledge and its uses and abuses are publicized. In this social/political code G means *geneticize:* define many medical problems as determined by abnormal genes, establish the genetic identities of individuals and groups and, if possible, correct genetic "defects." In this narrow purview, technical problems require technical fixes. The consistent refrain is that the Human Genome Project will find the genes involved in disease.[27]

What about the ethical, social, and political dimensions of this endeavor? Here is where A, T, and C come in. A is for *advertise:* the project gets credit for being concerned about possible negative consequences and for responding to public misgivings about ethical and political problems, and this helps to sell the overall endeavor.

T is for *trivialize:* make a list of problems involving privacy, insurance coverage, job discrimination, medical care, and abortion and show that these problems are already with us; argue that genetic engineering is merely an extension of existing medical technologies and raises no new moral issues; reduce complex controversies to simplistic terms; focus on the most extreme scenarios of abuse and provide reassurance that they are either in the realm of science fiction or are too far in the future or too far in the past to worry about now.

The fourth letter, C, is for *compartmentalize:* create a committee to stimulate study of these issues and to prepare society to deal with them so that science will not be slowed down and its researchers will not be distracted from their necessary work.

The Human Genome Project's approach to ethical and social issues was emphasized by Eric Lander, a leading advocate and participant in the project, in his testimony at an April 1990 congressional budget hearing:

> With our deepening knowledge about human heredity come difficult ethical issues—including questions of privacy, insurance coverage, job discrimination, medical care and abortion. Fortunately, the human genome project includes—in addition to its scientific mission—a serious program designed to try to identify the ethical and social issues *before* they arise and to identify possible solutions.
>
> I have heard it suggested that we could avoid these ethical problems by simply eliminating (or postponing) the human genome project. This is simply false: The genie is already out of the bottle. With or without the human genome project, the numerous ethical issues related to human heredity are already being posed by research findings throughout the length and breadth of NIH—concerning cystic fibrosis, heart disease, mental illness, and diabetes.
>
> The human genome project at least offers the prospect of addressing these questions on an organized basis—rather than letting them arise in the haphazard fashion in which they are currently proceeding.
>
> Today, biomedicine is saying: The ethical issues surrounding human genetics will not go away. Let us face them squarely, before they are fully upon us.[28]

The testimony in support of increasing the project's funding ended with this statement: "In summary, the Human Genome Project involves building infrastructure, nurturing technology, addressing ethics, and sustaining momentum."[29]

A few weeks earlier, James Watson's public explanation of his motivation for addressing ethics had appeared in *Science* magazine:

> Beginning with my opening press conference at NIH, and later through other meetings with the press, I made clear my concern for the ethical and social implications raised by an ever-increasing knowledge of human genes and of the genetic diseases that result from variations in our genetic messages. On the one hand, this knowledge undoubtedly will lead to a much deeper understanding of many of the worst diseases that plague human existence. Thus, there are strong ethical reasons to obtain this genetic knowledge as fast as possible and with all our might. On the other hand, the knowledge that some of us as individuals have inherited disease-causing genes is certain to bring unwanted grief unless appropriate

therapies are developed. So it is imperative that we begin to educate our nation's people on the genetic options that they as individuals may have to choose among.

I believed we should put money behind these convictions and suggested that, at the start, at least 3% of the earmarked genome funds should go to support the ethical and social implications area. In doing so, we must be aware of the terrible misuses of the incomplete knowledge of human genetics that went under the name of eugenics during the first part of this century. There exists real fear among many individuals that genetic reasons will again be used to make the lives of the underprivileged even more disadvantaged. We must work to ensure that society learns to use the information only in beneficial ways and, if necessary, pass laws at both the federal and state levels to prevent invasions of privacy of an individual's genetic background by either employers, insurers, or government agencies and to prevent discrimination on genetic grounds. If we fail to act now, we might witness unwanted and unnecessary abuses that eventually will create a strong popular backlash against the human genetics community.[30]

It is clear from the content and context of these statements that they are meant to reassure Congress and the public that the project's leaders are aware of the ethical and social implications of their work and are acting to confront potential abuses by educating society to prevent them.

Beyond "the Ethics Thing"

How does the Human Genome Project's approach to ethical issues differ from approaches of the past? Although there are many similarities, one apparent difference is that the project is making an effort to identify the ethical, legal, and social issues in advance, preparing society to deal with the "nonbeneficial" uses of the vast amount of genetic information the project is designed to produce. But if this effort is compartmentalized and insulated from the main mission of the project, rather than influencing its policies and priorities, then once again it separates the technical from the ethical and defers the ethical issues, defining them as a societal and not a scientific concern.

Yet, within this limited framework, the Ethical, Legal, and Social Implications program of the project is making a serious effort to stimulate research, public education and, in some cases, legislative action and public policy on some of the issues it has identified, including health insurance, privacy, and prenatal diagnosis. ELSI has funded a number of regional conferences and forums where these and related issues are discussed by experts in many fields. An unfortunate pattern at some of these meetings is that scientists in the genome project often lead off the program with an explanation of the technical issues and then leave without participating in and perhaps learning from the subsequent sessions dealing with the ethical implications of the work. Clearly what is needed is not only "scientific literacy" for the public but also "public literacy" for the scientists.

George Annas observed in 1989 that "ethics is generally taken seriously by physicians and scientists only when it either fosters their agenda or does not interfere with it. If it cautions a slower pace or a more deliberate consideration of science's darker side, it is dismissed as 'fearful of the future,' anti-intellectual, or simply uninformed."[31] Fortunately there are notable exceptions to this criticism.

These issues need to be discussed by scientists and others who care about such questions, provide public funding for the research, and have a stake in the outcome. However, the reward system in science and the training of scientists does not encourage such efforts. In the 1968 congressional hearings Arthur Kornberg stated that "there are absolutely no scientific rewards, no enlargement of scientific skills that accrue from involvement in public issues."[32] This perception is still widely shared among scientists today and is reinforced by competitive pressures and institutional cultures.

Another difficulty is the frustration many scientists feel in approaching the issues. Witness, for example, a biologist's response to my question about the meager discussion of ethical issues at a small conference he attended in the early 1980s on the prospects for human gene therapy. He answered:

> I wanted more discussion on it. . . . I did, and I didn't. There's a sense in which it's more fun to talk about the science. You're actually doing things in science. . . . I think everyone who lived through the Asilomar period in the late '70s and the regulatory period came to recognize that at the end of the day, when you're working with scientific things, you're in control. You, yourself, are

in control of what you're doing, of your laboratory, or of your scientific environment in advance. When you get involved in regulatory, ethical, or political issues, you have to share that control and
often you have very little input into what happens. I think that
scientists like being in control. I think all of us find such situations
at best ambiguous and at worst profoundly unsettling.[33]

A great deal of work remains to be done in order to encourage, train, and provide professional incentives for scientists to
consider seriously the social and ethical dimensions of their
work and to participate in the public discussion and resolution
of such issues in a manner that transcends their professional
and financial self-interests.

Albeit sporadically, Congress has expressed a concern to
avert potentially harmful results, having been prodded into action by anticipatory warnings from some scientists and public-
interest groups. The organizers of the Human Genome Project
have responded by proposing to devote at least 3 percent of the
project's massive budget to steer society away from harmful
uses of the expected genetic data. The 3 percent solution, even 5
or 10 percent, may produce valuable insight and information to
help society *adapt* to the expected applications and to help prevent "nonbeneficial" uses. The operating assumption is that the
production of vast amounts of human genetic information is inevitable and should be completed as soon as possible.[34] But the
results of this "technically sweet" enterprise will be applied in a
context of burgeoning genetic determinism in an increasingly
commercialized field. Discussions of the ethical implications of
the results are likely to be bypassed by market-driven actions, as
in the case of commercial pressures and projects for cystic fibrosis carrier screening. This is occurring despite warnings from
some researchers and an NIH panel that it is premature to
launch such programs because they will provide misleading or
false results and will raise expectations that cannot not be ful-
filled.[35]

True anticipatory action would have been to study the ethical, legal, and social implications of the genome project *before* it
was launched. Now that the project is well under way, the
knowledge gained by the ELSI studies should not be compartmentalized but should be integrated into the project—to influence its policies and priorities, so that "avoiding harm" does not

yield to "technical sweetness." At the same time, changes in scientific training and professional incentives must be pursued in order to encourage scientists in the field to consider seriously the ethical, social, and political implications of their research choices and to acquire greater "public literacy." As in the past, some may say that these are societal and not scientific issues. Some may continue to say that it is too soon to act before the project's results are in. But it soon may be too late.

Chapter 3

Vital Language

RICHARD DOYLE

*And whosoever was not found in the book of life
was cast into the lake of fire.*
Revelation 20:15

Like Thomas Pynchon's V-2 rocket state, where technicians work day and night "coding, recoding, redecoding the holy Text," molecular biologists and technicians work furiously to map and eventually sequence what has come to be known variously as the "book of life," an "ancient hard disk," or a "computer operating system." The genome. According to the contemporary rhetoric of "the" genome, we lick our fingers as we now turn the first pages of the book of life. Those pages, pages of a thousand thousand-page phone books, can provide us with the tools to decipher the mysteries of existence. "Humanity," the nature of humans, has been written in a cryptic language, a language secret and, to the initiated, transparent.

So the story goes, anyhow. In this brief text, I want to highlight the fact that the discourse of human genome projects—what we could call, following Michael Fortun, "genomics"—*constitutes a story,* one story among others that could be told about our genes and our identities.[1]

The discourse of the genome projects is varied and diffuse, but one metaphor that seems to be persistent, powerful, and unexamined is the notion that it is sensible and reasonable to describe DNA as the "book of life." How did we come to describe a mechanism of *heredity* as the "book of life"?

The philosopher Jacques Derrida has pursued the difficult task of mapping out the ways in which "nature" came to be seen as a "book."[2] Derrida highlights the theological and metaphysical implications of this identification of "nature" with the Word, implications that are enormous and varied. He points to a central irony of the "book of nature": the fact that such a book,

"natural" as it is, still must be written, is itself a somewhat unnatural and technological activity. For now, I will point to only
two crucial moments in the history of biology where our "natures," genes, came to be described via the metaphor of "code,"
a metaphor that is compatible with this tradition of seeing nature as "written." I do so to underscore the fact that the stories
we tell about and with "nature" are not simply scientific; they
are bound up with other historical, political, and theological narratives that are deeply ingrained in our cultural practices. The
ways in which we talk and write about genomes form an integral part of the human genome projects, a literary technology as
vital to the endeavor as the other, more obvious technologies of
mapping and sequencing.

Metaphors of Phenotype

Heredity has always been metaphorical. As the mechanism of
the begetting of like by like, heredity depends conceptually and
rhetorically on the mechanisms of comparison, simile, and analogy. The claim, for example, that I have a nose "like my
mother's" is quite literally metaphorical, in that its claim of re-
semblance relies on the simile "like my mother's." Of course, if
we claim that I have a nose "like a toucan" we could probably
(hopefully) say that this is a more metaphorical statement than
the comparison with my mother, but this would be a change in
degree and not in kind. Thus, even Mendel's straightforward
comparison of a "wrinkled" pea with a "round" one is, literally
speaking, a metaphor in that it fulfills the Aristotelian definition
of performing a "transfer from species to genus or species to
species or genus to species" in ascribing the "genus" pea to the
"species" wrinkled or round.[3]

Of course, to claim that heredity has a metaphorical or,
more broadly, rhetorical basis tells us nothing of the kinds and
flavors of metaphors available to describe the similarities and
differences of the kin of any given age or discourse. The description of the nose above, for example, is a metaphor of appearance, a phenotypic rhetoric that foregrounds one of the lay
markers of ethnicity and "character" in the United States of the
late twentieth century. All sorts of codes can be metonymically
and synecdochically read out of the nose, so to speak, and for

this reason the nose is seen as an important site of comparison between children and parents, as well as an important site for surgery.[4] The rhetorical and historical shift that I would like to mark, however, is the shift from the metaphors of phenotype to the metaphors of genotype, a shift that will help make feasible such metaphors as the "book of life." Although both "phenotype" and "genotype" are "equally" rhetorical, different rhetorics foreground different aspects of living systems.

From Phenotype to Genotype

Although he was a physicist, Erwin Schrödinger made a profound impact on the metaphorics of the genetic substance. Having made a mark in his own field, Schrödinger turned his attention to biological questions in his popular account of the physical basis of vitality. *What Is Life?* provides a rhetorical model of the gene that would influence Francis Crick's interest in DNA and provide the groundwork for George Gamow's reframing of the DNA–protein relation in 1954. An analysis of Schrödinger's text will provide us with a view of both Schrödinger's dependence on the traditional metaphors of heredity and his break with them, which allowed him to formulate the notion of a hereditary "code."

Schrödinger's rhetoric relies much upon the traditional metaphors of genetics in his "summary" of that subject. Indeed, because of his position as a "dilettante," Schrödinger's characterization of genetics gives us a very general picture of the nature of the rhetorical reservoir available to the geneticist of the 1940s. It is also this position as dilettante that allows Schrödinger to reinterpret some of these common metaphors. For example, his discussion of genetics begins with the notion of "pattern":

> Let me use the word "pattern" of an organism in the sense in which the biologist calls it "the four-dimensional pattern," meaning not only the structure and functioning of the organism in the adult, or in any other particular stage, but the whole of its ontogenetic development.[5]

Here Schrödinger employs what I called above a phenotypic metaphor, in that the notion of "pattern" refers to the "shape" of a developed organism and not just to the genotype, the shape, as it were, of its genes. Note that Schrödinger is careful to mark the importance of nomenclature by his use of quotation marks and the definitional gesture with which he begins. From here, however, the rhetorical pattern shifts and displaces; from the detail and complexity of the living organism, Schrödinger moves to the chromosome. Since this "four-dimensional pattern is known to be determined by the structure of the . . . fertilized egg," and since that cell itself is "essentially determined by the structure of only . . . the nucleus," Schrödinger turns his attention to genotype:

> It is these chromosomes, or probably only an axial skeletal fibre of what we actually see under the microscope as the chromosome, that contain in some kind of code-script the entire pattern of the individual's future development.[6]

No longer, then, is "pattern" to be seen in the exhibited characteristics and functioning of the individual. Rather, it is now something that is "contained" in the coded and scripted chromosome. No longer a reflection or even a production of genotype, "pattern" is now literally inside genotype. By shifting the meaning of "pattern" from a metaphor of phenotype to a rhetoric of genotype, Schrödinger literally and grotesquely turns "pattern" and the "organism" inside out. This fantastic and impossible twist in the history of the genetic substance must be seen as a fundamental reprogramming of the rhetorical "software" of genetics and, by extension, molecular biology. Schrödinger was able to redescribe a scientific concept through recourse to a kind of dream work. As in one of Freud's "absurd dreams" in which a patient "failed to distinguish the bust and the photograph from the actual person," Schrödinger mistakes or displaces the pattern of the organism by its "code-script."[7]

Thus, despite Schrödinger's care in his deployment of the terms of his summary, "pattern" takes on an essentially different meaning, as the developmental and physical complexity of the "four-dimensional pattern" is displaced by the genetic instructions for that pattern. Since we are dealing with "scripts" or texts, an analogy drawn from literary theory might illuminate for us the nature of this textual problem. Paul de Man describes an analogous slippage that arises in theories of discourse:

> It would be unfortunate, for example, to confuse the materiality of the signifier with the materiality of what it signifies. . . . [N]o one in his right mind would try to grow grapes by the luminosity of the word "day," but it is very difficult not to conceive the pattern of one's past and future existence as in accordance with temporal and spatial schemes that belong to fictional narratives and not to the world.[8]

This passage speaks precisely to the "pattern" of Schrödinger's move. By placing a spatiotemporal series of events "within" a code-script, Schrödinger is effectively put in the position of trying to grow grapes by the light of "day." More precisely, he confuses the "organism" and its development with its "essence" or its "recipe." It is precisely this confusion that de Man labels "ideology."

Schrödinger, at least in part, is aware of the possibility for confusion. Always attentive to the need for careful definition, he offers a more precise reason for the "code-script" metaphor:

> In calling the structure of the chromosome fibres a code-script we mean that the all-penetrating mind, once conceived by Laplace, to which every causal connection lay immediately open, could tell from their structure whether the egg would develop, under suitable conditions, into a black cock or a speckled hen.[9]

The code is thus at once secret and transparent. The ideal, god-like reader would be able to read the future of any given organism from the text of its stable and indelible "code-script." But Schrödinger seems to realize that this is not an entirely satisfactory metaphor. After all, "real" codes do nothing; they require a reader, or at least a reading:

> The term code-script is, of course, too narrow. The chromosome structures are at the same time instrumental in bringing about the development they foreshadow. They are law-code and executive power—or to use another simile, they are architect's plan and builder's craft—in one.[10]

In his careful attempt to articulate his description of the genetic substance, Schrödinger ironically falls prey to what Freud located as a "verbal foolishness" and what de Man labeled "ideology." If Schrödinger had posited the chromosomes as only a code-script that required a reading or a translation to produce an organism, his model could be accommodated to the more complex developmental model of "pattern" while offering a useful heuristic or metaphor for the specific function of the chromosomes within that pattern. With this last move, however, Schrödinger places all of the power within the code and none within the development of the organism. The insertion of "builder's craft" into the "plan" of genotype represents the deletion of the organism and phenotype.

Of course, the mere fact that Schrödinger's rhetoric encodes the genetic substance, and indeed life, as a written code does not account for why this rhetorical move was attractive, nor does it prove that this articulation had any "real" impact. To jump to such a conclusion would be to perform Schrödinger's error of mistaking a text for a complete development of an organism or a concept. It does, however, demonstrate that this articulation was both feasible and available. It also demonstrates historically where at least some of the plausibility of tropes like the "book of life" comes from, as well as the importance of attending to the written, rhetorical displacements that make up scientific discourse. That is to say, Schrödinger's use of metaphor, a metaphor that does not seem to be entirely in his control, highlights the way in which the life sciences can be seen to be made up of rhetorical techniques as well as scientific ones.

The power of this formulation is clear, as Schrödinger's location of life inside the code-script inspired Francis Crick:

> A major factor in his [Crick] leaving physics and developing an interest in biology had been the reading in 1946 of *What Is Life?* by the noted theoretical physicist Erwin Schrödinger. This book very elegantly propounded the belief that genes were the key components of living cells and that, to understand what life is, we must know how genes act.[11]

What is particularly instructive about Watson's formulation here is that it draws attention precisely to the conflation that I analyzed above. While it is perfectly predictable that the virtual founders of molecular biology would emphasize the role of the genetic substance in "life," this quotation strikingly illustrates the effect, both scientific and rhetorical, of Schrödinger's description. Not only did it provide the motivation for a migration of physicists into the life sciences, but it also helped frame the question of life within a reductionist framework that sought and found the secret of life—"what life is"—in a crystallograph and not an organism. "Absurd" or not, Watson and Crick's dream of understanding "what life is" includes a Nobel Prize and the beginnings of a research program to read the "book of life" whose ultimate logic leads to the genome initiatives. That is, the notion that "life" is best understood through a mechanism of heredity can be traced to the equation of "what life is" with the action, or *agency*, of a gene. This notion that genes can have agency, outside their place within the complex matrix of an organism and its development, can be traced in part back to Schrödinger's substitution of metaphors of genotype for metaphors of phenotype with the language of "code-script."[12]

Thus Schrödinger did not, in some sense, go awry. Rather, this episode in the constitution of molecular biological discourse brings into relief the other narratives at play within scientific discourse. Science is shot through with writing and rhetoric, and rhetoric is saturated with differences, displacements that make possible the moments of invention that, ideological or not, make plausible different scientific regimes and researches. Scientificity itself is at least in part a rhetorical effect, an effect of the possibility of the displacement and exchange of meanings and models both within and across discourses. Schrödinger's (metaphorical) exchange of the trope "phenotype" for the trope "genotype" was not merely Freud's "verbal carelessness"; it was a rhetorical possibility condition of molecular biology. It made it possible for Watson and Crick, among others, to equate life with the structure of DNA and, eventually, to seek to "decode" it.

And yet, Schrödinger's rhetorical invention is still far from the Laplacian readers of the book of life peering over electrophoresis gels today. The trajectory of the "code" metaphor was far from simple. While it is true that codes were literally "in the air" during the years of World War II, the impact of the specific metaphorics of the "code" were less than clear. The reductionist "deletion of the organism" discussed above was made possible by the notion that the essence of life was contained in a discrete unit of code-script, but it is only after the articulation of the structure of DNA that the rhetorics of "code" get played out. In Watson and Crick's "A Structure for Deoxyribonucleic Acid," which outlined the now-familiar double-helical structure of

DNA, no mention of the "code" metaphor is made. However, in their next article, "Genetical Implications of the Structure of De-oxyribonucleic Acid," they write:

> in a long molecule many different permutations are possible, and it therefore seems likely that the precise sequence of the bases is the code which carries the genetical information.[13]

Yet just what was meant by this "code," besides the fact that it somehow related the sequence of DNA to proteins, remained suitably enigmatic. How this "genetical information" synthesized proteins was still uncertain.

Even before Watson and Crick's announcement, A. L. Dounce, a biochemist, had proposed a template model of protein synthesis, a model more beholden to the metaphorics of "patterns" than of "codes":

> If we accept for the purpose of argument the suggestion that genes are composed of deoxyribonucleic acid, then it could conceivably happen that the deoxyribonucleic acid gene molecules would act as templates for ribonucleic acid synthesis, and that the ribonucleic acids synthesized on the gene templates would then in turn become templates for protein synthesis in the nucleus or cytoplasm or both.[14]

Here Dounce drew on a long tradition of the concept and metaphor of the "template," a tradition that extended at least as far back as 1930. As a model for protein synthesis, it has provided great explanatory power. Unlike the metaphor of the "code," however, the template metaphor has not been extended to a description of the genetic substance as a whole. Rather, it is an aspect and a feature of an overall entity which is characterized as the code, blueprint, or book of life. The template itself requires a mediation, a mechanism of translation. It remained for George Gamow to frame the DNA–protein relation in bookish terms.

In 1954, less than a year after Watson and Crick's "wish" to suggest a structure for deoxyribonucleic acid, a short, seemingly unambitious text appeared in *Nature*. George Gamow, cosmologist, physicist, and cartoonist, suggested a conceptual model for the DNA–protein relation in which the production of proteins from nucleic acids could be explained. Previously, Dounce had articulated in rough form the now-familiar DNA–RNA–proteins troika, but the question of how nucleic acids were "decoded" into proteins was still a mystery. Gamow's text, "Possible Relation between Deoxyribonucleic Acid and Protein Structures," included a proposal—the so-called diamond code—that ultimately proved to be wrong, but his conceptual and we might say rhetorical influence can be seen in the ultimate configuration and solution of what Crick in 1957 would call the "coding problem." Gamow's conceptualization of the coding problem—how four different bases produce or determine twenty different amino acids—as a problem of textual translation played a key part in research on the code, and it can be seen as a metaphorical shift from the previous emphasis on the metaphorics of "templates." What I will trace here is Gamow's precise discursive description of this "relation" as a "translation," an articulation that begins with "numbers" and ends with "organisms." As such, I will attempt first to foreground the precise ways in which Gamow's text "works" rhetorically. I will then attempt to foreground the ways in which Gamow's account relies on other, extrascientific narratives, stories that may help us to map some of things we are saying when we claim to read the "book of life."

Translating Gamow's Translation

In our unwinding of the rhetorical knots that structure Gamow's text, we will first tug on a thread, more specifically, a "fibre":

> In a communication in *Nature* of May 30, p. 964, J.D. Watson and F.H.C. Crick showed that the molecule of deoxyribonucleic acid, which can be considered as a chromosome fibre, consists of two parallel chains formed by only four different kinds of nucleotides.[15]

Thus, we pull on a fibre and end up in chains. Close analysis of this brief communication will show that it is bound by a logic of textuality. That is, this short article is "about," among other things, the production and practice of science through texts, in this case *Nature*. We see, for example, that in this book of nature, one must open with the book *Nature*. It is also written that in *Nature* is a communication, a communication that itself concerns communication (or at least, as we shall see, "alphabets," "words," and their natures). In the beginning, then, this is an intertextual affair, one that concerns communication between the book(s) of *Nature*. The very fact of the naming of this journal "Nature," of course, speaks to the close proximity if not identity of texts and nature in the scientific practices described within its covers. One practice of science is thus literally the communication between volumes of nature.

The communication "between" texts is, of course, what is at stake here:

> The hereditary properties of any given organism could be characterized by a long number written in a four-digital system. On the other hand, the enzymes (proteins), the composition of which must be completely determined by the deoxyribonucleic acid molecule, are long peptide chains formed by twenty different kinds of amino-acids, and can be considered as long "words" based on a 20-letter alphabet. Thus the question arises about the way in which four-digital numbers can be translated into such "words".[16]

Between these two hands Gamow deals—the "digit" and the "word"—there must be a "translation." Gamow's articulation of what will only later be referred to as the "coding problem" by Francis Crick codes the "relation" between DNA and proteins as a "translation," specifically a translation between mathematical and nonphonetic, alphabetic language. The order of the mathematical sign must be replaced by the order of the linguistic sign. This trajectory—from the mathematical to the linguistic—reflects the historical double articulation of nature as both a mathematical text and a linguistic one: nature, Galileo writes,

> is written in a mathematical language, and the characters are triangles, circles, and other geometrical figures. And Descartes wishes only "to read in the great book of Nature."[17]

The local protocols that govern these (and many more) invocations of the book of nature should not be overlooked, but for our purposes here I will stress the dual (even dueling) languages of nature, mathematics and prose. It should not be surprising that Gamow's text finds itself between two orders of signification, two different books of nature, two different codes. With Gamow's text, the dream of understanding "what life is" becomes a reverie about the translation of numbers to words.

Returning to Paul de Man's insights, we can see that the very framing of the "coding problem" by Gamow depends upon a slippage between what de Man called the "materiality of the signifier" and the "materiality of the signified." In fact, the gap between DNA and proteins, between Gamow's "digits" and "words," is precisely the space between the materiality of a sign and the materiality of its signified. As de Man points out, no one in his right mind would try to grow grapes by the light of the word "day," and Gamow quite sanely limits his task to a translation. And yet the question of how the DNA words become flesh requires an answer that goes beyond the "materiality of the signifier," the double helix of DNA; it requires a coimplication, a translation not of one sign to another, but from signs to organisms. The gap between the "organism" and its "code-script," obliterated by Schrödinger, returns to haunt molecular biology in the form of the coding problem. In order to sustain the idea that the relation between DNA and protein structures, genes and life, is a "translation," the difference between DNA and an organism must be effaced and rhetorically managed just as anyone attempting to grow grapes by the luminosity of the word "day" would need to cloak the distinction between a three-letter word and solar bombardment. The story of Gamow's rhetorical management of this impossible translation can be read right out of "Possible Relation between Deoxyribonucleic Acid and Protein Structures." In this reading, I will attempt to show that the framing of the DNA–protein relation as a translation of numbers to words proceeds by effacing the radical difference between a text—numerological or alphabetic—and an organism.

The two orders of signification are themselves translated both textually and "visually." To translate the gap between the digital and the linguistic, a gap that Gamow himself identifies as the central problem of his text, Gamow borrows from or relies upon a third order of signification, the icon or diagram—more precisely, two diagrams that, in the language of circles and triangles, help to tell the story of the translation of the genetic code into proteins. What Gamow feels cannot be represented in the textual realm gets drawn as a diagram. Thus, the diagram fills a certain "hole" in the text; what the text "itself" cannot bring to light is filled in by the diagrams. Not unlike Watson and Crick, Gamow calls upon a visual model to aid him in his telling of the story of DNA and proteins.

But this hole in the text, while briefly filled by the diagram, returns, as the diagram itself requires a textual narrative, a narrative built on the description of the "schema" as full of "holes." Thus, the narrative gap that is bridged by the diagram opens up again. Far from translating the gaps in Gamow's text, a text that itself seeks to effect translation, the diagram calls forth more translation, a translation itself full of gaps or holes:

> Fig. 1 shows schematically the structure of the deoxyribonucleic acid molecule. . . . We see that each "hole" is defined by only three of the four nucleotides forming it. . . . It can easily be seen that there are twenty different types of such "holes" as shown in Fig. 2.[18]

Clearly, in some sense we do not "see" a "hole" in the diagram; Gamow must translate the diagrams for us in terms of metaphors, metaphors that, it so happens, themselves name a gap— in this case, the diagrammatic and the textual—which always lead to more translations, more metaphors. The chain of polypeptides and its relations are described in terms of a chain of metaphors continually in need of translation.

But every code has a key, so these "holes" turn out to be keyholes:

> It seems to me that such translation procedures can easily be established by considering the "key and lock" relation between the various amino acids and the rhomb-shaped "holes" formed by various nucleotides in the deoxyribonucleic acid chains.[19]

The metaphor of the "hole," as well as a hole in the text, leads to a "lock." The attempt to close the gap on translation, which began as an arc from digits to words, has been finished and put under lock and key. This particular metaphor of confinement is instructive. While the alleged discrepancy between the order of language and mathematics made Gamow's text possible, opening up the question and its translation in terms of icons and metaphors, the metaphor of the "lock and key" opposes the "freedom" of translation to the finitude of the code. Indeed, even the metaphorics of capture are invoked:

> One can speculate that free amino-acids from the surrounding medium get caught into the "holes" of deoxyribonucleic acid molecules, and thus unite into the corresponding peptide chains.[20]

It would be tempting at this point to argue that Gamow's text, through its choice of metaphors, allegorizes its fate as a text, a fate that could be characterized as the attempt to achieve closure, an accomplishment that is possible only through the very deployment of metaphor which calls this into question. Like the book of nature, the point at which Gamow's text seems to have become "true" is in fact the point at which it is the "most" rhetorical. The solution to the problem of translation outlined by Gamow, which is itself a solution to the problem of how to get an organism from a text, flesh from a number or a word, can be named only by metaphor, a metaphor that no less than the gap between DNA and proteins requires translation. The solution, in fact, given the absence of experimental evidence, depends at least in part on the persuasive power of the metaphor of "lock and key," a metaphor which suggests that everything fits together securely, that the problem of translation can be contained. The plausibility of the cryptographic method for the dream of knowing what life is, in which "each sign can be translated into another sign having a known meaning, in accordance with a fixed key,"[21] is dependent upon precisely those "fictional narratives" which de Man reminds us are so difficult to avoid, narratives of transcendence achieved through the transparent and translated Word.

This, I think, is a very inviting reading, and not an inaccurate one. But it is also possible that this allegory of textuality allegorizes vitality:

> It is inviting to associate these "holes" with twenty different amino-acids essential for living organisms.[22]

While the metaphor of the "lock" encourages us to think the case is closed on the matter of the translation of code into proteins, of "digits" into "words," Gamow reopens it and invites in "life" and organisms. Thus far in the text, this has been a simple matter of translation, a matter reducible to "words," "numbers," and "keys." Indeed, I have argued that the very framing of the coding problem required the effacement of the difference between texts and organisms through the model of numerical-to-linguistic translation. Now Gamow asks us to translate this into living organisms, organisms deleted under the regime of the code-script. And yet, this is not the subject of this text. As we have pointed out, "Possible Relation between Deoxyribonucleic Acid and Protein Structures" relates the story of the translation of "digits" into "words." What on first glance would seem to be a surreptitious introduction into this text of yet another problem in translation is rather, for Gamow, not treated as a translation at all. The gap that necessitates a translation between numbers and words, DNA and proteins, simply does not exist "between" proteins and living organisms. Between "proteins" and "life" is the relation of "essence." This would seem to be in accord with the antivitalist impulse, which by some accounts has provided much of the conceptual drive of molecular biology, if by "essential" we interpret the relation as being one of "importance" if not identity:

> The ultimate aim of the modern movement in biology is in fact to explain all biology in terms of physics and chemistry. . . . I believe the motivation of many of the people who have entered molecular biology from physics and chemistry has been their desire to *disprove* vitalism.[23]

Thus, Gamow's insight was to abstract the problem of the relation of DNA and proteins from the chemical and developmental complexities of organisms, much as Schrödinger abstracted and retooled the notion of "pattern." This insight was therefore partly a rhetorical one; Gamow framed the problem with a new (recovered) metaphor of translation. Why, then, is the "living organism" dragged into this simple exercise in translation? If the relationship between proteins and organisms is simple and direct—that is, not in need of translation—what role does the invocation of the "living organism" play, rhetorically, in Gamow's text?

Our answer, as we might expect, calls for another (but not opposed) translation of the "essential" relationship between proteins and the living organism. Turning to the *Oxford English Dictionary*, the key for the code we are working in, we see that

> the "fifth essence" was a supposed substance distinct from the recognized four elements. What this fifth essence was, and where existing, was much disputed. Originally, it seems to have been the material of the starry heaven, as conceived by those who hesitated to identify it with "fire". Among the alchemists, it was usually supposed to be latent in all bodies, and to be capable of being extracted

from them by some recondite process; many thought that alcohol
was one of its forms. Others regarded the discovery of the "fifth
essence" as one of the unrealized aims of science, and attributed to
the hypothetical substance all sorts of miracle-properties. Hence
fifth essence or quintessence was used loosely in the various
senses "highly refined extract or essence" and "universal remedy."

At the same time that Gamow invokes the simple, seamless relationship between protein and living organisms, an entirely different and perhaps strangely complementary resonance is
produced. This is not, of course, to say that Gamow's use of the
metaphor of "essence" is only or wholly consonant with the alchemical definition offered above. But it is to say that the many
meanings of "essential" allow it to perform a very substantial, if
not alchemical, rhetorical function. It allows the relationship between this "translation" and the tremendous, if not vital, complexity of the living organism to be transformed into one that
invokes the "vital" nature of this enterprise while simultaneously effacing the distinction between reading and life, textuality and vitality. It also performs the double function of
allowing for the "coding" of life while preserving the attraction
of an ontological mystery. This double relation, which emerges
as an effect of the implosion of life and molecules, can be seen in
the rhetoric of contemporary research, a rhetoric that claims genome projects have only scientific and medical interest, while at
the same time they are sold as ontological research:

> One of the strongest arguments for supporting human genome
> projects is that they will provide knowledge about the determi-
> nants of the human condition. One group of scientists has urged
> support of human genome projects because sequencing the human
> genome will provide one of the most powerful tools humankind
> has ever had for deciphering the mysteries of its own existence.[24]

The "living organism" is the space or "hole" in which
Gamow's entire discussion takes place, its condition of possibility. Even while the explicit aim of Gamow's text, indeed of
molecular biology generally, is to determine and articulate the
fundamental chemical and physical mechanisms that make up
the "secret" or "book" of life, it is the very allure of the "essence
of life" that helps drive the investigation. The sense of "se-

crecy," "numerology," and religiosity that is invested in the "essential" relationship between DNA (numbers), proteins (words), and living organisms (life) provides at least a rhetorical tension between the project of demystifying "vitality" and discovering its "essence." It also provides a rhetorical tension within Gamow's text itself, as the possibly banal project of translation is explained by recourse to the most encrypted, untranslatable concept—life. By this I mean, of course, not that in any sense life is "really" immune to translation; rather that its definition is fraught with the kinds of metaphysical and fictional narratives that have made life, as an entity, opaque and endlessly available to investigation. Michel Foucault has shown that historically

> life does not constitute an obvious threshold beyond which entirely new forms of knowledge are required. It is a category of classification, relative like all other categories, to the criteria one adopts. And also, like them, subject to certain imprecisions as soon as the question of deciding its frontiers arises.[25]

The gap and border between DNA and proteins, numbers and words, codes and organisms is both the site of imprecision and the site of metaphorical intervention. The problem of translating "life" is one possible way of deciding on and effacing the border between textuality and vitality, a translation that appears within a historical moment in which life becomes "one object of knowledge among others," an object in and of language. It is a solution made possible by the simultaneous rhetorical displacement of the question of the organism and its return, a haunting trace of life that stalks the border between codes and bodies.

What, finally, is the effect of this scientific text on our present configuration as soon-to-be readers of the book of life? To the extent that the bookish or textual rhetoric of the genome functions as a popularizing and scientific metaphor for the Human Genome Initiative, Gamow's construction of the nucleic acid–protein relation as a process of translation provides the project at the very least with an unconcealed (so unconcealed that it is concealed) Christian rhetoric of the Word. Under this rubric, Gamow's metaphorics and their subsequent translation cast the genome mappers as scientific guardians of the Word. As the epigraph heading the present text should indicate, along with Gamow's description of the four-digital system of the DNA molecule as "the number of the beast," the writing of the genome as code and finally as "Book" makes Revelation possible. It also promises the possibility of an ending, a closure, an answer if not a complete or final solution. The metaphor of the book of life promises us that we can, after all, "understand what life is," if only we have the patience to read through till the last page. Unless of course we find that it reads, à la *Finnegans Wake*, "See page one."

Chapter 4

Tools for Talking
Human Nature, Weismannism, and the
Interpretation of Genetic Information

JAMES R. GRIESEMER

Too much has been taken for granted in the framework for describing biological "facts," and this makes it difficult to see clearly the implications of the Human Genome Initiative (HGI). The history of biology has much to teach about the social, ethical, political, and philosophical controversies raised by this initiative in biotechnology. The following are the main points I shall address: (1) the historical division of biology into sciences answering "how" or "why" questions lends the false impression that only one or the other kind of solution to a given problem is needed; (2) one root of this division is reflected in the distinction between germ and soma, leading to the false conception of reproduction as a flow of information; and (3) a significant social danger of the HGI is that it may slight further the role of organismal and population biology in interpreting molecular mechanisms whose control offers hope with respect to problems of human health.

I

Insofar as it has a biological basis, human "nature" has been interpreted in two fundamentally different ways: according to our (presumed) common underlying form and function, or according to our (presumed) common origin and subsequent diversification. Ernst Mayr has aptly sorted these two biological perspectives in accordance with two kinds of explanation: proximate and ultimate.[1] Proximate explanations answer "how" and "what" questions: how we as organisms function on the basis of what kind of material and organization. Ultimate explanations answer "why" questions: why we are as we are and for what historical reasons. In biology, proximate explanations are the province of sciences like embryology, anatomy, physiology, and genetics. Ultimate explanations are the province of evolutionary biology.

Explanations of human nature in biological terms tend toward either the proximate (how) or the ultimate (why) to the extent that they rely on one of two conflicting insights: that we are all essentially the same or that we are all essentially different. Identification of our nature in our biological similarity focuses attention on mechanisms (genetic, developmental, physological) that explain how similarities are generated. Identification of our nature in our biological differences focuses on the history of the origin and fate of variation in evolution. Because different biological sciences address the similarities and the differences, conflict can arise between scientists attempting to interpret biological research projects from differing perspectives.

Some controversial interpretations of the implications of the Human Genome Initiative depend on such conflict. Most of the scientists contributing to the HGI are molecular biologists who ask "how" questions about "the" genetic system in humans. For them, differences between people are anomalies or defects. For an evolutionary biologist, differences are the variation that fuels evolution. By linking arguments for pursuing the HGI to its "applications" (consequences for human health, understanding of ourselves as human beings), biologists have brought the conflict of perspectives on human nature to the center of the justification of the HGI. Where the molecular biologist finds a basis for the essence of human nature in the complete description of "the" human genome, the evolutionary biologist finds a basis (or, better, the lack of a basis) in the discovery of variation *wherever* one looks into human genomes.

Society and life have become increasingly "medicalized" and "reduced" to biology; and for all practical purposes, that means biology in response to "how" questions. While the HGI may result in new evolutionary insights, its avowed purpose and basis for federal support is its promise for medicine and society. Medicalization and reductionist thinking go hand in hand with the new prospects for manipulating our biological makeup and environmental conditions, medical diagnosis and therapeutic treatment.[2] But it is important to examine the HGI for *all* of its intended as well as unintended consequences, and not treat the consequences as spin-offs or side effects of a project in "basic" or fundamental biology.

Full examination requires consideration of the conflict between proximate and ultimate biological perspectives on the nature of human nature. To treat the HGI's implications for medicine, society, and our understanding of ourselves as spin-offs, as the Teflon of a government program to explore inner space, is to accept reductionism as a moral or political position. To argue this way one must assume that social problems have biotechnological solutions.[3] Philosophers try to minimize the number of assumptions lacking arguments, and this is one reason the HGI is of more than passing philosophical interest.

Compartmentalization of thinking into "how" versus "why" explanations, promoted by the historical division of labor in the biological sciences, exacerbates the problem of resolving controversy over genetic technologies. Compartmentalization suggests that the formulation of social problems in biological terms is relatively easy, while the solutions are complex and nearly intractable unless these are sought in terms of the lowest-level, proximate biological sciences. Disease? Eradicate it. How? Find a vaccine.

The proximate biological sciences have succeeded in no small measure because they have identified problems that concern relatively simple phenomena and require relatively simple solutions. "How" questions are formulated most simply if complexities are relegated to "context." One makes a mess of the question "How does the heart pump blood?" by starting with facts about human social structures critical for food production sufficient to nourish functioning human hearts. But these are nonetheless factors in a complete explanation of the pumping of blood. Biological "systems" are simple only if their environments are not included in the description. "Why" questions in biology are always comparative and can never avoid descriptions of context or environment for long.

Genetics is commonly offered as an example of a successful proximate science. Early in the twentieth century, the relatively simple problem of explaining how genes are transmitted from parents to offspring was distinguished from the vastly more complex problem of explaining how transmitted genes contribute to the developing organism and why they exist in the combinations produced by evolution. Thomas Hunt Morgan won a Nobel Prize in 1933 for his solution to the transmission problem—his "physical" theory of the genes as beads arranged on linear chromosomal threads—but the main problem of gene expression and distribution is with us still.

Similarly, the complexity of ecological, developmental, and evolutionary systems sometimes leads biologists to look with envy on the successes of physicists who are able to put their explanations in tractable, mathematical order. In both the development of organismal form and the dynamics of ecological systems, it seems clear what the problems are, but satisfactory solutions are lacking because of their descriptive complexity. These problems are even greater in humans, where the complexity of organismal interaction is compounded by extreme sociality.

The success of geneticists in simply describing the process of gene transmission by extracting a "doable" problem from the many interesting, but intransigent, ones is a tempting model for the treatment of social problems, especially those for which genetic technology has been developed: for example, cure or prevention of disease, protection of the species from the reproduction of the unfit, identification of criminals by DNA "fingerprinting," and a host of other "eugenic" measures that have fallen in and out of favor in this century as well as the last. The trouble with this strategy is that what *counts* as doable at any given time itself depends on the very social processes and problems the genetic technologist purports to engineer. For example, in order for a simple screening test for a genetic disease to be an effective means of reducing the incidence of that disease in a population, most of the population must be screened, those identified as having a predisposition to the disease or as carrying a certain gene must be counseled, and they must make the "right" decisions with regard to reproduction. But for this elaborate and complex social process to occur on a populational scale requires a substantial amount of *social* engineering: development of the biotechnology infrastructure to produce affordable screening kits, establishment of social and cultural institutions and norms that support screening and counseling, education in support of the "right" reproductive decisions, and so forth. Thus, genetic technological "fixes" do not circumvent the social solution of social problems; they serve only to focus our attention elsewhere in our *description* of the solution.

Numerous recent anthologies and symposia outline abundant ethical, moral, legal, medical, economic, and social problems raised by the Human Genome Initiative.[4] Unfortunately, the wealth of question-raising exercises has not been accompanied by sufficient challenging of assumptions to give much hope of progress. Too much is taken for granted in the framework of biological "facts" to see clearly the implications of the Human Genome Initiative.

The crucial insight underlying "how" explanations of our biological nature is that there is a common genetic system through which our heritage is passed to us as individual organisms, through which that heritage is displayed in development, and by means of which we pass it on to our children. Put differently, what is common to us all, what is native or innate, is genetic.[5] One sort of interpretation of human nature thus tends to focus on the possibility of a biological universal for humans: we all are caused by the same kind of genetic machinery.

The central insight of "why" explanations of our biological nature is that we are all different. The crucial ingredient of evolutionary change is variability. Whenever organisms are studied carefully variation is found, raising doubts that any *essential* similarity—even in our genes—can be found in our biology. Evolutionary explanations of human "nature" focus on our differences and lead to a view of our nature as inherently social and historical, rather than individual and mechanical: our nature is bound up in our participation in a certain sort of historical population as contributing parts. But this idea also leads evolutionists toward "population thinking" and rejection of the quest for essential properties: biological species are not the sorts of things that have essences.[6]

This conflict of perspectives on human nature seems built into biology itself. Evolutionary change can occur only if there is variation, and yet for the change to result in adaptation it must be heritable. Organisms must differ from, and yet resemble, their parents if evolution is to work. The opposition between "how" and "why" explanations also seems to bear this tension; yet they must work together, since they explain the same entities.

The opposition is illusory, however, and the illusion seems to grant authority to whichever perspective holds sway at any given moment in history. The nineteenth century after Darwin was a time of great interest in "why" questions and ultimate, evolutionary explanations. The twentieth century records the technologization and mechanization of biology and a shift toward "how" questions and the control of mechanisms, both as a method for investigating biological processes and as a way to improve the human condition.

Genetics and evolutionary explanations in biology appear to be autonomous only until the details of each are probed. The apparently universal genetic system, operating according to Mendel's laws and the principles of molecular genetics, seems to be a fixed basement upon which our explanations of particular human behaviors, physiologies, and morphologies must be built. But this system must itself have evolved: it is inconceivable that it sprang into existence fully formed. Its form and existence must be explained in evolutionary terms, probably in the context of no-longer-existing variants.[7]

By the same token, evolutionary theory depends upon the momentarily fixed facts of proximate biology, including genetics. While Theodosius Dobzhansky's famous adage is true, "Nothing in biology makes sense except in the light of evolution," it is also true that evolution does not make sense except in the light of the rest of biology.[8] Without stable concepts of genetic system and ecological context, evolutionary explanation of lineages of organisms related by descent would be meaningless. Put generally, evolutionary explanation occurs against a field of fixed proximate explanations; genetic, embryological, physiological, and morphological explanation occurs against a field of fixed ultimate explanations. That the two are intertwined should not surprise us, but the implications of this hybrid character of biological explanation for our reasoning about human nature are both profound and hard to discern in the specialized and compartmentalized discussions of professional biologists.

II

Let us turn to strategies of reasoning about human nature in terms of current biological theories and the background of biological "facts" used to trace the implications of the Human Genome Initiative. This is one place where philosophers have an important role to play: interpreting the impact of biological theories underpinning such major technological programs as the HGI. The elements of this ambitious international project have been well described elsewhere.[9]

It is worth reflecting on the history of biological theory because the perception is strong that the *combination* of theories and concepts we have today grew coherently from one concerted techno-scientific effort to increase biological knowledge; this perception reflects a belief that scientists know and accept biological theory as a single whole. Our image of the body of scientific knowledge and its implications for society, murky though it is, is a good deal clearer than our image of the scientific work that went to make it up. Clarification of history and its philosophical interpretation is one antidote to facile conceptions of scientific knowledge and is therefore an important first step toward properly tracing the wider implications of the development and possession of that knowledge.

Our scientific image supposes that evolutionary theory describes how natural selection favors individuals with certain genes over those with other genes. It further supposes that molecular genetics describes the common system by which genes act as their own agents, copying themselves in the process of DNA replication as well as coding for those proteins which make the bodies that act on the genes' behalf in the Darwinian struggle. Genes make more genes, and genes make the body. This dual causal role lends support to the metaphorical description of genes as "master molecules" governing all the significant events in the body, which passively abides.[10] The body is slave to its molecular masters, and the fields of science *describing* the body are also slaves (i.e., derivative, reducible) to the master field, genetics. The impression that genes are master molecules is strengthened by their apparent theoretical robustness: they *must* be important if they are central players in the "how" explanations of molecular genetics *and* in the "why" explanations of evolutionary biology. Historically, though, genes were not always the central players, and the route by which they have become so depends not only on the development of biological theory per se, but also on the guiding metaphors used to *express* theory in a manner useful to proximate and ultimate biologists alike.

One of the most important guiding metaphors of late-nine-teenth-century biology is "Weismannism." This is the doctrine of the continuity of the germ cells and discontinuity of the body cells, or somata.[11] August Weismann, like many of his contemporaries, sought a unified theory of heredity to explain how organismal characters and form are generated as well as how such features are transmitted from one generation to the next.

Weismann thought of the cell as containing a hierarchy of determining units, with simple molecules at the lowest level. He thought that different genetic determinants would be sequestered in different daughter cells when each parent cell divides during development. To explain genetic transmission Weismann postulated that, unlike the somatic cells that form the bulk of the body, those destined to form germ cells (sperm or eggs) would carry an entire complement of genetic determinants and so pass on the total hereditary legacy of the parent to the offspring. Since only the germ cells, not the body—or somatic—cells, contain the entire complement of genetic material and since only they pass on their genetic material to offspring, only alterations to the germ cells (mutations) can produce hereditary modifications in offspring. Thus, according to Weismannism, the continuity of germ cells from generation to generation is required to explain the phenomena of heredity.

Weismannism is the basis for much of our causal talk in theoretical and applied biology, but the history of Weismannism as a guiding metaphor suggests a gradual impoverishment of the conceptual tools available for expressing the cause–effect relations investigated by modern science. Some of this impoverishment traces to a reliance on certain visual representations of Weismann's ideas. The substitution of a simple, abstract visual representation for a complex theory is commonplace in science, but the consequences of such substitutions are rarely examined.

It is often observed that technical advance frequently outpaces our ability to comprehend its consequences.[12] Genetic engineering provokes predictions of dire ethical, social, and political ills in addition to promises of new basic knowledge and medical treatments. Some fears expressed in the recombinant-DNA debates of the 1970s already reveal such a "comprehension gap." The reason given is usually the failure of old scientific, moral, political, legal, medical, and social concepts to encompass the new developments. But this is only a partial truth. An important additional cause is a gap that arises when the representational repertoire of technologists is not sufficiently developed alongside the techniques, skills, and practices that contribute to new technology. In other words, the lagging means to *express* concepts may cause comprehension (and dissemination) to lag behind innovation.

The rate of progress in molecular biology since the 1940s is great enough to have caused a comprehension gap between biologists' experimental procedures, technical capacities, and understanding of basic biological mechanisms, on the one hand, and the relatively outmoded language and visual representations used to describe and interpret their advances, on the other. The most commonly used language of cause and effect is inadequate to describe and analyze the conduct and results of empirical biological research, much less to present interpretations of its social, ethical, and policy implications to the public. As the technology required to complete the Human Genome Initiative becomes more sophisticated, this gap will widen and increase the difficulty of translating technological capacity into sound—and just—social policy. Examining the historical development of tools for talking about causality is a step toward narrowing the gap between technological capability and understanding.

Weismannism's most influential form of expression is cause–effect diagrams. The great historical influence of diagrams produced by Weismann's commentators depends on a number of factors. One is that diagrams (and visual displays generally) are typically treated as representations rather than hypotheses.[13] Visual representations in science substitute a fixed structure in place of a dynamic process of argumentation and evaluation of evidence; they concentrate power, in the sense that the roles of many elements of a network of ideas, people, places, and phenomena are attributed to the few elements appearing in the visual display.[14] Insofar as diagrams of Weismannism are taken to represent Weismann's ideas, they can be treated as surrogates for those views and the arguments that led to them. More important, the biological *phenomena* to which Weismann directed his attention are then also taken to be represented by the structures depicted in the diagrams. So, the historical circumstances in which diagrams of Weismannism came to be accepted as representative of Weismann's ideas are critical for understanding those diagrams' power. One aspect of the accumulation of power by a diagram is the degree of simplification it offers in comparison to the things it represents.

In its diagram form, Weismannism has become standard for describing biological causality and for attributing causal agency and responsibility in biological explanations. With the decline of Lamarckism, the Weismannian core of neo-Darwinism (the combination of Darwinism, Mendelism, and Weismannism) is rarely challenged. The core of neo-Darwinism is in need of reexamination and most probably in need of revision: Weismannism is a guiding metaphor that both gives a false picture of the theory it is supposed to depict and straitjackets modern talk about biological causation and agency.[15]

The current weight placed on genes in the interpretation of biological causation, and hence the weight placed on genetic technology in future solutions to human health problems, depends on two historical facts: the separation of problems of heredity and development at the turn of the century, and the role of Weismannism in rejecting the inheritance of acquired characteristics.[16] There is little doubt that genetics made progress as a science owing to the idealization of genetic transmission as autonomous from development, and that Weismannism secured the separation of these problems in the domain of evolutionary biology. This separation is maintained in part because of the convenient but misleading visual logic of biological causation inherent in diagrams of Weismannism drawn by geneticists.

The noninheritance of acquired somatic characteristics is an implication of Weismann's theory of the continuity of the germ-plasm and the discontinuity of the soma.[17] This theory has been "summarized" in a famous diagram in E. B. Wilson's widely used textbook.[18] Wilson's diagram is a vast simplification and idealization of Weismann's theory. It depicts causal arrows from germ cell to germ cell in a continuous causal history, causal arrows from germ cells (zygotes) to somatic cells, but no causal arrows from somatic cells back to germ cells. Somata form a discontinuous "line of succession," and the two modes of causation, autocatalysis and heterocatalysis, both emanate from germ cells. In such a scheme, it only makes sense to attribute responsibility for control of both gene transmission and development to germ cells: they are the only causal agents depicted. Even if somatic cells are altered during the course of development,

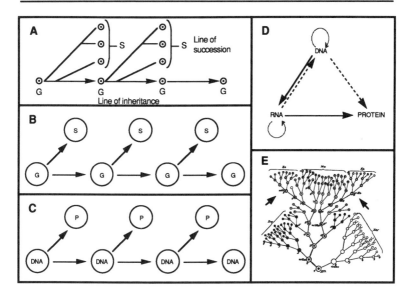

Figure 4.1. Weismannism in Diagrams. *A*. Structure of E. B. Wilson's representation of Weismannism, after Wilson (1896, p. 13, fig. 5; see note 18). S = soma; G = germ cell. *B*. A simplification of Wilson's diagram. *C*. A modern molecular representation of the central dogma of molecular biology, showing isomorphism with diagram B. Diagrams B and C are after Maynard Smith (1965, p. 67, fig. 8; see note 20). *D*. The central dogma, after Francis Crick (1970, p. 561, fig. 2; see note 19). *E*. Representation of the continuity of the germ plasm and discontinuity of the soma, reproduced from August Weismann (1893, p. 196, fig. 16; see note 17), showing a zygote (*bottom*) dividing into the cells of the three germ layers, continuity from zygote through cell generation 12 (*top*), and differentiation of germ cells in generation 9 (*at arrows*).

there is no causal propagation of such alterations beyond that particular individual (see Fig. 4.1*A*).

The theory expressed in Wilson's diagram was given modern form in Crick's "central dogma" of molecular biology.[19] Genetic information flows from nucleic acids to proteins; once it flows into proteins, it cannot get out again (see Fig. 4.1*D*). Maynard Smith has compared Weismannism to the central dogma, making the historical connection between the two explicit.[20] The central dogma forms the basis for many of our current attributions of biological causality, agency, and even responsibility.

While it was originally characterized in terms of *information* flow, the central dogma is now widely read as a statement about material agency, reflecting its visual isomorphism to Weismannism: DNA *makes* more copies of itself and also *makes* protein. This reading attributes the same causal asymmetry to genes and proteins that Wilson's version of Weismannism attributed to germ cells and somatic cells (cf. Fig. 4.1*B, C*). Nucleic acids are the only causal agents depicted in Crick's and Maynard Smith's diagrams.

Wilson's original diagram, however, distorts Weismann's theory in important ways and, by simplifying, Wilson has inadvertently impoverished the language of biological causality. In his later publications, Weismann expressed his theory as the continuity of the germ *plasm* and the discontinuity of the soma, not as the continuity of the germ *cells*. The germ plasm is the molecular material (later found to be genes on chromosomes) that is carried inside the nuclei of germ cells. Its continuity is ensured by the normal process of cell division.[21] Weismann took great pains to distinguish his theory from the one Wilson's diagram depicts.[22] Germ plasm may be continuous even while germ cells are not if the cells carrying germ plasm undergo differentiation in development. Weismann's own depiction of his theory is quite different from Wilson's.[23] It shows only an idealized part of a single organism's development. Moreover, it shows that the first germ cells arise *as products of somatic differentiation* in a given cell generation. There is a hiatus of some number of cell generations between the germ cells of the parents and the germ cells of the offspring. In contrast to the discontinuity of germ cells in Weismann's view, his diagram shows that the germ *plasm* is continuous in its passage from zygote to primordial germ cells (*UrKeimzellen*) through somatic intermediates, while the somatoplasm is a discontinuous product of germinal plasm (see Fig. 4.1*E*).

Acceptance of the causal structure of Wilson's diagram or its modern molecular counterpart has spread widely and influenced the thinking of most biologists. Because of its simplicity and portability, Wilson's diagram is likely to exert strong social influence through its representation of our deepest understanding of biological causation and the need to simplify when biologists interpret their work for the public. Weismannism is entrenched in our thought in part because its diagrammatic representation is clear, simple, easily expressed, and portable. But Weismann's original argument, using diagrams to *illustrate* ideas previously formulated has been inverted. Now we use language to formulate a theory on the basis of the abstraction previously expressed visually in Wilson's diagram. Because the diagram Wilson produced is wrong, its entrenchment in biological thinking has led to strange contortions as developmental biologists try to express what is wrong with Weismannism while relying on the very causal framework it expresses. Developmental processes are often much more complex than the simple picture given by Weismannism, but expressing such relations is made more difficult by the entrenched language assigning a dual causal role to germ plasm (genes) and no causal role to the soma (body). The difficulty is compounded in the Crick–Maynard Smith equation of flow of genetic information and flow of genetic matter, for it permits interpretation of the purely abstract information relation as causal.

In the end, biologists trying to bring development and genetics together in a more adequate picture of proximate biology are *reinventing* aspects of Weismann's theory, but they (and the public) are hobbled by Weismannism, which girds the framework of our biological thought and language. As it has receded from view in the wake of interest in molecular phenomena, and therefore from explicit discussion, Weismannian assumptions have become difficult even to detect and therefore to question.

Emerging from the contrast between Weismannism and Weismann are several critical facts with implications for the interpretation of the Human Genome Initiative, whose goal is to increase the quantity of genetic information. First and foremost, Weismann's theory implies that heredity is a problem *of* development, not an autonomous problem. This is familiar ground for biologists, but it is difficult to express using the language of Weismannian diagrams. The continuity of the germ plasm but not of the germ cells is a fact that can be understood in terms of the developmental process of somatic differentiation, as Weismann saw. It is also a fact that must be explained evolutionarily, since the point at which germ cells differentiate in the soma is an evolved property critical in the evolution of individuality itself: Weismannism is true only in those rare cases where germ cells differentiate in the first cell generation of development.[24] Thus, the truth or falsity of Weismannism, like the truth or falsity of

Mendelism, is a *consequence* of evolution, not its cause. As a result, proximate explanations of genetic information make no sense except in the light of evolution.

Second, since the continuity of germ plasm is a function of somatic differentiation, the Wilson diagram of Weismannism is fundamentally wrong: there *should be* causal arrows from soma to soma. The body *is* a cause in inheritance, a fact that is fundamental to evolutionary biology. Proteins and other cell components are causally responsible for the events of cell division and DNA replication. The problem of interpreting genetic information is thus more subtle than either Weismannism—stated in terms of cells and protoplasm—or the central dogma—stated in terms of informational macromolecules—can express. The problem is to explain how the causal path from soma to soma influences the *flow* of genetic information without violating the facts of molecular biology. While the abstract heredity relation may be aptly described in molecular terms as a flow of genetic information, reproduction—the process that causes inheritance—is not a flow of information but, rather, a flow of information-bearing matter. This flow has to do with both populational change in the distribution of genes and developmental control of gene expression. Understanding the flow of genetic information should therefore be a *joint* concern of proximate and ultimate biology, not the exclusive province of one sort of science or scientist vested with sole authority for interpretation. Pronouncements by molecular biologists on the topic of "human nature" must be tempered by responses of evolutionary biologists on the significance of molecular information and variation.

Part of the fear that attends support for the Human Genome Initiative is that as we push toward molecular-technological solutions to health problems, we will cede further authority to specialized scientists who are ill-equipped to trace the consequences of their technologies out of the laboratories and into the complex world of a modern society. Scientific reductionism seems to lead to changes in the social, moral, and political balance of power. But to evaluate the consequences of putting trust and faith in molecular biotechnologists, consider the problem structures and discipline structures described in the present essay. "How biologists" (a.k.a. mechanism or proximate biologists) formulate solvable problems by dividing the world into a relatively simple "system" and a relatively complex, but ignorable, "environment." "Why biologists" (a.k.a. comparative or ultimate biologists) formulate solvable problems by comparison among multiple entities, whether simple or complex. For the social, biological, and health problems served by the HGI, the genome is treated as a simple system in a complex context (the body, the population, the society, the world).

III

When it comes to anticipating the future consequences of the HGI, we tend to examine claims made about the "systems" constructed by the advocates and to assess how these systems will be received in the somatic, populational, or social context *as defined by the molecular technologist*. But such contexts can change in ways that make anticipated outcomes meaningless. The real issue in evaluating the HGI is not whether the sequence data will be produced (which seems inevitable) or whether it will be put to use in any particular way or to any particular end. Rather, the issue is whether authority to define the parameters of the evaluation—specifically, what assumptions to make about the social contexts in which the sequence data will be interpreted—should rest with the technologists or with others in society. Put baldly, should Walter Gilbert, or James Watson, or Leroy Hood be permitted to characterize the *relation* between gene and body, or gene and population, or gene and society that will form the basis of public assessment regarding whether or how the HGI should go forward or not?

The risk in accepting molecular technologists' predictions rather than taking into account evaluations of other scientists (in particular, population and evolutionary biologists, let alone nonscientists), can be seen by building upon some recently discussed examples.[25] The naiveté of eugenicists early in this century, who thought that genetic defects could be removed by selective-breeding programs, has long been dismissed as the mistake of an era in which scientists failed to take into account the complexities of their subject and the limitations of their theories. The fact that most genetically caused diseases are recessive means that there are always many more carriers of apparently normal health in a population than there are afflicted individuals. Selection against the afflicted can at best reduce the frequency of such genes to that found in carriers. Selection against carriers based on molecular detection of recessive genes (pressure not to reproduce, selective abortion, sterilization) can at best reduce the frequency of such genes to that produced by new mutation, not eliminate such genes altogether. The greater caution of modern geneticists, owing to their historical loss of innocence as a result of the disasters of eugenic social policy, would *seem* to warrant greater confidence in their current pronouncements about the likely health benefits of the new genetic technologies.

Likewise, it is well appreciated that the health benefits of the anticipated increase in knowledge about genetic disease will depend on the extent to which information can be communicated to consumers and translated into "correct" reproductive decisions. Until the day of mandatory universal gene therapy has come, the main mechanisms for prevention and "cure" of genetic disease will remain counseling of prospective parents and elective abortion. The predictions of technologists as to the future health benefits of the HGI rest on the assumptions that genetic counseling will be effective and that abortion will be available. That these assumptions are well known and widely discussed seems to justify further confidence in the prognostic abilities of technologists: whether such assumptions are true or not, the technologists at least seem to be taking the right (i.e., familiar) kind of assumptions into account.

If the perspectives of organismal and population biology are ignored, however, other kinds of issues regarding the social context in which genetic information is received are not so clear. A molecular technologist might predict that genetic diseases will increase over time owing to an increase in mutation rates associated with the fact that mothers (in most Western countries) are tending to have children later in life. Since older mothers are more likely to have children with genetic defects than younger ones, it might be expected that the rate of mutation—and with it the rate of genetic defects in a population—would go up. But this is a case where simple extrapolation from the individual case to the population misleads. Delaying reproduction till later in life certainly increases the risk to a given fetus, but one must also consider the whole reproductive span of mothers in order to extrapolate to the population. It appears that not only are mothers having children later, but having children is becoming more concentrated in the middle of the period of fertility. Thus, *average* age at reproduction (and with it, possibly, the average rate of genetic damage) is declining.[26] The details of this demographic story are complex, but the lesson is simple. The consequences of the molecular technologist's story about genetic damage increasing with the age of the mother cannot be extrapolated to society without considering the whole demographic pattern of reproduction. The issue has as much to do with the distribution of reproduction within and among parents in a population as it does with the molecular mechanisms by which genetic damage increases with the age of the mother. One wonders whether gene sequencers know any more demography than the ordinary nonscientist knows genetics.

Another population consideration in predicting the incidence of genetic disease concerns patterns of mating. Since most genetic diseases are caused by recessive genes, "outbreeding"—mating with a genetically unrelated individual—can decrease disease incidence while *increasing* the total number of genes for a disease in a population. Partly this is because outbreeding lowers the chance of two carriers from the same population mating and producing an afflicted offspring. Consideration of only a single population might lead to the inference that if measures such as genetic testing and counseling and elective abortion are not taken to reduce the number of carriers, then the number of afflicted cannot be reduced. But the problem clearly concerns patterns of migration and interpopulation marriage as much as it does the molecular mechanisms behind "recessive-caused" disease. Who in the mid-1980s, when the HGI was initiated, would have predicted the fall of the Soviet Union, or the consequent changes in global migration rates and patterns, or the possible increase in the ratio of outbreeding to inbreeding this might cause? How often is migration of peoples considered in arguments for or against the health benefits of HGI?

The lesson of these examples is clear. While genetic research advances by dividing the world into simple systems and complex environments, social problems are not solved merely by the control and manipulation of such isolated systems. One must take into account, explicitly or implicitly, both system and context; and molecular biologists have not the expertise, nor should they have the authority, to impose their beliefs and assumptions about context in a social evaluation of the HGI.

The articulation of joint concern is important for interpreting our biological nature(s) precisely because it will (and should) shape how we understand biological causation and will thus constrain how we attribute biological agency and responsibility to various entities. If the soma causes the continuity of the germ plasm by causing a flow of genetic material in reproduction, it seems implausible to think of genes as master molecules and implausible to attribute causal responsibility—for behavior, intelligence, or disease—to them alone rather than to the network of interacting parts.

The Human Genome Initiative promises a revolution in the quality and quantity of our information about human genes. Much is already known about which genes are where and what a few of them do, but the revolution in quality that the HGI may bring will be owing to its promise of completeness. A complete map of the human genome will revolutionize two spheres. Scientifically, complete genetic information will enable basic, applied, and clinical research in a degree of detail and precision not possible with incomplete information. Socially, the *idea* of the information, of a complete book of human "nature," will transform our conception of ourselves as we discover what scientists, clinicians, corporations, and governments do with the information.

The Human Genome Initiative's "book of human nature" will mean different things to scientists and to the rest of the public, just as other books mean different things to writers and readers. For scholars, books afford starting points for fresh investigation. The main impact of the HGI for scientists will lie in its role as a tool in the construction of new knowledge about genome organization, gene expression, development, and disease. For all but the biotechnologists whose research is to improve the tools, the work of DNA sequencing and mapping is tedious and scientifically uninteresting, its results being only intermediate steps on the way to interesting and important questions about fundamental biology and human health. For the public, books embody the state of knowledge of the experts. Their significance lies in the sense of completeness they afford, in their summation of worldly knowledge as a "body." The HGI will index what scientists know about us as genetic beings and will guide how we think about ourselves.

Nonscientists must be careful, however, not to let the per-

ceived causal role of genes and the consequent authority of geneticists over other biological specialists be interpreted as
justifying a moral or political authority on the part of geneticists
over public consumers of the products of genetic research. The
triple analogy—gene is to body as geneticist is to biologist as
genetic knowledge is to the body politic—fails in each of its
terms. The dual role of genes depicted in Weismannian diagrams is a misreading of Weismann's theory relating heredity,
development, and evolution. The modern gloss of reproduction
as a flow of genetic information shields genetic explanations
from significant complexities of development and, through its
prevarication on causality, simultaneously shields arguments
for biotechnological solutions to social problems of human
health from complexities of social engineering. The authority of
geneticists as both producers and interpreters of genetic information—the heritage of the Wilsonian reading of Weismann—
is challenged by the facts of development. These facts have so
far defied "reduction" to molecular biology, and they give pause
to most scientists about the enthusiastic rhetoric of HGI zealots.
The conception of science as serving two distinct roles—as
autonomous, objective producer of knowledge and also as interested solver of social problems—is challenged by the observation that the former is an interacting, integral part of the latter,
not an autonomous agent: genetic engineering is *social engineering by other means,* and it is up to society to determine whether
the biotechnological approach is acceptable.

Weismannism's pivotal role in reshaping the perceived social implications of biology in the nineteenth century may, if it
continues to guide interpretation of biological causation, play a
continuing role in shaping our scientific and public perceptions
of the importance of genetic information. By the same token,
reform of the guiding metaphor could be an instrument for social change: a new metaphor, diagram, or analysis of biological
causation could reinterpret the triple analogy, allowing us to envision different roles for the public, scientists, and other would-
be users of biological information, genetic or otherwise.

The concept of genetic information must be deeply embedded within an evolutionary framework if the errors of Weismannism are to be corrected. If Weismannism is wrong because it
attributes causal efficacy in genetics and development to genes
and not to the soma, an alternative causal picture may displace

genes from their status as master molecules and raise anew questions about how "genetic" information "flows." This displacement in turn might help to empower individuals as biological agents whose autonomy is threatened by a reductionist view of organisms at the mercy of their genes.

The acceptance of Weismannism is one critical step along the way toward accepting the triple analogy, which in turn is a step toward allowing scientists to speak for us by virtue of their authority to interpret causality. But the basis for their authority in the first place is their success in establishing the asymmetrical causal relation between gene and body and the consequent success of the analogy between gene and body, on the one hand, and analyzer of gene (geneticist) and analyzer of body (other biologists, social scientists, citizens, etc.) on the other. If the analogy fails because geneticists have failed to establish the causal asymmetry between gene and body, then there is no reason to accept their claim to political, social, or moral authority on that basis. Empowerment of the nonscientist follows from a denial that the scientist has sufficient knowledge to decide social questions.

The implications of substantial changes in ways of talking about biological causes for how the public (and, probably, scientists as well) would interpret the significance of the Human Genome Initiative are potentially enormous. If the body or the social group (rather than the genome alone) is causally responsible for our nature, then the book of human nature is far from being written just by virtue of the complete specification of human genetic information in the Weismannian sense. Many proponents of the Human Genome Initiative believe its value lies in the advances in developmental genetics research it will afford. Reshaping the guiding metaphors used to interpret the genome's causal significance will supply this enlightened perspective to the rest of society.

Chapter 5

Master Molecules

EVELYN FOX KELLER

The idea that organisms, even human organisms, are reducible to—and hence representable by—their genes surely goes back to the early days of genetics. But with the successes of modern molecular biology and its identification of DNA as the molecular constituent of genes, the concept of the DNA as a "master molecule," controlling the structure, behavior, and development of living organisms, has earned the status of the "master concept" of biology. For the past three and a half decades, this concept has controlled the development of biological science as forcefully as genes themselves have been presumed to control the subjects of that science. The emergence of the Human Genome Initiative in the late twentieth century is surely a manifestation of the success of this concept; at the same time, its advocacy has served to further that success dramatically, promising, as it does, that the sequence of our DNA can reveal to us who and what we are—that is, "what it means to be human."

The current success of genetic determinism, rampant today not only in biology but in the culture at large, suggests a need to reexamine both the logical and the empirical content of this very notion of genes as master molecules. Accordingly, I want first to review briefly some elementary considerations about what genes can and cannot do (even in principle) and about what genetics can and cannot, even in principle, study. In this context, I then want to look at what modern molecular genetics has actually taught us about how genes function in practice; and, finally, at the end of my essay, I want, also very briefly, to consider some of the implications of these observations for the role of molecular genetics in medicine and human health.

Genetic Determinism

The principle of genetic determinism, especially when taken to imply that the organism can be its genetic constituents, depends on a prior notion of genes as active agents. Yet, for all organisms, even for organisms lacking in the complex sorts of behavior that we often attribute to "minds" or "souls," indeed even for bacteria, this notion can be—in fact, generally is—highly misleading. Genes may well encode the vital information required for the unfolding of the organism in development, but they do not in themselves constitute sufficient cause for that unfolding, and in no sense can they be taken to be adequate physical or conceptual proxies of the organism in question. Take, for example, the idea of locating "a gene for X" in the exceptionally simple case of a gene identified with a particular enzyme. What we mean by that expression is that we have identified a stretch of DNA which, when inserted into a system, is capable of (1) locating and translating into a protein some particular sequence of nucleotides contained in that stretch of DNA, and (2) utilizing that resultant protein in the expression of what we call a trait. Only then can a given stretch of DNA be said to "code for" that trait. In other words, the idea of "a gene for X" already presupposes the existence of an organism capable of identifying, translating, interpreting, and making productive use of a particular gene.

Similarly, genetics is a science that proceeds through the analysis of functional failures in an already existing organism, through the analysis of departures from some preexisting functional norm. Genes are identified and located by their failure—that is, through the study of mutations, which function, if you will, as maps for misreading. We might even say that mutations "cause" such misreadings. But the further claim that the normal allele (that genetic form which is not mutant) "causes" a proper reading does not follow, either logically or physiologically. Such an inference appears to make sense only to the extent that the entire physical-chemical apparatus of the organism and its environment are effaced.

It was precisely this problem that caused such massive resistance from embryologists in the early days of genetics, and that helped maintain so large a gap between embryology and genetics in the first half of the twentieth century. The familiar argument made by many embryologists—that genes could not account for "fundamental" traits, but only for "trivial" ones— was based on their commonsense observation that the mutations geneticists studied represented, virtually by definition, mere modifications of an already existing functional form. Somewhat astonishingly (at least in retrospect), geneticists were able to counter such arguments successfully by pointing to mutations that affected vital functions (e.g., respiration) even while they were unable to address the underlying complaint.[1] Today, however—now that the basic role of genes is no longer contested—this intuition of an earlier generation of embryologists can be readily granted—if not by geneticists, then at least by molecular biologists.[2]

A more general point central to the issue of the causal role of genes is that all biological functions are composite functions, involving the correct "reading" of many genes. The more complex the function, the more genes are likely to be involved. What genetics can and often does enable us to do is to identify aberrations in some component part that lead to failure of the composite function—always, however, relative to the other components of that function and almost always relative to particular environmental conditions.[3]

One might conclude, and indeed for many years geneticists did so conclude, that what I am describing as an insufficiency of genetic analysis for the understanding of normal function is merely a consequence of the fact that we have not yet identified all the relevant genes. If a single gene can give only part of the story, then all we have to do is to locate more genes. But this kind of thinking seems to reflect what I might call a "beanbag" conception of the organism, harking back to what Ernst Mayr long ago—and somewhat disparagingly—described as "beanbag genetics." If the organism is seen as a beanbag of traits, corresponding to a beanbag of genes, with one gene corresponding to one trait (the model that in fact prevails in quantitative genetics), then normal function, indeed health, merely requires a beanbag of normal genes. The problem with this model is that it cannot generate an organism. A pot of normal genes can generate only a pot of enzymes, and even this requires the preexistence of the requisite machinery for translation and enzyme synthesis. More seriously, however, the ultimate measure of whether such enzymes are or are not functional must be provided by the organism itself. This simple fact, so conspicuous to developmental biologists, and so peculiarly irrelevant to the history of genetics and molecular biology, lies at the core of all efforts to represent organisms by the sum total of their genes—that is, at the core of the program of genetic reductionism.

The reason this problem has been irrelevant to the history of genetics and molecular biology is that, until now, it has in no way interfered with the remarkable successes of these disciplines, at least in their own terms. Surely, the high point of this history was the identification of DNA as the genetic material, alongside the discovery in 1953 that the double-helical structure of DNA provides a simple mechanism for genetic replication and that its nucleotide sequence provides an equally simple mechanism for encoding the information that could specify sequences of amino acids. By 1960, the successes of molecular biology included, as well, accounts of the processes of transcription and translation required in the actual mechanics of protein synthesis. These staggering accomplishments swept the entire domain of biology. Not only had mechanisms for the replication and transcription of DNA been elaborated, but in 1961 François Jacob and Jacques Monod had also demonstrated an elementary mechanism for regulation (the operon) which, even though worked out for only the lowly bacterium *Escherichia coli*, was widely seen as providing a prototype for regulatory processes in all organisms, even the elephant.[4] Emboldened by such success, Jacob and Monod could conclude their historic paper by writing:

> The discovery of regulator and operator genes, and of repressive regulation of the activity of structural genes, reveals that the genome contains not only a series of blueprints, but a coordinated program of protein synthesis and the means of controlling its execution.[5]

Everyone, it seems, was convinced, including even many biologists of development. Joseph Needham was of the demurrers. In 1968 he reminisced:

> I remember saying in lectures that "the genes certainly determine whether an organism has brown eyes or blue eyes, but do they really settle whether it has a liver or a hepatopancreas?" . . . We were not sure in those days that "the specific, generic, and even

class characters of organisms" with all their profound differences
in fundamental bodily pattern and function, could be attributed
entirely to their genetic equipment without cytoplasmic responsibility; and, if everyone nowadays accepts this, is it not an act of
faith rather than a proven scientific doctrine?[6]

To most readers of the time, however, such an "act of faith"
appeared to have been overwhelmingly borne out. Indeed, although the operon model did not in fact offer any resolution at
all to the problem of how the orderly differential activation of
genes in space and time is effected, the mere fact that Jacob and
Monod were addressing the issue of regulation seemed like
something of a lifeline.

An earlier generation of embryologists had warned of the
"Wanderlust" of geneticists[7] and the "powers of appropriation"[8]
of genetics; by this time, though, such overt expressions of resistance had largely disappeared. In the face of the overwhelming success of molecular biology, fifty years of resistance were
now being supplanted by strategies of accommodation. The renaming of "embryology" as "developmental biology" in the late
1950s and early 1960s provided one such strategy. The history of
this renaming, along with the adoption of genetic determinism
as an "act of faith" by developmental biologists, clearly merits
study in its own right, but for my purposes here, a few brief
comments should suffice. First of all, the term "developmental
biology" was new and untainted—either by the prejudices of its
predecessors or by the charges of mysticism that had in the intervening years descended on these once great names.[9] Equally
important, it had the ring of universality. Free of the distinctly
metazoan bias explicit in the term "embryology," "developmental biology" was far better suited to the new ordering that posi-
tioned E. coli as representative of the entire biotic domain. In
such a climate, any reminder that the work of Jacob and Monod
did not actually bear on chickens and eggs, but only on single-
celled organisms that do not undergo basic processes of differentiation, seemed a minor and inconsequential carp.

For the present discussion, however, the principal point is
that, by the end of the 1960s, proclamations of a convergence
between genetics and developmental biology were both widely
heard and widely believed. Yet, Needham was right: this confidence, despite the "one gene, one enzyme" hypothesis of

George Beadle and Edward Tatum, and even despite Jacob and Monod's analysis of the operon, was more an "act of faith" than it was a demonstrable proposition. In fact, well into the 1980s, molecular genetics still had little to say about the thorny and stubbornly recalcitrant problem of what differentiated the regulatory processes, or the DNA, of some cells from those of others.

Over the past ten years, thanks largely to the development of recombinant-DNA technology, the influx of the techniques and mind-set of genetics into developmental biology seems finally to have begun to pay off. Extraordinary progress is now being made in our understanding of the mechanics of regulation, of how particular genes get turned on and off, and even in the identification of genes involved in developmental processes. Developmental genetics is today the hottest field of biology, and the work now being done suggests that the long-awaited rapprochement between developmental biology and genetics is on its way. For many, current successes in this area are taken as a vindication of belief in the power of genes to "control" development. A closer look, however, suggests that the terms of this rapprochement are turning out to be rather different from those envisaged in the one gene, one enzyme hypothesis of Beadle and Tatum, or even in Jacob and Monod's operon, and certainly different from those of beanbag genetics.

Indeed, it is one of the great ironies of the Human Genome Initiative that, while relying on and fostering both the notion of DNA as master molecule and the conception of genes as exclusive loci of biological control, this program has actually contributed to a shift in focus: away from genes as causal agents and to genes as components of more-complex networks that implicate the entire organism. There are even indications that some of the experimental work this very program sponsors has already begun to subvert the simplistic model on which it relies.

After three decades of faith in the unidirectional control exerted by genes on the organisms they "direct," the language of developmental geneticists has begun to shift increasingly to the control that organisms exert on their genes. In a recent article in *Scientific American* titled "Smart Genes," the author tells us that

> the mystery of *how developing organisms choreograph the activity of their genes* so that cells form and function at the right place and at the right time is now being solved. Hundreds of experiments have

shown that *organisms control most of their genes, most of the time, by regulating transcription,* which is used to make the myriad proteins that make one cell different from another. "That gene control is achieved by regulating transcription is the main lesson of molecular biology in the past 20 years," says Eric H. Davidson . . . at the California Institute of Technology.[10]

A few sentences later, the author again quotes Davidson, who coined the term "smart genes," describing his search for the "brain of the smart gene" not in the genes themselves, but in a complex of proteins (known as the transcription complex), a "sloppy computer" that is now seen as the locus of decisionmaking. Molecular genetics has clearly come a long way since the days of beanbag genetics, and possibly even since the days of master molecules.

Why, then, am I so concerned about an article of faith that may in fact be on its way out? Partly, I am interested in the historical force that the language of master molecules and genetic determinism has been—and still is—exerting, even in those areas where it is being subverted. More generally, though, I am concerned about the extent to which such language has taken on a life of its own, more or less independent of the subversive potential of actual experimental findings. The very rhetoric invoked to sell the Human Genome Initiative, at a time when much of the work on regulatory mechanisms had already begun to undermine that rhetoric, bears this out. And it is the old rhetoric, rather than the shift in language demanded by current research, that has done so much to support the rise of confidence in genetic determinism within popular culture. It is also this older rhetoric that has exerted so worrisome an influence on general, and even medical, conceptions of health and disease, and it is to this issue I want now to turn. Indeed, it may be that a critique of genetic determinism (or reductionism) has its greatest relevance for discussions of disease (especially genetic disease) and its relation to health or normality. Let me therefore turn to the question of what we mean by health and disease.

Health and Disease

Disease is a concept that has traditionally functioned in relation to the healthy organism in somewhat the same way as the concept of the mutant functions in relation to the normal allele. That is to say, the tacit (and necessary) referent of disease is the organism (generally speaking, a human organism). Disease, then, refers to a departure from a normal state as perceived or reported by a patient. Genetics is a powerful tool for identifying particular components of the causal sequence that leads to particular diseases. But only for very exceptional diseases can these genetic components be considered apart from the environment. For such cases (e.g., cystic fibrosis and Huntington's disease) there is no question but that molecular genetics provides powerful and unambivalently welcome tools. Most diseases, however, are not so simple; it might even be said that cystic fibrosis and Huntington's disease provide particularly misleading models for thinking about disease.[11] For the vast majority of diseases, the impairment of function requires as well the right (or wrong) environmental conditions. Thus, the notion of "disease-causing genes" is a euphemism, not unlike the euphemism "a gene for X." DNA sequencing enables us to identify aberrant nucleotide sequences, and insofar as some of these aberrations lead to abnormal function, DNA sequencing can contribute to the diagnosis of conditions experienced as diseased. What it cannot do is "reveal" whether or not a patient *has* a disease.

Finally, just as we cannot properly infer the genetic basis of a trait from the identification of a mutant aberration of that trait, neither can we infer the genetic basis of normal function from the identification of a genetic contributant to abnormal function. To the extent that we subscribe to the "beanbag" conception of the organism, we might be tempted to think that the normal state is the absence of (all) "disease-causing genes," but such a notion of "normal" is necessarily an abstraction—an ideal perhaps to be longed for but, statistically at least, highly abnormal, and possibly as meaningless from a biological perspective as the absence of all "death-causing genes."[12] Over the past thirty years, the category of genetic disease has grown astronomically. Today, genetic diseases number close to four thousand for single-locus syndromes alone; the ailments that are described as multilocus have not even been counted. The most rapid growth is probably to be found among behavioral conditions, with large numbers of new entries made to every edition of the official catalog of mental illness (*The Diagnostic and Statistical Manual of Mental Disorders* or, more familiarly, the *DSM*). Not only are we on the hunt for genes "causing" alcoholism, schizophrenia, and manic depression, but also those for reading disabilities" and "attention deficit disorders," PMS, perhaps even "homelessness." Only partly can this expansion of the category of genetic disease be attributed to the development of scientific knowhow. In part, it is a result of the ideological and institutional expansion of molecular genetics; in part, it is simply a result of the cultural triumph of genetic reductionism.[13]

One last point: genetic reductionism invites a far more radical depersonalization of medicine than that initiated by the earlier and more general march of medicine from art to science. It invites the effacement not only of the environment and history of the patient, but also of the patient him/herself. To the extent that we accept the conflation of organisms with their genes, it is perhaps inevitable that we seek the cause of ills in our genes, and their solution in genetic technology. But even beyond the inappropriateness of blaming all our ills on our genes, we face the threat of what may be an even more serious problem: a shift in the very criteria of what constitutes "illness," from symptoms of unhealth as experienced by an individual patient to whatever is revealed in his or her DNA sequences. Increasingly, genes are seen not only as causing disease, but as the very locus of disease. With this move comes the invitation to shift responsibility for the detection of disease from patients and their physicians to sequencers and their database managers. There are many problems associated with the geneticization of health and disease, but perhaps one of the most insidious is to be found in its invitation to biologically and socially unrealistic standards of normality, threatening not a return of the old eugenics, but a new eugenics—what the Office of Technology Assessment itself has called a "eugenics of normalcy."[14] But what is meant by the term "normalcy," surely one of the most fraught and insistently ambiguous in the human language? Ian Hacking usefully traces its ambiguity back to Auguste Comte, who, Hacking writes,

> expressed and to some extent invented a fundamental tension in the idea of the normal. . . . On the one hand there is the thought that the normal is what is right, so that talk of the normal is a splendid way of preserving or returning to the status quo. . . . On the other hand is the idea that the normal is only average, and so is something to be improved upon.[15]

Inevitably, this ambiguity permits all of us a certain latitude in our hopes and expectations for a "eugenics of normalcy." In ways too obvious to spell out, it also clears a large field for the operation of distinctly nongenetic, ideological forces. Where so much is at stake, it behooves us to think more seriously, and more carefully, about the social and individual bodies on which the very meaning of health and disease, normal and abnormal, depends.

Chapter 6

Normality and Variation

*The Human Genome Project
and the Ideal Human Type*

ELISABETH A. LLOYD

Certain issues involving science are widely regarded as ethical or social—the appropriate moral and medical responses to abnormal fetuses, for example. The "concept of abnormality" *itself* is not usually one of these social or ethical issues. It is assumed that science tells us what is normal or abnormal, diseased or healthy, and that the social and moral issues begin where the science leaves off.

For many purposes, such an understanding of science is appropriate. In this chapter, however, I would like to challenge the "givenness" of the categories of normality, health, and disease. By understanding the differences among various biological theories and the distinguishing features of their respective goals and approaches to explanation, we can analyze the way in which scientifically and socially controversial views are sometimes hidden inside apparently pure scientific judgments.

I am not suggesting that the misleading nature of some of the scientific conclusions I discuss implies some unsavory *intention* on the part of the scientists involved. On the contrary, my point is that there are sincere scientists working among different theories and subfields, each with their own standards of explanation and evidence. The diversity of theories and models involved in implementing the Human Genome Project provides a unique challenge both to the producers and the consumers of the DNA-sequencing information. I contend that the problems arising from this diversity have not been recognized or addressed.

In drawing attention to some important differences among the biological theories involved in the Human Genome Project, I will explore several possible misunderstandings that may be arising from viewing biology as a monolithic and completely integrated science. Further, I raise some concerns about the risks inherent in biological and medical reasoning about genetics.

Health and Disease

Judgments concerning health and disease inevitably involve questions of classification. "Health" encompasses the thriving, fully functioning, or normal states of the organism, while "disease" includes states of malfunction, disturbance, and abnormality. States of organisms do not announce themselves as desirable or undesirable, healthy or diseased, normal or abnormal; such classifications are inevitably applied by comparing the state of the organism to some *ideal* which serves a normative function. Where does this ideal come from?

Roughly speaking, our notions of the ideal state of an organism are informed by our understanding of the "proper" or appropriate functions of various parts. The function of the kidneys is to clean the blood; if the blood is not cleaned thoroughly, and the organism loses the benefits of the "proper functioning" of the kidneys, then the kidneys are "diseased." Overall, the organism does not function as well as it once did. But suppose instead that an organism with badly functioning kidneys never had kidneys that effectively cleaned the blood? Then the comparison must be made not to the prior state of that individual, but to a more abstract notion of "proper functioning" of kidneys in people. In other words, the ideal is *normal* kidney functioning, where "normal" signifies the function in a thriving person.

The difficulties of classifying diseases are well known, having been faced by every theory of medicine in human history. The range of definitions of "normal functioning"—from proper balance of the four humors, to clear flow along the chi meridians, to freedom from cohabitation with microorganisms—has also received a great deal of attention. It seems, therefore, that it would be a major scientific advance, and a significant relief, to be able to understand disease and proper function on the molecular level, and it is just this that is promised by many proponents of the Human Genome Project.

Renato Dulbecco, for example, argued that significant advances in cancer research would be made possible by knowledge of the exact human DNA sequences.[1] Similarly, Nobel laureate Jean Dausset has defended the Human Genome Project by arguing that it will allow us to predict when a person will develop an illness, or at least when he or she will have a predisposition to that illness. Early diagnosis and preventive measures are also emphasized. Dr. Jerome Rotter, director of the Cedars–Sinai Disease Genetic Risk Assessment Center in Los Angeles, says, "[I]t's more than just knowing you're at risk. You can take steps to prevent coming down with the disease or be able to cure it at an early stage."[2]

The descriptions of disease promised by the Human Genome Project are intended to be on the biochemical and, sometimes, even the molecular level. James Watson, codiscoverer of the structure of DNA, and later director of the National Institutes of Health segment of the Human Genome Project, asserted that genetic messages in DNA "will not only help us understand how we function as healthy human beings, but will also explain, at the chemical level, the role of genetic factors in a multitude of diseases, such as cancer, Alzheimer's disease, and schizophrenia."[3] The geneticist Theodore Friedmann has proclaimed that, "molecular genetics is providing tools for an unprecedented new approach to disease treatment through an attack directly on mutant genes."[4] Once diseases have been pinpointed on the molecular level, treatment can begin: "inherited diseases can be identified with biochemical as well as genetic precision, often detected *in utero*, and, in some cases, they can be treated effectively."[5]

The promise is that diseases will finally be subject to truly scientific classification, analysis, and treatment. Detailed descriptions of the molecular causes of disease will enable medical researchers to develop more precise preventive and therapeutic techniques. Once the human genome is sequenced, we will have a library of genes with which any potentially abnormal gene can be compared. Abnormal genes will be isolated, altered, replaced or, in case they are present in implantable embryos, simply discarded.

In many ways, this picture of medical promise and possibility is undoubtedly positive. It is also inadequate and misleading. The primary problem is that the picture of disease most often presented in discussions of the Human Genome Project is oversimplified. Specifically, the presentation of genetic disease and abnormal gene-function as self-announcing is unjustified, except in the most trivial sense. General physiological notions of normality, health, and disease are defined according to a *different* set of standards that go beyond molecular-level descriptions. Describing genes as "causing" diseases is, on a basic scientific level, to confuse at least two distinct levels of theory and description. While a genetic classification of disease may indeed be desirable and useful, it also involves a series of judgments about the ideal forms of human life. Moving the level of diagnosis down to the molecular level does *not* succeed in avoiding the fundamental value judgments involved in defining health and disease, contrary to the suggestions of the genome researchers.[6]

So while molecular techniques will certainly aid in the diagnosis, identification, and analysis of disease processes, they cannot replace the profoundly evaluative and essentially social decisions made in medicine about standards of health and disease. In fact, molecular techniques should be understood as offering an unprecedented amount of social power to label persons as diseased. Hence, it is more important than ever to gain insight into the normative components of judgments about health. The potential submersion of normative judgments under seas of DNA-sequence data should not persuade anyone that conclusions concerning health and disease have now, finally, become scientific. Any appearance to the contrary is a result, I will argue, of some rapid and illegitimate shifting between biological subtheories. Once the structure of the theories involved has become clear, it will be easier to see how and where evaluative decisions are being made.

Molecular Descriptions

Let us begin by taking a closer look at the description and explanation of disease at the DNA level. The typical form of the model used in explanation is described by T. H. Jukes: "[I]nherited defects would be caused by changes in the sequence of DNA, perhaps a change in a single nucleotide. Such change might result in the replacement of one amino acid by another in a protein at a critical location, making the protein biologically useless."[7]

A paradigmatic case of genetic disease, sickle-cell anemia,

fits this general model well and is an early, compelling, and fairly complete case of medical genetics. The original mystery was why certain populations had a high incidence of a type of red blood cell that seems to cause health problems. The red-cell abnormality stemmed from a difference in the hemoglobin molecule which impeded its ability to carry oxygen, hence damaging the bodily capacities of a person with these cells. An analysis of the biochemical causal pathway revealed that the genes that code for the hemoglobin molecule in these people were different from other people's hemoglobin genes in a particular way, thus affecting the ability of the hemoglobin to pick up oxygen. The differences in genes contributed to a difference in the proteins made according to the pattern on those genes, and these protein (hemoglobin) differences had systemic and detrimental effects on health.

This *biochemical causal-pathway model* traces an isolated chain of events that yields the effect of interest. In the standard genetic/biochemical model for the production of hemoglobin, the hemoglobin gene codes for a protein that is included into the red blood cells, cells that, in turn, serve the function of carrying oxygen to the cells of the body. The model presents, in detail, a picture of "normal or proper functioning."

There is not much room for simple variation in this explanatory scheme using the standard model.[8] But why should there be? The purpose of the basic explanation is to explain *how it could be* that hemoglobin is produced and operates effectively in the body. The goal of the explanatory theory is to delineate at least one causal chain that could proceed from the initial state—DNA arranged on chromosomes in a zygote—to the final state—iron arranged in hemoglobin molecules carrying oxygen around the body. The final model of hemoglobin abnormality in sickle-cell anemia represents an astonishing piece of detective work, since it assumes an understanding of each chemical reaction involved in the "normal" causal chain. The abnormality itself is explained through isolating the points in the sickle-cell causal chain that are different from the model of normal functioning.

Watson, in motivating the genome projects, presents a similar picture: "The working out of a bacterial genome will let us know for the first time the total set of proteins needed for a single cell to grow and multiply."[9] Such a goal is perfect for a biochemical causal model: what is desired is some complete set of causal steps yielding a living organism. But variation plays no role in this model. It is an uninteresting, and even distracting, feature of the processes on which the explanatory theory is focused.

In other words, under a biochemical causal model, there is no obvious approach to dealing with variation. One could classify all variations on this main scheme as "abnormal." Owsei Temkin, in ridiculing a definition of disease based on genetic origins, teased that "there should also be as many hereditary diseases as there are different genes representing abnormal submolecular chemical structures."[10] Temkin argues against classifying diseases on causative principles in general, "lest specific diseases be postulated which have no clinical reality."[11] More sensibly, we would prefer to define a variant as abnormal or diseased only if it interfered with "proper function." Proper function, however, cannot be defined within the molecular genetic model itself: it must be defined in terms of the physiological functions of the resultant protein.[12] Here, proper function could involve simply the presence of an *effective* hemoglobin for carrying oxygen around. But there could be (and are) different degrees of effectiveness. How should we divide these up into abnormal and normal?[13] Simple variations and undesirable variations? Some differences in DNA lead to large changes in function, while other differences are imperceptible with regard to oxygen delivery in a normal person.

A friend was exposed to this problem personally. Having gone to a physician who was up-to-date on all the most recent screening techniques, my friend's slightly red eyes prompted the doctor to run a blood test. The results of this test were positive, and my friend was informed by his doctor that he had "abnormal" hemoglobin and liver functioning, something called "Gilbert's disease." When my friend asked about the health consequences of this abnormality involving an essential protein in his body, he was told that the disease was "nonfunctional," and the only known effect was a reddening of the whites of the eyes.

The point is this. If normality is defined at the level of the biochemical causal model, all variation in the DNA of the hemoglobin genes is abnormal. As such, however, the genetic abnormality tells us nothing about its effects on physiological function in the larger organism.

Another example emerges from recent research on human

breast tissue. "Fibrocystic breast disease" exists in approximately 45 percent of the female population over age thirty-five. In one sense, the relevant phenomena are called "fibrocystic disease" because they involve the process of encystation, which is additional to the usual physiological *functions* of breast tissue, such as milk production. On the medical and physiological level, however, it seems that the fibrocystic condition is completely "normal" for the average adult woman; furthermore, the condition does not impede or alter the usual physiological functions of the breasts. In what sense, then, is the fibrocystic condition a "disease"? This is a case in which refined understanding at the cellular level leads to the classification of a condition as an "abnormality" or "disease," while at the functional, medical, or physiological level it is unclear what sense can be made of labeling nearly half the women over the age of thirty-five "diseased."

Again, if normality is defined according to some model of physiological function, molecular information alone cannot decide whether a certain person is normal or abnormal. The DNA information itself is potentially revealing about the functional state, but only potentially.[14] Abnormality in the DNA or in the causal chain may or may not have health consequences that we would consider significant. Carl Cranor, in his discussion of genetic causation and Hartnup disorder, emphasizes the contingency of the emergence of disease on other factors.[15] He also reviews the various types of confusion that can arise regarding genetic causation. I offer here a diagnosis of the underlying mechanism that produces the kinds of confusion discussed by Cranor.

Proper Function

The second type of biological model involves reference to proper function on an organismic level. This level of model is usually considered most appropriate to medicine, and it could be called a *medical model*. Generally speaking, the medical model tends to be on the level of the whole organism, rather than on the cellular or molecular level. Take the example of the common cold. While part of the explanation of how a person contracts a cold is that they were exposed to a cold virus, the rest of the explanation requires taking account of the body as a whole: one does not get a cold simply from exposure to the virus; failure of the immune system to fight the virus invasion effectively is necessary, as is multiplication of the virus within the cells. Similarly, cancer cells are recognized as such on the microscopic level, but their undesirability is because of the damage they do to organ function. The presence of cells simply growing in the wrong place may not impair function—witness the innumerable cases of benign tumors that lie undetected until death occurs from other causes.

The first important aspect of the medical model, then, is its *organismic basis*. A second feature, one that has far-reaching social and policy implications, is that the medical model must rely on *socially negotiated standards* of what counts as the proper functioning of a human being.[16] What range of functional performance is normal? Any answer involves a picture of what a human body should be like.[17] Probably the clearest recent demonstration of the social negotiation of categories of health and disease is the battle, in the past two decades, over the medical classification of homosexuality.[18] Peter Sedgwick, for example, argued persuasively that classifying homosexuality as a disease is clearly not just an empirical assessment of biological function.[19]

To see the force of this argument, take the claims made in 1991 concerning differences in brain structure between homosexual and heterosexual men.[20] Suppose, for the sake of argument, that these anatomical differences arise (in this environment) from genetic differences. (There is no evidence for this; the differences could just as well be caused *by* homosexual activity as be the causes of it.) Suppose, further, that we were able to isolate some genes whose functions included structuring this part of the brain, and that people with a particular sort of brain structure were more likely to be homosexual. Should this genetic character be considered an "abnormality"?

To answer the question, we would need to assume some "proper functioning" of the brain structure, and we must also align this proper function with a particular environment. (It could be that the same genes produce a different brain structure in a different environment, and that this brain structure is not correlated with a tendency to practice homosexuality.) What can we conclude about these genes? Only that they yield particular results in particular environments. But is this normal functioning? Clearly, the answer depends on something *outside the genetic causal story*: it depends on whether we think homosexual behavior should count as normal functioning in human beings. In other words, this distinction between normality and disease depends on how we envision human life ought to be. This story introduces a further problem. If homosexuality is not seen as normal functioning, it is unclear which approach would most successfully move the population toward a higher incidence of normal functioning—changing the environment in which this gene is expressed, or doing something on the genetic level to select out or replace this gene.[21]

The example of homosexuality brings out the profound value decisions involved in labeling certain functions as normal or abnormal. Without such evaluations, genes cannot be labeled as normal or abnormal in any but the most trivial respect—that is, insofar as they differ from the paradigmatic biochemical causal pathway currently accepted for that gene.[22] And such a weak classification system cannot do the work in medical genetics that has been advertised for the Human Genome Project.[23] The issue of defining the *standard* of health and disease is as open as it has ever been. Indeed, there is now the additional challenge of applying it to unimaginably fine biological differences.

Population Genetics Models

Very different types of description and explanation are used in population genetics, where the emphasis is on the analysis and maintenance of variation in populations. Population geneticists have posed persistent challenges to the grander claims made for the Human Genome Project, urging that a biological account of variation in human populations must accompany the DNA-sequence information that was originally targeted.[24] On average, any two human beings differ from each other in approximately 10 percent of their nucleotides. Critics argue that any complete understanding of the functions of human DNA must be able to describe and account for this variation.[25]

Consider the meanings of "normal and abnormal" in the context of population genetics theory. Since the state of a population at a given time is given in terms of the distribution of different types of genes, a great deal of information is needed to delineate what is normal and abnormal, including (1) the range of the types of genes, (2) the range of phenotypes and functions associated with these genes, (3) and the range of environments and the related norms of reaction. Finally, some decision about what will count as adequate functioning in a specific environment is also needed; only then can a specific type be categorized as *diseased*. Clearly, such information is not going to be provided by the biochemical causal models that are prominent in molecular genetics.

Development and Embryology

A fourth type of biological theory is needed to understand genetically based disease. The models of embryology, epigenesis, and developmental biology, though often confused with biochemical causal-chain models, are distinct from them, since they are designed to describe different things and to answer different questions. Specifically, epigenetic models describe the process of what actually happens with genes in environments; ideally, the end result is a description of the emergence of a phenotype in an environment. In this context, "normal" usually means that you get, at the end of the process of development, what is expected given those genes in that environment. Something is labeled as "abnormal" if it is not what is expected.[26]

The fundamental importance of environmental considerations in interpreting traits as normal or abnormal can be seen in the case of New Guinea highlanders, who often have urinary potassium/sodium ratios 400 to 1,000 times the "normal" Western ratio. Daniel Carleton Gajdusek argues that this difference is a metabolic response to a sodium-scarce, water-poor environment.[27] Notions of proper physiological function, then, depend fundamentally on the related environment.[28]

Genetics and Disease

Having considered these four types of biological theories, with their corresponding notions of normal and abnormal, we are ready to return to the specific issues surrounding the Human Genome Project. In the genome project, certain genes are labeled as abnormal, and the decision to do so is made by using as a comparison the DNA sequence of a gene that appears in an accepted model of the biochemical causal chain. What is abnormal under the biochemical model is not necessarily abnormal under a medical model. Nonetheless, researchers interested in the genome project routinely slip from a DNA level of description to a medical usage of "abnormal."

P. A. Baird, for example, promises that the genome project will yield a "new model for disease," in which we will be able to diagnose on the basis of causes, and not simply treat symptoms.[29] Carl Cranor points out that Baird's view exaggerates the role of genetic causes in disease.[30] I would add that Baird is assuming the appropriateness of applying the biochemical causal-chain model to all people carrying the gene; the implication is that the gene will produce disease 100 percent of the time, which, as Cranor emphasizes, is very rarely true for genetic disease.

Victor McKusick, former head of the international Human Genome Organization, also tends to overstate the case for genetic causation: "Mapping has proved that cancer is a somatic cell genetic disease. With the assignment of small cell lung cancer to chromosome 3, we know that a specific gene is as intimately connected to one form of the disease as are cigarettes."[31] Showing the genetic basis for one cancer, is, of course, not the same as showing that every cancer is best understood as a genetic disease.

A similar problem arises in the study of a gene region linked to liver cancer. This study found a region of the DNA where the gene is especially sensitive to exposures to toxins; the toxins induce mutations in that spot, which then prevent the gene from performing its usual physiological role.[32] This is a significant advance, especially since this gene has been implicated in many types of human cancer, including tumors of the breast, brain, bladder, and colon. This case seems to support Friedmann's claim that "human cancer should be considered a genetic disease" because "it is likely that most human cancer is caused by, or is associated with, aberrant gene expression."[33] But the toxins appear to be a necessary condition here, in addition to the presence of the sensitive gene region. So in one sense, the disease is genetic; in another, it arises from environmental causes.

The differences in biological models I outlined above can help with this case. Under a biochemical causal model, the mutant gene is a necessary link in the biochemical causal chain of this liver cancer. Hence, the liver cancer has a genetic cause.[34] Under a physiological model, the usual presence of particular proteins is interrupted through the exposure to toxins in the cellular environment. Hence, the abnormal functioning of the body is dependent on the interaction of environment and cells.

The implication in discussions of genetic bases of diseases is that an abnormal gene leads to abnormal functioning which is itself deficient. But this, of course, is not shown from the strict biochemical description. Both a developmental and functional model are necessary to support the identification of the genetic difference with what we traditionally identify as disease. One problem is that entities on the medical level, such as alcoholism, may be very difficult to pin down genetically. While a gene believed to be implicated in some severe cases of alcoholism has been found, researchers are more convinced than ever that (1) many genes are involved in the disease and (2) they are *different genes* in different groups of individuals.[35] As Vicedo has argued, "all the meaningful questions will *start* when all the sequencing is done."[36]

What about the presumption of genetic bases? Many researchers will cite Huntington's disease, or cystic fibrosis, or Down's syndrome, as clear-cut cases of disease versus normality. But there are more than a hundred mutations cataloged that will produce cystic fibrosis as a clinical entity; and Down's syndrome is diagnosed as trisomy 21, although such a chromosomal arrangement can yield people with a very wide range of abilities. While some researchers are quick to cite the clear, deterministic cases, out of the total number of genetic screening tests available now, nearly all are for gray areas, where the genetic difference is a risk factor, or provides a vulnerability, to develop a specific physiological disease. How is this vulnerability to be understood?

Developmental models are crucial. Gene expression depends inextricably on environment, and environmental responses to knowledge of genetic predispositions can guide development away from dangerous outcomes.[37] Suppose that a person learns she has "the gene for arteriosclerosis" and modifies her diet and exercise regime as a result. We cannot say she will develop arteriosclerosis; in fact, having changed her environmental circumstances, she may well have a *reduced* probability of developing arteriosclerosis in comparison to the population at large. The point is that having a gene for something does *not* imply having that phenotype. "Abnormal" genes may or may not yield "abnormal" or "diseased" organisms. Dr. Henry Lynch, director of a cancer genetics program in Nebraska, is worried that genetics programs will emphasize genetics over simply life-style factors that are much more causally influential.[38]

Professor Bernard Davis and his colleagues in the Department of Microbiology and Molecular Genetics at Harvard Medical School have been visible critics of the Human Genome Project. They argue that studies of specific physiological and biochemical functions and their abnormalities will be much more useful medically than the sequencing of the human genome.[39] Furthermore, only through the refinement and application of developmental biology and population genetics studies of gene distributions can *susceptibility* be studied and interpreted scientifically. Public and scientific misperceptions of susceptibility are probably one of the most prominent problems facing those interested in the development of genetic medicine.

There is a tempting and widespread error in reasoning which is exacerbated by the slippage back and forth between distinct biological meanings of "normal." Under a biochemical causal model, let us suppose a person in whom arteriosclerosis is damaging their health and whose phenotype is clearly "abnormal" and "diseased" according to the medical model. The desired biological explanation traces a causal chain from the genes through the expression and development processes to the resulting pathological state. When asked, "How does arteriosclerosis happen?" the answer is given: "There's a gene for this, which, under these environmental circumstances, takes part in such-and-such a causal chain, resulting in buildup on the arterial walls."

So far, so good. The problem arises when we attempt to understand what it means if a person tests positive for that gene. It is tempting to think that this means they either have or will have arteriosclerosis. But this would be to mistake a contributing cause for a sufficient condition.[40] Exposure to a cold virus is a contributing cause for coming down with a cold, but it is not sufficient; the immune system must also fail to control the spread of that virus in the body. Similarly, having a certain gene might contribute to getting arteriosclerosis, but it is not sufficient; the environmental conditions must also be right in order for arteriosclerosis to become a health problem.[41]

So, take persons with "the arteriosclerosis gene." Are they abnormal? If we define the standard biochemical causal model of fat metabolism as "normal," then they are "abnormal," and the cause of that abnormality is genetic. Are they abnormal on the phenotypic level? Are they diseased? Not necessarily, if we are using the medical model. Inferences that slip from a discovery of genetic abnormality to conclusions of medical abnormality or disease are fundamentally mistaken and unjustified. It is not that the two levels are unrelated or irrelevant to each other; it is just that slipping from "abnormal" in one to "abnormal" in another without evidence is not defensible scientifically.

Conclusion

Claims that the Human Genome Project will give us "the recipe to construct human beings" or the keys to understanding "human nature" are misleading at best.[42] The usefulness of molecular- or DNA-level descriptions by themselves is extremely limited. Genes whose descriptions on the DNA level differ from an accepted paradigm of the biochemical causal model may or may not be physiologically significant. Regarding the medical uses of the Human Genome Project, then, the only relevant form of variation is determined by a medical or physiological model. It is important to understand that the medical model of health and disease is just as subject to value judgments as it ever was. Its necessity has not diminished, it has simply gained a wider scope for use. Deciding how human beings *ought* to function is still a negotiated social decision. Proponents of the medical uses of the Human Genome Project have ignored the problems arising from the social nature of disease, but these will not disappear. On the contrary, biotechnology has new powers to implement and *enforce* codes of normality. Molecular biology cannot provide an objective and scientific code of health and normality. The scientific ability to make fine discriminations of variation and the technological power to act on them makes it imperative that *variation itself* be the focus of a searching public debate and educational effort.

Chapter 7

Errare Humanum Est
Do Genetic Errors Have a Future?

CAMILLE LIMOGES

Proponents of the Human Genome Project (HGP) have repeatedly emphasized the relevance of its projected results and achievements for medical practice and therapeutics,[1] and they continue to do so: "Mapping and sequencing the human genome will not in itself provide a complete biologic understanding of life. . . . But the medical benefits of the mapping and sequencing we do in the 1990s and the first decade of the twenty-first century will be profound and immediate."[2] Indeed, in the discourses directed to decisionmakers, and to other audiences as well, in view of promoting and explaining the program, medicine is providing most of the rhetorical justification.

The connection between molecular biology and medicine, of course, is hardly new. For instance, even before the benchmark 1953 papers on the helical structure of DNA, Linus Pauling had identified sickle-cell anemia as a "molecular disease."[3] Another instance was George Beadle putting forth the British physician Archibald Garrod as the privileged forerunner on the path he had himself followed with Edward Tatum: Beadle credited Garrod's work on the "inborn errors of metabolism" as "representing the beginning of biochemical genetics"[4] and also attributed to him the then-controversial idea conveyed by the dictum "one gene, one enzyme."[5]

This chapter will explore some historical relationships between molecular biology and medicine, as well as their purport for the future. It will also examine some issues, hinging on the notion of "genetic error," that bear upon the genetic makeup of individuals in relation to the normal and the abnormal in medical contexts. Finally, it will suggest that some matters of "ethical" significance might already have been given shape in actual scientific processes.

"Error" in Medicine and in Molecular Biology

Despite Beadle's claiming Garrod as his forerunner, the notion of "inborn error" did not undergo any revival in the early years of molecular biology "Genetic error" was reborn in a new context—not the older one of metabolic diseases, but that of DNA replication.

Erwin Schrödinger, who introduced the notion of a "hereditary code-script" to account for the multidimensional "pattern" of the organism in its structure, functioning, development and reproduction,[6] also considered the term "error" to be "too narrow," the chromosomal structures being at the same time "law-code and executive power." Moreover, he did not conceptualize mutations as errors of copying or replication, but rather as different "readings" or "versions" of the "code-script." He actually even emphasized that "while it might be tempting, it would nevertheless be entirely wrong to regard the original version as "orthodox," and the mutant version as 'heretic.' " In principle, he wrote, we have to regard them as being equally right—for the normal characters have also arisen from mutations.[7] Schrödinger also pointed out, however, that the "comparative conservatism which results from the high degree of permanence of the genes is essential." Interestingly, though, he did not support this view by appealing to the requisites of an informational code-script but, rather, on the basis of the metaphor of testing innovations in a factory one by one, so as not to disturb unduly the performance of the production process.[8] Only from the second half of the 1950s on were the metaphors of the code and its reading to be taken more literally and systematically, giving prominence to the notion of "genetic error."

Crick's "central dogma" was couched in terms of a unidirectional flow of "information," "information" being defined as "the *precise* determination of sequence, either of bases in nucleic acid or of amino-acid residues in protein."[9] It is in this context, during the years dedicated to the "breaking of the code," that the language of "genetic error" or "mistake" first gained widespread currency. In 1959, Ernst Freese described mutations as "induced by mistakes in base pairing."[10] By 1963 this new language had become so firmly established that Vernon Ingram's classic paper of 1958, explaining how sickle-cell hemoglobin is produced by the substitution of one of the glutamic-acid residues by valine in each of the half molecules, could be read as unraveling a case of "genetic error."[11] This is all the more interesting because Ingram never mentioned the word "error" in his paper and had rather continued to use the more classic language of "mutations" and of "differences" between the polypeptide chains of "normal" and "abnormal" hemoglobin.[12] The notion that DNA "like a tape recording, carries a message in which there are specific instructions for a job to be done," and that "exact copies can be made from it . . . so that the information can be used again and elsewhere"[13]—a notion convergent with work conducted simultaneously on the regulation of the "transfer of information" and the "messenger RNA" by Jacob and Monod (1961)[14]—had created something like an irresistible trend in favor of the informational view and its associated notion of mutations as "genetic errors."

At the present time, mutations continue to be viewed as "errors," particularly when they occur in the course of the DNA-replication process, or as "damage," particularly when caused by environmental factors between the replication cycles. The recourse to two different and overlapping domains of reference, the informational and the mechanical, in order to address the issue of mutations in molecular biology becomes particularly obvious in the discussions of "DNA repair," making use of notions such as "slippage errors" and "proofreading," "frameshift mutations," "mismatch corrections," and the interestingly conflated "error-prone repair."[15] This sort of conflation of the informational and the mechanical, which has become current, is even better exemplified in a phrase taken from the latest major texts in the field: "DNA is the only cellular macromolecule capable of being repaired after sustaining structural damage. Moreover, it encodes the machinery for effecting a wide variety and large number of repair processes."[16] This might seem to suggest that information theory—after having been probably more a metaphorical resource for molecular biologists than a deeply embedded structure of molecular biological theory—is now giving way to modes of discourse closer to biotechnological engineering. However, even though such a shift—if real—might eventually prove to be of some significance in medical terms, be it "error" or "damage," the connection between medicine and molecular biology runs no risk of being relaxed. Both "error" and "damage" call for "correction" or "repair."

From Genetic Error to the Understanding of Diseases

The HGP, in the discourse of many, provides an enticing picture of medicine becoming truly radical, empowered to eradicate disease at its root, where lies the "defective gene,"[17] or "molecular lesion."[18] Yet this still remains, for the time being, entirely programmatic.[19]

What is already actual and at stake, however, is the need for a common understanding of the relationship between the genetic and the pathological, and of the relationship between the genetic and the therapeutic. This is now the object of much debate, after a period during which, according to some, a clear cleavage existed (and was up to a point respected) between the genetic and the cultural,[20] or during which, according to others, precedence had been given to the "external determinants."[21] The practical significance of the shifts and the ultimate consequences of a redirecting of attention to genetic causation are at this stage far from clear.

Indeed, some of the most strident, urgent, and confident claims regarding genetic therapies come from people who seem quite remote from the clinical wards and who have little or no therapeutic experience. There is no need to think that the most simplistic approaches are those which will effectively prevail. In fact, I take it as a telling manifestation of the present turmoil of ideas over genetics, genetic error, genetic defectiveness or abnormality, and related therapeutic issues that—almost half a century after its contrivance—the foundational myth of biochemical genetics is being debunked and its subject, Archibald Garrod, "rediscovered," though simultaneously transformed, and now again made uniquely able to serve new purposes.

George Beadle, as noted earlier, created the image of Garrod as founding father of biochemical genetics and patron of simple-linear genetic causation (the "one gene, one enzyme" hypothesis). This image has fitted well with the approaches adopted by molecular genetics: far from being questioned, it gave rise to a very substantial literature purporting to explain the neglect of Garrod's views up to his Mendel-like "rediscovery" by Beadle.

Quite interestingly, this historical reconstruction of Garrod's contribution has, from different quarters, recently and suddenly been contested. A historian of science, Jan Sapp, has devoted one whole chapter of his recent book to a critical analysis of the myth of Garrod as founding father of biochemical genetics.[22] One year before, in his biographical sketch of Edward Lawrie Tatum, Joshua Lederberg had characterized as a "misconstruction" the notion of Garrod's anticipation of the "one gene, one enzyme" hypothesis. Garrod, Lederberg pointed out, "had no comprehensive theory of gene action" and "never quite made the leap from the anomaly provoked by the mutant gene to the positive functioning of its normal allele."[23] In his foreword to the reprint of Garrod's second book, Inborn Factors in Disease (1931), Lederberg again expressed the view that it is "difficult to divine exactly what he [Garrod] believed to be the scope and function of the normal gene(s)," concluding that in any case Garrod's conception "is not yet the direct one to one mapping of genes to enzymes later insisted on by Beadle and Tatum."[24] Even more assertively, two admirers and editors of Garrod, Charles Scriver and Barton Childs, write that he "has been given credit by Beadle for being the first to propose a direct relationship between a gene and an enzyme. . . . But, in fact, Garrod could not have made any such proposal in 1909 and there is no evidence in Inborn factors or in the lectures given in the 1920s that he came to that conclusion later on." But Garrod's editors do not stop there. No more the epitome of the researcher asserting the power of simple-linear genetic causality, Garrod now rises, however, under a new guise—that of the physician-researcher uncovering "chemical individuality" and drawing attention to the complexities of "genetic predisposition."[25]

Garrod's notion of "chemical individuality" had been paid some attention to before,[26] but essentially from a historical viewpoint, whereas it is now being reasserted as relevant in current discussion and research on medical genetics.[27] Garrod thought that the detectable, particularly striking "inborn errors of metabolism," such as alkaptonuria or albinism, were just the tip of the iceberg, "extreme examples of variations of chemical behavior which are probably present everywhere." There is, he stressed, "no rigid uniformity of chemical processes," and the "individuals of a species do not conform to an absolutely rigid standard of metabolism"; in brief, all human organisms manifest "chemical individuality." Such a view involved some scrutiny of the notion of disease. For Garrod, an "inborn error of metabolism" did not necessarily entail a disease: alkaptonuria, for instance, "is not a manifestation of a disease but rather an alternative course of metabolism."[28]

Rather than leading to an ontological notion of disease, such as the one often related to uses of "genetic error" or "defective gene," Garrod's metaphorical notion of "inborn error of metabolism" resulted in an emphasis on chemical individuality providing the foundation for a renewed understanding of the notion of "diathesis," or individual inborn predisposition, and the assertion that "there is . . . no fixed standard of normality and health."[29] It is in this context of asserting the primary significance of genetic factors, which, however, express themselves in the experiential singularity of an individual human being—against a tradition of a more rigid genetic determinism and in contrast with the concept of the normative determinism of a standard genome (somewhat implied by the notion of "genetic error")—that Scriver and Childs want to reclaim the figure of Garrod.

They emphasize, for instance, that the "polymorphism in DNA greatly exceeds that which we would have predicted from phenotype," this polymorphism being the base of "what Garrod might have called the ultimate chemical individuality."[30] Also, they account for the occurrence of a disease by the incongruence, or "mismatch between individual versions," of a biological endowment and an environmental experience.[31] Further, they assert that "a gene associated with disease in one person may not represent a real risk in another . . . and not simply because of absence of provocative experiences. Rather, since any phenotype represents the effects of all the genes entering into its origins, modifiers may nullify the potentially bad effects of any one."[32] On that backdrop, it is understandable that even though they favor the HGP, Scriver and Childs nevertheless maintain that even "a complete map of the human genome . . . every gene sequenced, its product identified, and its expression understood" would only "have given us a detached analysis of our parts." For "to have the knowledge of molecular genetics and biology is one thing and to have the knowledge of physiological genetics is another."[33]

Physiological genetics is not biochemical genetics. In the end, having rejected Beadle's and Tatum's foundational construction of Garrod and having reappropriated this founding father for their own purposes, Scriver and Childs indeed do not make their way back to an equation of physiological and bio-chemical genetics. They are, quite the contrary, very explicit about their determination to forward a different research program: "While Beadle and others did what was obvious to them, when they reversed the thinking of their era by looking for the gene mutations that influenced known chemical reactions (and in so doing paid homage to Garrod), it will be our turn to want to know how the chemical reactions modified by mutations produce their effect on the phenotype of the whole being."[34]

Such views are predicated upon crucial changes undergone in the understanding of gene action during the past forty years. In Tatum's classic presentation of the "one gene, one enzyme" hypothesis[35]

1. all biochemical processes in all organisms are under genetic control;
2. these biochemical processes are resolvable into series of individual stepwise reactions;
3. each biochemical reaction is under the ultimate control of a different single gene; and
4. mutation of a single gene results only in an alteration in the ability of the cell to carry out a single primary chemical reaction.

The evolving representation of gene action has now become somewhat more complex. It is now understood that genes may also code for proteins that are not enzymes, or for RNA products, and that proteins composed of nonidentical polypeptide chains depend upon the action of cistrons, subunits of DNA. It is also known that the activity of a given enzyme may require many subunits from different genes, or that a given polypeptide chain may have multiple enzyme activities. Moreover, post-translational cleavage of a peptide may occur, as well as DNA rearrangement prior to transcription, and so on. It has also become clear that not all mutations result in dysfunctional proteins: given the redundancy in the genetic code, some 23 percent of point mutations are synonymous mutations producing an unchanged amino acid. Finally, gene expression has been shown to be controlled not only by regulatory genes but also by a class of proteins, regulatory proteins, generally encoded by other unlinked genes.[36] As molecular biology research moved from prokaryotes to eukaryotes—bringing molecular biology closer to medical relevance—much attention has been paid to the complex processes through which the same set of genes accounts for the development of the diverse tissues that compose an individual. Despite a single genomic constitution, not all genes are transcribed in the different classes of cells; investigating the location, rate and timing of this transcription has led to exhibiting the key role of distinctive proteins, some of these transcription factors acting, moreover, through protein–protein interactions and not by binding to a DNA substrate.[37]

Indeed, changes have been so profound that we may well have to revise such very basic notions as that of the "gene." This has happened before: the gene of the Mendelians, that of the molecular biologists, and that of some evolution theoreticians do not map neatly one onto another.[38] In this regard, Paul Berg has recently expressed the view that a reexamination of this fundamental concept is needed, and that a gene ought not to be conceived of only as DNA coding segments: "A more appropriate view of a gene is that it consists of the entire transcription unit (exons plus introns) and the regulatory regions involved in governing that unit's expression under a variety of conditions. By that definition, current data suggest that about 50% of the genome's sequence is comprised of genes."[39] It remains unclear here, however, why regulatory proteins would remain subsumed under the "variety of conditions" rather than as an integral part of the transcription unit.

Be that as it may, in this new context the unidirectional model exemplified in the "one gene, one enzyme" dictum does not appear to be of much help anymore, although it no doubt did play a major heuristic role in the earlier development of molecular biology. This also means that some discourses celebrating the "profound and immediate" benefits of "reverse genetics" for medicine might have to be toned down.

No doubt, at a time when the HGP is so widely and strongly promoted, it is inviting to suspect some global imperialism of molecular genetics over medicine. Indeed, some "molecular crusaders" have not deemed it ridiculous to depict their own endeavor as a search for a biological "holy grail," a rhetoric that has brought sharp attacks from countercrusaders (or should one say Saracens?) determined to fight anything that might smack of a portentous genetic determinism. This, however, may be at least partly unwarranted. As Stephen Jay Gould quipped in his review of an apocalyptic book relative to biotechnology, "The domino theory does not apply to all human achievements."[40] This might well obtain in the case of the HGP. Although, to be sure, simplistic statements are quite easy to come by, it simply is not true that the "molecularization" of biology irresistibly leads all of medicine toward ever more simplistic forms of genetic determinism.

To be sure, the language of radical molecular genetics still flourishes (taking so-called molecular lesions or errors for more than the questionable metaphors they are), and it may even have found reinforcement in the wake of the HGP movement. Certainly, however, such language does not appear to be unproblematic for all scientists.

Allelic variation does not need to be seen as abnormal, or as an error, otherwise than through the application of an arbitrary a priori categorization. Even genes involved in causal processes resulting in an abnormal phenotype are just that, one of many causal factors. This point is often now made forcefully even by some of the strongest advocates for medical genetics. Let us compare, for instance, statements from the last two editions of the "bible" of medical genetics, *The Metabolic Basis of Inherited Disease*. In 1983—that is, before the very idea of a Human Genome Project had emerged—the editors of the fifth edition emphasized the foundational significance of genetics. They stated: "The first edition . . . was published in 1960, a time when the 'inborn errors of metabolism' were being rediscovered and slowly converted to 'molecular disease.'"[41] Furthermore, "The intimate relation between genetics and metabolism is symbolized by the title of this volume: *The Metabolic Basis of Inherited Disease*. In the 1980s, it could just as easily be: *The Inherited Basis of Metabolic Disease*."[42] No doubt. Six years later, in the next edition, the new editors stressed among the new features "evidence of molecular genetics in one chapter after another."[43] However, the basic science chapter of the same edition emphasizes that, even in so-called Mendelian or monogenic disorders, "there are relatively few . . . where the single locus *entirely* determines the disease phenotype"; the phenotype is also subject to modification by genes at other loci as well as by environmental factors.[44]

The unraveling of genetic causes of disease, then, did not

lead these authors to assume that they are sole causes—quite the contrary. Indeed, I take it as significant that the senior editor of this sixth edition also wrote: "Molecular genetics is a powerful way to solve biological problems and most of us, myself included, willingly join the cadre of reductionists who use 'reverse genetics' as an interpretive paradigm in biology. But in some ways molecular genetics is a welcome respite from the difficult task of dealing with phenotype paradigms."[45] Far from being reducible to the gene as their ultimate single key, "even Mendelian diseases are multifactorial" and have an experiential or environmental component.[46] For instance, among probands presenting the same "Hartnup" mutation in an autosomal gene, some suffer from the disease while others do not at all.[47]

At least it should be clear that those actors in the field of medicine who are interested in and related to the science the HGP is promoting are far from homogeneous or monolithic. Possible erosion of the dominance of the informational mode-of-representation of matters genetic; attempts by scientists at reconstructing historical genealogies of scientists in relation to realignments of research perspectives; requestioning of basic scientific and biomedical notions—these, as alluded to above, may be signs of a field now more fluid and less firmly and definitely stabilized than is usually acknowledged, especially by those who fear the consequences of the HGP. If this view is correct, if positions among researchers cannot be always subsumed under simple notions of unlinear genetic determinism, but on the contrary exhibit a diversity of critical conceptual stands, the time may be ripe for opening a new round of questions of some social and ethical significance.

Concluding Remarks: Debating Normality in the Course of Science

Much energy has been spent debating the relative merits of whether to practice ethical judgment according to stated principles—as is now generally done in medical ethics in the wake of the Belmont Commission[48]—or by application of ethical theory. So much so that it seems to have prevented paying sufficient attention to the fact that much reflection and explicit decision-making comes much too late in the day. It is not correct to assume that matters of social and ethical significance are raised and decided upon only after the research is done—when the time will come to decide whether or not to put some results into practice, to discuss the proper uses of a given technology. In fact, some of the most decisive and significant of these issues are already being given form and substance in the very process of doing science; they are largely resolved and embedded in procedures or technology, when these are passed on to consumers and other users.

In the matters that occupy us here, the course of action is already given shape in scientific research as concepts such as "genetic error," "genetic lesion," or "normal gene" are being contrived and put to use. Some of the most crucial ethical issues are implicitly decided upon not in the context of philosophical discussions using the conceptual tools of ethicists, but in that of scientific research and discourse itself. It cannot be otherwise.

That the scientific construction and use of concepts may have social or ethical implications, beyond their scientific consequences, does not escape the attention of many scientists and physicians. Indeed, the cases are numerous where some of them show unease toward the notions they utilize. For instance, concerning the detection by screening programs of genetic diversity in hemoglobin genes, some authors will say that "*a gene may be 'abnormal'* (a mutant) but no disease is produced." Despite their characterization of "abnormal hemoglobin," these same authors write: "This counseling problem will persist until there is a new understanding among physicians and the public that '*normal' includes a great deal of genetic diversity*," and "the lay public is at present almost totally uninformed concerning the concept that *genetic diversity is frequent but not abnormal*." If genetic diversity is frequent and not abnormal, why then characterize each instance of mutation as "abnormal," as these authors themselves do? Indeed, they conclude that "our definition of normal must be revised."[49]

This example was chosen because the notion of "normal" is centrally at issue for the questions that interest us here. It is a notion of crucial ethical significance, although it is not per se one pertaining to the realm of the ethicists. It is no doubt a notion that ought to retain their attention, but it is foremost a scientific and medical concept.[50]

To be sure, concepts deemed significant in scientific theorizing will not be abandoned by scientists simply because some uses may have questionable social consequences in the eyes of some, or because they raise acute ethical dilemmas. Still, the critical examination of concepts is a requisite certainly no less for the researcher than for the philosopher. Questions relative to normality, to the biological differential characteristics of our species, to the characterization of mutations as genetic "errors" or "lesions," to the polymorphisms that contribute toward differentiating each of us as individuals, to what counts as normal or abnormal variation—these are questions to be dealt with in the process of doing science. When language—and much more than language—equates genetic variation with error or the abnormal, scientific consistency may be questioned. After all, it is genetic "errors" that made us as a biological species: we humans are integrated aggregates of such "errors." Genetic variation is the source of evolution; it is the reason why there could be primates and not just protists or their precursors. Indeed, if in the narrow context of replication mechanisms it is understandable why the notion of "error" emerged—though even there it involved rather loose language, as Schrödinger had pointed out earlier[51]—drifting from error (mutation) to the abnormal is untenable. In a Darwinian world, there is no longer any norm of a species beyond its relations to its environment, physical and biotic. Normality has no stable referential meaning: the *reference is in the experience* of the individuals in the population. The notion of "genetic error" in that regard is a regression to typological thinking or, as Charles Scriver would say "categorical thinking." There is no such thing as a standard genome.

Accordingly, it would seem that some issues of considerable social and ethical relevance are to be examined far *upstream* from where most ethicists intervene. This is no call for the operation of moral vigilantes in the midst of scientific work; it is just pointing out that the search for conceptual consistency is intrinsic to the scientific process. It also underscores the limited effectiveness of a *downstream* bioethics conceived of as a rational discussion to help delineate a course of action regarding the suffering individual, or regarding the use of a technology. Key questionings occur, and ought to, *upstream*, while and where the science is being done, in the scientific process itself: before the technologies and procedures have been packaged and black-boxed, crucial conceptual decisions, as well as strategic choices, are already being made.

Chapter 8

Genetic Causation

CARL F. CRANOR

The idea of causation plays a crucial role in assessing some of the moral and social implications raised by new developments in genetics, genetic technology, and the Human Genome Initiative (HGI). More specifically, the idea of genetically caused diseases is a critical area of discussion. Already researchers have cataloged some three to four thousand "single gene-caused diseases."[1] Next, they will turn their attention to multiple gene-caused diseases, so-called polygenic disorders.

Identifying genetically caused disorders opens the possibility of "individualized medicine." Physicians of the future, instead of identifying manifestations and symptoms of disease, making an accurate diagnosis, and developing appropriate treatments, may be able to turn their attention to genes as one of the "internal causes" of disease for at least some diseases. Such information may enable them "to interfere earlier in the cascade of events leading to overt disease and clinical manifestation"[2] and to design individual therapies appropriate to the cause in question. Early intervention can take many forms, but a prominent one of concern to many is gene therapy: "directing treatment to the site of the defect itself—the mutant gene—rather than to secondary or pleiotropic effects of the mutant gene products."[3] Physicians will take a sample of a patient's blood, perform a DNA analysis to identify the disease-causing genes, and design an individualized treatment for each patient's particular disorder(s) and genetic makeup. A drop of blood, a diagnosis, a treatment, and voilà, a new and better you. Of course, such suggestive scenarios will not soon, if ever, be realized. Nonetheless, because ideas capture our imaginations and guide our research, technology, and medicine, we should seriously consider some of the key elements of such scenarios and subject them to critical analysis, for otherwise we may become their captives.

Genetic causation is one concept in need of understanding. Critics as well as advocates of the new genetic tools are tempted to distort causal notions in order to argue for their positions.[4] Also, this idea has become one part of the intellectual turf over which there are disputes; it occupies a central role in discussions about the desirability of various research strategies as well as therapeutic options. Genetic causation—rather than the pros and cons of various research and therapeutic strategies—sometimes seems to be a major focus of debate. This is unfortunate because one often reads discussions of causal connections or the lack thereof between genes and diseases without any explicit debate of alternative research strategies or various therapeutic options. Causal notions do the work of normative debates. Thus, in order to understand some of the broader research and therapy issues, we need to understand better the background notion of causation. Once causation is clarified and despite its importance, however, the focus should be less on it and more on the scientific, moral, and social considerations that bear on research strategies and choices of therapy.

The underlying issue that gives rise to the concern about causation has to do with claims about the causal role of genes in disease which may lead research scientists and medical practitioners to focus on genes rather than on other biological processes as the important contributors to disease. Such a focus may or may not be insightful for so-called single-gene disorders; that remains to be seen. However, critics claim that even such optimism about single-gene disorders is misplaced, for researchers looking for *the* cause or *a* cause of a disease have too simplistic an idea of biological processes.[5] Polygenic disorders, they claim, are another and potentially more serious matter, because focusing on the genes in such cases may be even more misleading. Scientists may too quickly invoke the notion of the "abnormal" gene or focus on the gene(s) as *the* cause or the important cause. This may lead scientists and physicians to address illnesses by reference to genetic explanations, technologies, and therapies, instead of trying to understand the issues in alternative ways, and instead of relying upon alternative therapeutic strategies. While I am in no position to adjudicate the biological disputes, progress can be made by clarifying the complex notion of causation, understanding what it can and cannot do, and then recognizing explicitly the various considerations that bear on choosing research strategies and medical therapies.

Causation

Consider ordinary, commonsensical notions of causation with which we are familiar. Sometimes we seek to explain the normal course of events: the movement of tides or planets or the growth of a flower. At other times we seek to understand departures from the normal course of events: the existence of a drought in a normally wet climate, heavy rain in a normally desert environment, the explosion of a space shuttle, or the aberrant growth of a mammal. Sometimes we use causal explanations to identify features of complex events that we wish to control: Of the factors that cause rivers to overflow their banks, which can we control and engineer so that towns and people are not harmed in the future? Of the many factors that contribute to cancer, which do we pick out that we can most easily control and manipulate in order to prevent the development of cancer in others? Finally, for legal or moral purposes (or for metaphorical extensions of them), we sometimes pick out certain causes to *blame* for untoward results.

A common notion of causation—*a* or *the* cause of an event—is "one condition selected from a complex set of conditions which . . . are together sufficient to produce the consequence."[6] The jointly sufficient set of conditions that produces an effect may include negative conditions (e.g., the failure of a switchman to change the switches may cause the train wreck) as well as positive conditions (e.g., the switchman changes the switches the wrong way). Causes may be actions, events, states of affairs, failures to act, the nonoccurrence of an event, and the nonoccurrence of a condition; we can use the word "contingency" to range across these different types of causes.[7] In searching for causes we sometimes focus on *explanatory* notions and we sometimes emphasize *nonexplanatory* notions. Explanatory causal ascriptions tend to shed light on or provide understanding of phenomena, while nonexplanatory notions may fix blame or pick out causal factors that are easy to manipulate or handle for various pragmatic or engineering purposes.

Explanatory Notions of Causation

Sometimes we are merely interested in what "usually or normally happens" in the ordinary course of events, in "standardly recurring regularities" (e.g., why the wind blows, why flowers grow, or how a fertilized egg becomes a newborn mammal). Such accounts "require long stories involving descriptions of diverse states of affairs and the invocation of various laws of nature."[8]

A second, primarily explanatory, kind of causation in ordinary life, as in the law, "is most often prompted by the occurrence of something unusual: we ask for the causes of accidents, catastrophes, deviations from the normal or accepted course of events."[9]

> We may be presented with some contingency (a railway accident or someone's death) which we find puzzling: we do not know why or how it happened. In such cases to inquire for the cause of the contingency is to ask for an explanation which, when provided, makes what has happened intelligible, because it shows it to be, after all, something which exemplifies known general laws as to how things happen, though some considerable analysis of the facts of the situation and much further evidence beyond the initial information may be required before this causal explanation can be given.[10]

In these circumstances, we have a contingency that does not ordinarily occur, and we seek the causal explanation(s) to account for the departure or deviation from the normal course of events. Scientists may be interested in accounting for such unusual events as the extinction of dinosaurs or the causes of fifty-year floods. Lawyers are concerned with events whose causes might justify legal remedies.

Which contingencies we select from the set sufficient to produce the event depend upon the context and our interests. If slamming a door with eight glass panes in it breaks one of them, several different inquiries may interest us. If we are merely interested in why the glass broke, the slamming door may be a sufficient causal account. If we are interested in why one specific pane rather than the seven others broke, we should ask what distinguished the broken pane from those which did not break. If we are interested in why the door slammed in the first place, we might look to Sam's anger or, for a more psychological explanation, at Sam's relationship with his father. Causal explanations, then, are dependent upon context and upon our interests. It is, however, difficult to provide much in the way of general guidance for selecting "the" or "a" cause of an outcome.

Because causal explanations are so context- and interest-dependent, though, we should scrutinize causal ascriptions carefully for their contexts and for the aims such ascriptions might serve. When we consider claims about genetic causation, this is especially important; for that notion is frequently invoked to make a normative point, instead of arguing for the research or therapeutic point more directly.

Both kinds of causal inquiry described above are explanatory in that they seek to shed light on either normal (the first case) or unusual (the second case) events. Hence, we might think of the "criterion of selection in [such an] explanatory context . . . as *the Lantern Criterion*."[11]

Nonexplanatory Notions of Causation

Sometimes causal ascriptions are nonexplanatory or at least not primarily explanatory. Engineers and others interested in practical affairs may seek the cause factor to an outcome "that is . . . easiest to manipulate or control . . . [in order] to eliminate events . . . if they are harmful or to produce more of them if they are beneficial." These causal ascriptions are typically made with a view to identifying the "most efficiently and economically manipulable causal factor." Following others, we might think of this as "the handle criterion" because it selects for the causal factor that people can "get a hold of and manipulate."[12]

Identifying easily manipulable causal factors for engineering purposes may or may not aid causal understanding. Engineers were able to design airplane propellers that functioned well without having a complete or even a good theoretical understanding of optimal design.[13] It is even possible that one can have a good causal understanding of a phenomenon without necessarily knowing how to engineer it to produce certain results. Scientists appear to understand the genesis of AIDS, but they do not yet understand how to control it. Consequently, we must be careful about inferring causal understanding from easily manipulable causes of a phenomenon (and conversely). This distinction seems especially important in considering genetically caused diseases.

A fourth kind of causal inquiry, typical of the law or morality, goes beyond searches for abnormal antecedents of unusual events. Here we have, in addition to some loss, harm, or departure from the normal course of events, *suspect human behavior;* that is, some violation of the law (or, in morality, some moral shortcoming) is evident. In such cases, we want to know whether the suspect behavior is a causal contributor to the loss or harm. There are, as it were, two starting points for such inquiries: "some wrongful act (or other contingency defined by law) and (usually) some loss or harm, and the problem is to determine whether the loss or harm is *so connected* with the wrongful act that it is its consequence."[14] These are more typically *blaming* contexts, for we inquire whether the suspect behavior is so connected to some loss or harm that it should be blamed for the result. We might think of the criteria for attributing such causes as the "stain criteria," for the aim is to select a factor for purposes of allocating blame (or "staining") the person or event involved.[15]

In addition to the paradigm case of causal ascriptions in law or morality, we may also metaphorically "blame" suspect nonhuman events for bad outcomes. In such cases, we should be cautious in attributing causal blame, just as we are in law or morality, because we would be identifying a "suspect event" and then attributing causal efficacy to it.

When we consider the so-called genetically caused diseases, what kinds of causal claims are being assumed? Explanatory? Engineering? Blaming? In the present debate about genetic disease, such questions are important because causal notions can mislead us in various ways and disguise what should be important debates in defining biological research agendas and in developing genetic technologies.

The Temptation to Underestimate the Causal Role of Genes

One temptation in debates about genetic disease is to underestimate or even to deny a causal role to genes in order to make a normative point.[16] Thus, some commentators deny that genes "control" or "program" phenotypic disease,[17] and they challenge the biotechnological dream of manipulating genes in order to control the quality of infants born "because [such a dream] exaggerates the control genes exert over metabolism and development."[18] Moreover, this raises a concern that the "reemergence of eugenics, in the form of genetic engineering, is the most recent stage in the drama of genes as determinates or causes," as well as a concern about "replacing 'bad' genes with 'good' ones" or about changing or moving genes from one place to another on the chromosomes in order to treat genetic diseases.[19] The "power of the particles [genes] is exaggerated, while the contributions of the systems in which they operate are undervalued or ignored."[20] This view emphasizes the complexity of the biological system, where many components and conditions contribute to a given disease, and it hesitates to attribute causation to genes.[21] Thus, some argue, while sickle-cell anemia is known to be related to a single gene, that does not explain why some with this disorder are seriously ill from early childhood and others show only "minor symptoms later in life."[22]

While there is much good sense in calling attention to biological complexity, the case can nevertheless be overstated. Based on ordinary notions of causation there may well be reasons to acknowledge in at least some contexts that a gene is "the" or "a" cause of a disease. For so-called single-gene diseases, one could fully recognize that a disease in a human being is the "outcome" of a complex set of conditions and at the same time draw attention to one of those contingencies as "the" or "a" cause of the disease for purposes of *understanding, shedding light on,* the process. This does not differ from many other scientific or nonscientific causal inquiries we make about events in our lives (e.g., why the train wrecked). The fact that a complex set of conditions is sufficient to produce an event does not detract from drawing attention to one of the contingencies as "a" or "the" cause for certain purposes. What matters is the context and the purpose and that we do not lose sight of the complexity of the processes involved. Thus, if a malfunctioning gene is the unusual antecedent in an otherwise normal biology of people and a disease such as sickle-cell anemia results, it may be quite illuminating to call attention to this fact. (And it may be illuminating even if it does not explain all aspects of a disease.) We seek to draw attention to factors that are normally present, though absent in this case, or normally absent but present this time, and that "make a difference."[23] It may be that "single-gene diseases" that are a relatively direct product of a defective gene are rare, and thus not representative of what we might think of as "genetic" diseases.[24] Nonetheless, pointing to genes as causes, even if rarely justifiable in the end, may prove insightful and at the very least not conceptually odd.

Yet, such critics seem correct that it is important to acknowledge the biological complexity of diseases, because even for purposes of understanding, identifying one condition (e.g., a malfunctioning gene) as the cause could unduly influence research objectives and therapeutic efforts. Concepts, theories, experiments, and instruments developed to pursue one research objective may exclude or "close off possibilities of other programs"[25] or may cause us to ignore some of the complexity of the phenomena. Too much focus on one part of the disease-process "elephant" may divert attention from other equally or more important causal factors. And, as Ian Hacking notes, a more substantial risk may be not merely the temporary one of ignoring part of a complex process, but a misdirected long-term refocus of research:

> A science can develop among many possible paths, bringing into being different phenomena. Phenomena that we create on one possible historical path might not be created on another historical path, say because we have invented neither the instruments nor the theory of the instruments through which we could recognize or control them. Moreover any path that we do follow has its own momentum. Experimental techniques and instruments, when they produce what are taken to be stable results, themselves suggest further steps to take by analogy. Had we not started out on a path, we would not have created later on what we do in fact create.[26]

Whether this in fact happens, whether it is a serious distortion of research, and whether it should be rectified in particular cases are difficult questions to answer, requiring detailed knowledge of the discipline and considerable historical insight. The crucial point is a more modest conceptual one: we should be careful, especially as a branch of science such as genetics is developing, not to lose sight of the whole field and not, because of an enthusiastic focus on one particular development, to lose sight of the richness that field may offer.

Moreover, those who tend to underemphasize genes as causes are correct to call our attention to abuses that might result from an overemphasis on genes as causes. Just because we understand how a defective gene contributes to a disease, it does not follow that the gene should be our *therapeutic* target. Treating, repairing, inserting, manipulating, altering, or replacing genes should be undertaken, if at all, only after the most careful assessment of the risks and benefits of the process and of alternative means of treating the disease, including the no-treatment alternative. (Even for the paradigm single-gene disease, sickle-cell anemia, it appears that the indicated treatment relies on antibiotic drugs.)[27] Such therapies should be scrutinized for their social costs and benefits on persons and their biology—not only as individual treatments, but as general medical and institutional responses to disease. Addressing such issues raises complex factual and normative issues.

The concern about ascribing too much causal influence to genes appears to have even greater credence in relation to polygenic diseases, diseases that are by definition the outcome of a complex set of conditions, including the interaction among several or many genes as well as between those genes and the surrounding biological context. To focus on one or two genes as "a" or "the" cause of such diseases may be even more misleading than it is for single-gene disorders. Recent searches for the "genetic cause" of alcoholism may be just such a case of a search for genetic causes gone too far.[28] Not only may such ascriptions misdirect therapy, they may also distort research and understanding as well as our conception of ourselves.

These worries suggest there may be a second way to read the critics of genetic causation. While such critics recognize that genes are part of the causal process of disease and that genes may even provide a way by which to identify part of the causal process, they may be concerned that scientists are too quick to ascribe causes for *engineering purposes*, to get a handle on some manipulable part of the causal process in order to "correct" a person's biology. If a gene appears to be an easy "handle" to grab in order to modify the disease process, scientists may ignore other, less radical or less costly approaches to research and therapy.[29]

On the lookout for "suspect" factors in the causal process, scientists may tend to "blame" (in a metaphorical sense) a gene for the condition in question. They may quickly fix attention on genes simply because a particular gene is obviously defective and may make some causal contribution, however small, to the condition. If this is the case, then we should raise an analogue of the legal question about causation: Is the phenotypic disease *so connected* with the suspect (defective or blameworthy) gene that it is its consequence and thus worthy of therapeutic attention?[30] In the law, demanding standards of proof must be met before attributions of such causal connections to the suspect actions of a person are justified. Such evidentiary standards are designed to protect the interests of people charged with (blamed for) offenses. Similarly demanding evidentiary standards might be considered before "blaming" genes for disease—not in order to protect the "rights" of genes (a silly idea), but to caution the medical and research communities (and discourage them if need be) against too quickly pursuing radical therapeutic strategies when others may be available.

However one reads the critics' claims about genetic causation, to some extent these critics appear to misidentify the locus of concern. While many of their ideas merit attention, a good deal of the conceptual and normative work in their arguments is done by the idea of causation. This is not quite the right focus. Their view appears to be that if genes, even in the easy case of single-gene diseases, are not causes, then they cannot possibly "determine" disease and, thus, can neither be candidates for understanding the disease nor candidates for manipulation, alteration, or modification. They use a *conceptual* argument (genes are not causes) to try to prevent research and therapeutic approaches they think are mistaken. By adopting such an argument, they deprive a quite useful concept ("a" cause or "the" cause) of one of its typical, standard jobs in our conceptual apparatus in order to help blunt a normative conclusion they think is wrong. Conceptual claims invoking (or, better, not invoking) causation seem exaggerated as a basis for research and therapeutic recommendations.

Thus, even if one agrees with the ultimate concerns of these critics, they are purchased at the price of some conceptual distortion. A much better approach might be to recognize that genes, for at least some single-gene diseases (even if rare), appear to make discernible causal contributions to some diseases, but to deny that this settles all questions concerning scientific understanding, recommendations about research agendas, and the important normative and practical issues as to how such diseases should be treated or "engineered," if at all.

The Temptation to Overemphasize the Causal Role of Genes

At the other extreme, some advocates of the new genetic technologies are tempted to employ arguments that appear to *overemphasize* the causal role of genes in disease in order to support their recommendations. While critics of the new technologies appear to fear an overemphasis of genetic causation of disease (so they try to play down the causal contributions of genes), advocates appear to embrace the causal role of genes because of interests *they* have. This is also a mistake, although individuals holding this view are harder to pin down.

One such advocate, P. A. Baird, urges us to recognize the "internal causes" of, and to develop a new model or paradigm for, disease. Thus, he urges that we should focus less on "manifestations" of disease and more on the "cause" and "pathogenesis" of disease. Indeed: "Genetics will increasingly enable us to *interfere earlier in the cascade of events* leading to overt disease and clinical manifestations." He urges us as a society "to take advantage of this opportunity for prevention and avoidance [of disease]." This entails several steps. A first-level strategy is to identify genetic markers so that individuals can detect "*all* single gene disorders so that family members may plan reproductive options," or so that individuals with the gene may have appropriate management in order "to avoid the complications." Prevention might also take the form of dietary modification or drug treatment of individuals suffering from certain diseases. In short, "to be forewarned is to be forearmed."[31]

No longer need we limit ourselves to making the diseased person comfortable because we do not understand the pathogenesis of disease, or use "halfway technologies" in order "to compensate for later or in-stage effects," both of which can be highly sophisticated and extremely expensive responses to disease. Instead, we can understand "cause and pathogenesis."[32] Preventing or treating the causes of disease tends to be much less expensive, Baird claims, than either of the other two stages of medical treatment. Whether this cost argument is sound or not, of course, depends on a detailed analysis—not only an assessment of the costs of making people comfortable or using halfway technologies, but also a realistic estimate of the total cost of understanding and identifying the causes of pathogenesis

and the costs of appropriate "intervention" or therapy. Cost fig-
ures may be especially problematic where they rest on the intensive and possibly quite expensive sequencing technologies
that currently characterize genetics. Consideration of the plausibility of this cost argument, however, is beyond the scope of
my essay.

Still other advocates explicitly endorse gene therapy as a
plausible treatment option. Recent work "has firmly established
mutant genes as uniquely appropriate targets for therapy, for at
least some genetic disorders."[33] And some even advocate gene
therapy for *infectious* diseases, since these "result from the infectious agent's genes."[34] For example, one advocate, Theodore
Friedmann, places an emphasis on genes as causes of disease as
part of a deliberate persuasive strategy. He "calls something a
genetic disease to [get us to] think of particular kinds of therapies. It's [calling something a genetic disease] a kind of tool to
convince people to focus on certain therapies. Nothing is sim-
pler than treating a disease at its cause."[35] While such a conceptual move, deliberately labeling the cause of disease as "genetic,"
serves Friedmann's purposes, it is also misleading. He, like
critics of genetic technologies, appears to use a conceptual claim
in order to help argue for normative research and therapeutic
recommendations.

Causes and Cures

The preceding discussion should give us pause with respect to
the cavalier use of causal ascriptions. Although the agency of
causation in the biological world is complex, to identify a cause
for an event of disease does not seem conceptually odd. But our
commonsensical notion of causation, when analyzed, turns out
to be a complex one. This realization should help us to avoid the
temptation to utilize oversimple explanations of, and oversimple therapies for, complex phenomena. It is especially important
to keep this model of causation in mind when considering the
understanding of, and cures for, "genetic diseases." As we have
already noted, it is one thing to know the "cause" of a disease,
quite another to know its cure.

A more subtle view of the causes and recommended treatment of disease is suggested by Charles Scriver and Barton

Childs in their epilogue to *Garrod's Inborn Factors in Disease*. Discussing familial hypercholesterolemia (FH), phenylketonuria (PKU), and Hartnup disorder, they recognize that genes predispose individuals to these conditions and help identify the affected individuals. They then show how interaction between genetic and environmental factors, broadly conceived, produces these diseases. However, information about the particular gene(s) involved plays little or no role in the *treatment* of these conditions. Instead, Scriver and Childs focus on diet, drug therapy, and "prevention of birth" in response to these diseases. For example, they discuss two treatments of FH (hyperproduction of cholesterol), neither involving gene therapy: "one to reduce the overburden of cholesterol [by using nonabsorbable bile-acid binding resins] and the other to suppress overproduction [by administering drugs]."[36]

Similar points emerge from their discussion of PKU (an accumulation of phenylalanine that results in mental retardation) and Hartnup disorder (a kind of dermatitis with neurological symptoms following exposure to too much sunlight). The typical treatment for PKU consists in a low-phenylalanine diet or "prevention of birth" of a child with the disorder. Neither treatment, however, is free from significant personal cost: the life of a patient (and family) constrained to a low-phenylalanine diet is apparently not an easy one, and abortion may be a problematic solution. Appropriate treatment of Hartnup disorder appears to consist in avoiding a reduction in protein intake and providing "supplements of the affected essential amino acids."[37]

Thus, even though the three disorders Scriver and Childs discuss are heritable and predispose individuals to the conditions, the genetic component is not the only causal contributor to the outcome. There are "environmental" contributions to the conditions in each case. In addition, a genetic predisposition may not represent a real risk in the case of Hartnup disorder, because "[since] a phenotype represents the effects of all the genes entering into its origins, modifiers may nullify the potentially bad effects of any one."[38]

Moreover, treatment does not consist in gene therapy. Genetic information appears to help identify classes of individuals affected, and in some cases to identify defective receptors (for FH) or proteins, but treatment does not involve the genes. It is difficult to know how representative Scriver and Childs's examples are (part of a much larger problem in this area, it appears). But if they are typical of the wider class of "genetic diseases," then perhaps their examples should caution us against being too quick to turn to genetic fixes for so-called genetic diseases.

Of course, there is much that molecular biologists and geneticists do not yet know about genes and technologies that might permit genes to be the focus of cures. As they obtain a better understanding of genetic mechanisms and biological strategies for controlling and manipulating them, such treatment options may or may not become feasible.

However, distortions in research may result from too narrow a focus on genes. Ian Hacking (noted above) makes the general point. Elsewhere in the present volume (Chapter 4) James Griesemer makes a more particularized point about the focus on genes in the history of biology: a historical mistake may have distorted biological research. Griesemer suggests that there has been a gradual diminution of conceptual tools for expressing the complex cause–effect relations constructed and examined in modern biological research; and he notes the adverse effect this has had, and may continue to have, on developments in biology as well as on related social issues.

We are in the midst of a biological revolution. Genetics, genetic technologies, and genetic therapies appear to have a major role in explaining biological processes, developing treatment options (and even cures) for diseases, and developing preventive strategies and new products. What will ultimately be accepted as the proper role of genes in understanding biological processes and in treating diseases will be answered only as a result of biological research and developments in the field. This is not an issue to be settled by conceptual analysis. The analysis of causation that we have considered merely provides a vantage point from which to analyze tensions in the field that are somewhat disguised behind the concept of causation. And I have argued that a reasonable view of our ordinary notion of causation shows how it can be distorted to make certain recommendations more appealing.

The hopeful view is that some of these implicit disputes will be settled by future biological research because we will have a better understanding of the biological process and because therapeutic strategies will be available with the new understanding.

A less hopeful perspective, à la Hacking, is that we may not be able to assess adequately the correct view of the role of genes in understanding and therapy. The reason is that research paths and technologies developed now will greatly influence what the field becomes in one or two decades or a generation from now. Thus, if genes remain the focus of attention and genetic technologies are developed to serve research and to implement applications, two decades from now we might well have difficulty conceiving how the field could have been different. To return to the elephant analogy made earlier, if present research focuses on the head and trunk area, in a decade we may have difficulty pursuing research on the sides or tail or even thinking about these as appropriate areas of research. The reason: our attention, concepts, technologies, and the important questions to be pursued will have been influenced by choices made earlier. Given a kind of conservatism to the development of intellectual research, it may be difficult to rethink or reorient research once the whole field or most of it is committed to a particular research path.

In these circumstances, perhaps scientists should be cautious about committing themselves to a particular research path for a whole field to the exclusion of others. Simplistic causal claims can influence the debate and hide some of the complexity of the issues. Scientists should carefully evaluate research agendas and not exclude topics of research because of an unbridled enthusiasm for the focus of the moment.

What is needed, instead of either of the extreme approaches discussed above, is a clearer understanding of our ordinary causal notion so that we neither forget the complexity of the biological world nor forget that it is important to call attention to certain features of that complexity (causal contributors) for certain purposes. Moreover, we need as dispassionate an evaluation of research agendas and therapeutic approaches to disease as we can achieve, so that we do not inadvertently (or deliberately) commit ourselves to a particular view of the world or to particular therapies and thereby lose sight of (or even lose) other areas of research or other therapeutics options. Research, therapeutics, and technological commitments can take on lives of their own. We should self-consciously recognize that we are in the midst of a changing field and recognize how the choices we make now might markedly change the future.

A number of risk-assessment and cost-benefit questions should be asked about research and therapeutic alternatives:

- Are genes the appropriate causal foci for single-gene disorders in order to maximize research understanding and therapeutic options?
- What are the appropriate treatment options for a particular disease?
- Is gene therapy an appropriate option to be considered in the case of polygenic disorders?
- Should our research and therapy institutions be organized to focus largely on genetic research and gene therapy?

It will be difficult to step back, keep these questions and issues in view, and attempt to address them—especially the more fundamental ones—because research and therapy decisions are made by many different individual actors and institutions. The field may seem propelled by an invisible force not subject to organized control. Nonetheless, in order to anticipate and consciously choose our research and medical future we should make the attempt.

To a large extent, scientific research appears to be decentralized and atomistic. Scientists pursue research on topics that interest them and that seem worth pursuing as a means of adding to the stock of scientific knowledge. To the extent that research has this atomistic feature, and to the extent that there is no one person or agency controlling the direction of research, it seems odd to speak of "organizing our research and medical institutions." Although there may be something to this point in the abstract, research has suggested that scientific enterprises may be implicitly organized through the career goals and ambitions of leading scientists[39] and through the influence of "paradigm shifts" adopted by different generations of scientists.[40] To the extent that leading individuals influence the development of a field, they bear greater responsibility for the results. Some, of course, relish the opportunity and push particular research agendas. Perhaps the influence of such individuals should be moderated by others who take a broader perspective on the fields of research and therapy.

Even if such sociological and psychological forces did not

exercise some organizing influence on research and medicine, however, both are influenced in major ways in the United States by governmental and private funding agencies. The National Institutes of Health (NIH) and its funding priorities clearly shape much of the biological research in this country. Thus, since such groups can importantly shape the development of biological research and treatment therapies, they would do well to keep in mind both the complexity of causal claims and the complexity of the biological world. Perhaps the model of causation discussed above will serve as something of a reminder of that complexity and of the many research and therapeutic paths that could be followed, paths that should not be inadvertently foreclosed.

In addition, private foundations with organized constituencies of victims and researchers devoted to addressing, and ultimately to eradicating, various diseases (sickle-cell anemia, Huntington's disease, etc.) target research funding. Even if various income, race, class, and other factors did not lead to the proliferation of such foundations, which they might, the mere fact that some diseases rather than others are targeted for research and treatment surely influences research and therapy priorities. Moreover, in times of tight research budgets, the role of private foundations may become much greater and potentially more distorting. Graduate students are reported to pursue fields of research in which there is funding by private foundations, since such foundations may be a more reliable source than governmental agencies.[41] To the extent that private foundations which target specific genetically caused diseases fund a greater portion of all biological research, this will further draw scientific research away from fundamental research that has a chance of avoiding some of the narrow pitfalls described above.

Perhaps of greatest importance for genetic research and therapy, however, is the current U.S. governmental effort to promote and fund research on the human genome through NIH and the U.S. Department of Energy. These agencies aim to promote the geneticization of biological research. In addition to funding genetic research and the research into ethical questions that this might foster, they might also acknowledge the complexity of causal relations in biology and support inquiries into the social and scientific wisdom of emphasizing genetics in research and therapy.

Chapter 9

Eugenic Anxieties, Social Realities, and Political Choices

DIANE B. PAUL

Will developments in biomedicine prompt a "new eugenics"? Many people apparently fear that the answer is yes. A host of television programs, trade books, and scholarly and popular articles express their authors' alarm at the prospect of a eugenics revival. As Robert Wright has noted, "Biologists and ethicists have by now expended thousands of words warning about slippery eugenic slopes, reflecting on Nazi Germany, and warning that a government quest for a super race could begin anew if we're not vigilant."[1]

Their message is often buttressed with accounts of the American and German eugenics movements. These histories serve as cautionary tales, meant to remind us that genetics once served corrupt social ends and alerting us to the possibility it may do so again. They also tend to be remarkably similar, down to the slides. They constitute a catalog of the inane and appalling: "Fitter Families" contests at state fairs, immigrants turned back at Ellis Island, Nazi death camps. The moral is clear, if vague in respect to details. Genetics has been badly abused in the past. If we are not careful, it may happen again. Thus precautions need to be taken.

Perhaps understanding the past can help us chart a course through the dangerous shoals of genetic engineering although, as Michael Lockwood suggests, "that may be a little like looking to the history of the temperance movement for guidance on the contemporary problems of drug addiction."[2] It is in any case highly improbable that these canned histories, with their attitude of total contempt for the past, will promote a critical perspective on current developments in biomedicine. They are in fact far less likely to inspire self-criticism than self-congratulation. In comparison with our grandparents, who held inexplicably absurd and odious ideas, we look pretty good.[3] Indeed, making us feel good may be their chief function.

Consider the ritual injunctions to "be vigilant." What exactly are we to guard against? Few commentators believe that a new eugenics will simply repeat the mistakes of the past. We might therefore expect to be told in what guises eugenics actually appears today, or will likely appear tomorrow; however, these discussions are typically abstract and general. Concrete cases would of course provoke controversy. Thus we are cautioned to be on guard—against nothing in particular. The lessons of history turn out to be vacuous.

Perhaps the unthreatening character of the discussion explains why advocates as well as critics of the Human Genome Initiative acknowledge eugenics as a serious concern. Of course not everyone does. Some partisans of the project simply dismiss eugenic anxieties, while others view anxiety itself as the problem.[4] But the literature celebrating the project is replete with homilies about the need for vigilance lest abuses recur. Even James D. Watson, its first and very hardheaded director, thought the eugenics issue was real.[5] It has become, in effect, the "approved" project anxiety.

In comparison, other concerns receive short shrift. The past few years have witnessed publication of a raft of popular books celebrating the genome initiative. Most focus on its promise for medicine.[6] None questions whether mapping and sequencing the whole human genome represents a cost-effective way to prevent or cure disease. Their authors warn of the need to guard against a resurgence of eugenics. They do not say what they mean by eugenics or why it is bad. The answers to both questions are generally believed to be obvious. The burden of this essay is to show they are not—and to explore some political consequences of our failure to explore these assumptions.

The Multiple Meanings of Eugenics

"Eugenics" is a word with nasty connotations but an indeterminate meaning. Indeed, it often reveals more about its user's attitudes than it does about the policies, practices, intentions, or consequences labeled. (The problem of multiple meanings was recognized by the Commission of the European Communities when it omitted the word "eugenics" from its revised human genome analysis proposal on the grounds that it "lacks precison.")[7]

The superficiality of public debate on eugenics is partly a reflection of these diverse, sometimes contradictory meanings, which result in arguments that often fail to engage. Thus, for one party, "eugenic" properly applies only to intentions; for another, it may also describe effects. From the latter's standpoint, it makes perfect sense to call the practice of abortion following prenatal screening "eugenics." From the former's, it does not. Few if any women choose abortion with the aim of improving the gene pool. But private decisions may, taken collectively, have population effects. These consequences would appropriately be labeled eugenic (or perhaps dysgenic) given some definitions—and equally inappropriate given others.[8] And that is but one source of confusion.

Francis Galton, who coined the term "eugenics" in 1883, defined it as "the science of improvement of the human race germ plasm through better breeding"; also as "the study of agencies under social control which may improve or impair the racial qualities of future generations."[9] Both versions identify eugenics as science, rather than social policy. But if eugenics only implied *study*, it would hardly arouse such indignation. Some modern definitions are even more innocuous. According to the historian Mark Haller, eugenics is "the concern with the genetic improvement of mankind."[10] By this definition, virtually all medical genetics is eugenics.

Most definitions, both historical and contemporary, assume that eugenics involves an agent with a goal. This agent "attempts" or "promotes" or "interferes" with some process to bring about a desired population-level change. The following definitions are typical: eugenics is "the attempt to improve the population through selective breeding";[11] "the promotion of reproductive options favoring desired human genetic traits, especially health, longevity, talent, intelligence, and unselfish behavior";[12] "attempts to improve hereditary qualities through selective breeding."[13] On these definitions, eugenics is a conscious policy, pursued by the state or some other social institution, to alter the genetics of a population.

But, as noted earlier, eugenics may also be defined in terms of consequences. In this case, agency is attributed to individuals, as well as to the state or other social institutions. Motive is no longer relevant. Individuals do not necessarily (or even ordinarily) intend to produce population effects. The collective results of their actions may even be unpalatable to some of those individuals. A definition broad enough to include unintended consequences will necessarily incorporate medical genetics. Indeed, as Elof Carlson has noted, it will apply to ordinary acts of human reproduction.[14]

The notion of "back door" eugenics implicitly depends on a definition of eugenics in terms of effects. A number of recent critiques have warned of an indirect route to eugenics; that is, eugenics as the unintended result of individual choices. Thus, in Robert Wright's view, the real danger arises not from state policy, but from our increased capacity for homemade eugenics, where families *choose* the kind of children they want.[15]

We have seen that "intentions/effects" is one way of drawing the line between what is and is not eugenics. It overlaps with two other common, if tacit, lines of demarcation: the "coercive/voluntary" and the "individual/social." The last two are often combined, as in Neil Holtzman's definition of eugenics as "any effort to interfere with individuals' procreative choices in order to attain a societal goal."[16] Let us consider first the question of interference.

Eugenics and Coercion

It often turns out that what people object to in eugenics is not the goal, such as improving the health of the population, but the means employed to achieve it.[17] From this standpoint, in the absence of coercion (as reflected in law or obvious forms of social pressure), policies designed with the good of the population in mind are not properly labeled "eugenic."

There are, however, both historical and analytical problems with this approach. Many eugenicists stressed the voluntary character of their proposals. This was especially true in Britain. For example, the English socialist Havelock Ellis insisted that "the only compulsion we can apply in eugenics is the compulsion that comes from within."[18] It likewise excludes most "positive eugenics" (which aims to increase desirable traits rather than reduce undesirable ones), since these schemes are usually voluntary. Thus H. J. Muller's proposal to artificially inseminate women with the sperm of particularly estimable men would not, in this perspective, qualify as eugenics. Nor would William Shockley's similar project involving Nobel Prize winners. For the same reason, there could be no "back door" to eugenics. That route depends on women *choosing* to be tested and aborting their "defective" fetuses.

Moreover, it is no simple matter to determine whether a policy is coercive, and indeed there is no value-neutral way to decide. Coercion has different meanings in different political traditions: for classical liberals and contemporary (libertarian) conservatives, a decision is voluntary if there are no formal, legal barriers to choice. For liberals in the tradition of T. H. Green or for socialists, coercion is not simply a matter of removing legal barriers: we are free to choose only when we have the practical ability to agree or refuse to do something. Thus, in the former tradition, the potential parents of a Down's syndrome child are free to abort the fetus or bring it to term. In the latter, they are not, since the "downstream" costs of caring for a severely handicapped child are enormous.

Our language obscures this fact. We speak of "private, voluntary" choice as though individual choices are ipso facto free.[19] But this is true only if we define freedom as the absence of legal restraint. In some political traditions, whether parents are considered free to bring a severely disabled fetus to term is a matter not just of law but of economics.

Disputes about the uses of new genetic technologies cannot be easily resolved, since they are linked to more-fundamental values, about which people disagree. In the literature on social and ethical implications of biomedicine, we often find dictates like "Coercion should not be used."[20] Such injunctions miss the point. There is already general agreement that coercion is bad; the problem is a lack of agreement on what coercion *is*. The same point applies to the related axiom of respect for personal autonomy. Autonomy in respect to reproductive decisions has become a near-universal value. But this agreement masks fundamental conflicts about what it *means* for people to make their own decisions.

The Nazi euthanasia program and many of the U.S. state sterilization statutes were obviously compulsory. But some anxieties about coercion extend beyond the possibility of being segregated or sterilized or shot by the state. They include concerns about lacking realistic alternatives to the decision to undergo carrier screening or prenatal testing, or to abort a genetically imperfect fetus—as a consequence of cost-saving policies adopted by private employers or insurance companies or by physicians' groups promoting a new "standard of care" in response to fears of malpractice suits. In some political traditions, the exercise of this kind of social power calls into question the voluntariness of a woman's choice. In others, it does not. Thus, apparent social consensus dissolves once we begin to probe a bit.

Eugenics and Social Aims

Sometimes it is the rationale, rather than the means employed, that identifies a policy as eugenic. Programs are often tagged with the label if their intent is to further a social or public purpose, such as reducing costs borne by the sociomedical system or sparing future generations suffering. In this perspective, genetic counseling or support for biomedical research motivated by concern for the quality of the "gene pool" would be eugenic, while the same practices motivated by a desire to increase the choices available to individuals would not. This same criterion is also employed to distinguish the old eugenics from the new.

In his book *In the Name of Eugenics*, Daniel Kevles characterized postwar advances in medical genetics and biomedical engineering as a "new eugenics."[21] The phrase was bound to be provocative. After the Second World War, eugenics fell increasingly into disrepute. But many geneticists remained convinced that improving the biological quality of human populations was a worthy goal, and feared it would be abandoned in the backlash against establishment eugenics. They therefore searched for new and politically neutral ways to pursue their objectives. From these efforts emerged the field of genetic counseling and, ultimately, such medical techniques as prenatal diagnosis and experiments in gene therapy. Many who approve of these developments also abhor "eugenics." Hence the controversial character of Kevles's expression.

It was not, however, Kevles's intent to condemn these new techniques and therapies. Indeed, he is convinced that the "new eugenics" has jettisoned not only the social prejudices that marked much of the old, but the social *interests* that spurred the first generation of medical geneticists. In his view, some who developed (and funded) the field of medical genetics may have aimed to improve the quality of the gene pool. But in the 1960s, the ethos of genetic counseling shifted from concern with the welfare of populations to the welfare of individual families, as determined by families themselves. This change marks a welcomed, decisive break with the past. Previous abuses resulted, in his words, from elevating "abstractions—the 'race,' the 'population,' and more recently the 'gene pool'—above the rights and needs of individuals and their families."[22] In effect, old (bad) eugenics reflects interests that are social; new (at least potentially good) eugenics reflects interests that are private and individual.

This same individual/social criterion is often employed to distinguish what is genuinely "eugenic" from what is not. In this perspective, techniques and therapies that increase choices for individuals are not, by definition, eugenic—whatever the motives for these choices or whatever their social consequences. Hence the "new eugenics" is a misnomer. But there is less than meets the eye in this dispute. Both positions assume that pressures to limit individual choice should always be resisted.

Private acts do have social consequences, however. And it at least requires argument to show why social consequences should not be a matter of social concern. The conventional counterposing of the interests of individuals (which are good) to those of society (which are bad, or at least less compelling) ignores the fact that society is constituted by other individuals, and that individuals have social interests. For historical reasons, we have come to take for granted that the rights and needs of individuals (or individual families) should take precedence over rights and needs that are social. But these alternatives are more complex than current discussion admits: it is not so clear that all good is on the side of the individual; indeed, it is not so clear what it means to be on the side of the individual in the first place.

From a historical standpoint, the desire to draw the line here is certainly understandable. Whether or not we can agree on what eugenics really is, there have been policies associated with the eugenics movement that we now find abhorrent. And those policies were defended on the grounds that individual desires must be sacrificed to a larger public good.

In the extreme view, the individual was thought to count for nothing, the larger community all. The following passage from Madison Grant's influential 1916 book, *The Passing of the Great Race*, illustrates this perspective: "Mistaken regard for what are believed to be divine laws and a sentimental belief in the sanctity of human life tend to prevent both the elimination of defective infants and the sterilization of such adults as are themselves of no value to the community. The laws of nature require the obliteration of the unfit, and human life is valuable only when it is of use to the community or race."[23]

Few eugenicists spoke in so harsh a language. But the need for individual sacrifice on behalf of the larger social good was a belief shared by all eugenicists, whatever their other social and economic views. Thus the socialist Lancelot Hogben, whose views were generally shared by those on the Marxist or Fabian left, wrote that "the belief in the sacred right of every individual to be a parent is a grossly individualistic doctrine surviving from the days when we accepted the right of parents to decide whether their children should be washed or schooled."[24]

Because the raison d'être of eugenics was the sacrifice of individual desire to public good, it was often characterized as a "secular religion." The idea that science could, and should, function as a religion was first proposed by Francis Galton and later defended by various socialists, such as George Bernard Shaw.[25] Bertrand Russell also argues the point in his essay on eugenics in *Marriage and Morals*:

> The idea of allowing science to interfere with our intimate personal impulses is undoubtedly repugnant. But the interference involved would be much less than that which has been tolerated for ages on the part of religion. Science is new in the world, and has not yet that authority due to tradition and early influences that religion has over most of us, but it is perfectly capable of acquiring the same authority and of being submitted to with the same degree of acquiescence that has characterized men's attitude toward religious concepts. . . . Religion has existed since before the dawn of history, while science has existed for at most four centuries; but when science has become old and venerable it will control our lives as much as religion has ever done.[26]

Grant, Hogben, and Russell had little in common except their enthusiasm for an alliance of science and state that today

seems at least naive. Few people are any longer inclined to cele-
brate either. Indeed, the notion that individual desires should
sometimes be subordinated to a larger social good has itself
gone out of fashion, to be replaced by an ethic of radical individualism. In 1885, Jane Clapperton's assertion that the socialist
state would eventually have to restrain the sexuality of those
"who persist in parental action detrimental to society" was not
especially controversial.[27] Some people still talk this way. But it
is now considered shocking.

In the late 1980s, Dorothy Wertz and John Fletcher queried
medical geneticists in nineteen countries about their attitudes
toward ethical problems in genetic counseling, prenatal diagnosis, and screening. They found parental autonomy to be a
dominant value. More than 90 percent of geneticists in the
United States, and more than 80 percent in other countries, believe that counseling should be nondirective.[28] A statistic from
another recent study by Wertz, Fletcher, and John Mulvihill provides an even more striking illustration of the change in ethos.
In 1972–73, only 1 percent of genetic counselors in the United
States would perform prenatal diagnosis (or would refer parents) for selection of fetal sex in the absence of X-linked disease.
In 1975, the figure was 21 percent. In 1985, it was 62 percent.[29]
And in a 1991 survey, Deborah Pencarinha and colleagues
found that 85 percent of master's-level genetic counselors would
either counsel or refer patients desiring sex selection.[30]

There are complex reasons for this ideological shift. It is possible here to sketch only the most significant, one of which is
surely the reaction to abuses committed in the name of eugenics. Consider the history of attitudes toward sterilization of
retarded persons. In the 1927 case of *Buck v. Bell*, which upheld
the Virginia sterilization statute, Justice Oliver Wendell Holmes
wrote: "It is better for all the world, if instead of waiting to exe-
cute degenerate offspring for crime, or to let them starve for
their imbecility, society can prevent those who are manifestly
unfit from continuing their kind. The principle that sustains
compulsory vaccination is broad enough to cover cutting the
Fallopian tubes."[31]

The 1981 *Grady* decision provides a striking contrast with
both *Buck v. Bell* and the case of Karen Ann Quinlan. In *Grady*,
the parents of an adolescent girl with Down's syndrome feared
that their daughter, who was about to enter a sheltered work-

shop, would be raped or seduced. They asked their physician to sterilize her, but the local hospital refused to permit it. The parents then asked the court to authorize the procedure. When the judge ruled in their favor, the New Jersey attorney general appealed to the state supreme court, which confirmed the lower court's decision. But in contrast to the *Quinlan* case, where it ruled that the decision to terminate life-support systems could be delegated to family and physicians, the New Jersey Supreme Court held that sterilization of retarded persons always required judicial approval. The court explained its departure from *Quinlan* by reference to the "sordid history" of eugenic sterilization.[32]

Another factor is certainly the expanding jurisprudence of privacy, which has centered on sexuality and procreation. In the 1972 case of *Eisenstadt v. Baird*, the Court held: "If the right of privacy means anything, it is the right of the individual, married or single, to be free of unwarranted governmental intrusion into matters so fundamentally affecting a person as the decision whether to bear or beget a child."[33] The repudiation of the ethos underlying *Buck v. Bell* could hardly be more complete. This reversal has been the joint product of a liberal Supreme Court and of broader social movements, in particular feminism.[34]

But the claim that women have an absolute right to control their bodies also has implications that make some feminists uneasy.[35] Elizabeth Fox-Genovese has observed that contemporary feminist theory is marked by "the uneasy coexistence of communitarian and individualistic commitments."[36] Tensions arising from these dual commitments are especially evident in discussions of prenatal diagnosis for sex selection. Many feminists (including genetic counselors, most of whom are women) are made very uncomfortable by this practice. After all, as Wertz and Fletcher have noted, "gender is not a disease."[37] But if women have an absolute right to reproductive choice, they cannot consistently be denied the right to choose the sex of their offspring. And if it is acceptable to choose fetal sex, is there good reason to object to selection for other nonmedical traits? This is a question that opens troubling vistas to many feminists.

Another strand in the tapestry of arguments can be traced to Carl Rogers, father of "client-centered counseling," whose theories strongly influenced the ethic of genetic counseling in the 1970s.[38] From the 1940s (when heredity clinics were first established) through the 1960s, genetic services were generally provided as a sideline by physicians and research-oriented Ph.D. geneticists. It was only in 1969 that Sarah Lawrence College established the first master's level program for professional counselors. Thus the vast expansion in genetic services of the 1970s was accompanied by a shift both in the gender and the training of counselors. The new service providers were much more attuned to the psychological dimensions of the counseling process. They were influenced in particular by Rogers's view of the counselor's role as clarifying and objectifying the client's own feelings.[39]

Reproduction, the State, and the Market

The convergence of these forces in the 1970s ensured that, in respect to reproduction, autonomy would supersede other competing values. But the commitment to personal autonomy has obscured the fact that individual reproductive decisions do have social consequences, and that in a market system the privatization of those decisions will result in their commoditization. Robert Nozick's concept of a "genetic supermarket," a system that allows prospective parents to order (within limits) the genetic characteristics of their offspring, is the logical outcome of this trend, in which the power of the market ultimately replaces that of the state.[40] As Robert Wright suggests, the real problem is not the one we most fear: a government program to breed better babies. "The more likely danger," he writes, "is roughly the opposite; it isn't that the government will get involved in reproductive choices, but that it won't. It is when left to the free market that the fruits of genome research are most assuredly rotten."[41] He also notes (following Arthur Caplan) that those who now take advantage of prenatal screening are concentrated at the upper end of the income scale, while children with Down's syndrome are almost certainly being born disproportionately to those at the bottom.[42]

Wright calls this development "homemade eugenics." I do not think that labeling it eugenics helps to clarify the issue. The social structures and processes involved are not those envisaged in the eugenics literature or implicated in its historical practice. The word functions here, as it so often does, to mobilize anxieties. It says: no right-thinking person could fail to object to the process described. It is used, in effect, as a club. But the problem Wright identifies is certainly real.

We have essentially retreated to a position associated with nineteenth-century liberalism: that there are two spheres of activity—one in which the individual possesses absolute liberty, the other in which society might legitimately interfere. That distinction was originally asserted by John Stuart Mill. He thought there were two kinds of actions, those with and those without social consequences. Where one's actions affect others, society might intervene. But "over himself, over his own mind and body, the individual is sovereign."[43]

Few philosophers think this distinction workable; it is difficult to identify any activities devoid of social effects. But it is perhaps worth noting that reproduction and parenting were almost the only activities in respect to which Mill urged *greater* state responsibility. He wrote: "The fact itself, of causing the existence of a human being, is one of the most responsible actions in the range of human life. To undertake this responsibility—to bestow a life which may be either a curse or a blessing—unless the being on whom it is to be bestowed will have at least the ordinary chances of a desirable existence, is a crime against that being."[44] Thus, even Mill, who wished to grant the widest possible scope to individual action, and the least to society, thought reproduction and parenting inherently social.[45]

As the passage from Mill suggests, reproductive decisions have—at a minimum—consequences for another person. Our language conceals this fact. For example, we talk of "individual families" as though the interests of parents and children are necessarily identical. Yet potential conflicting interests within families are reflected in "Baby Doe" cases (where parents want their infants to die) and in the cases of parents who petition the courts to approve sterilization of retarded (usually female) children.

We do recognize potential conflicts in nonreproductive spheres. Thus, in respect to the issues of child labor or child abuse, we grant that the rights of individuals (as exercised by some individuals) may threaten the interests or freedom of other individuals in the absence of some intervening social choice. Consider the latter case. While ignoring the interests of the child, what if it could be shown with sufficiently persuasive evidence that violent and abusive treatment of children produced violent and abusive adults? Would there not then be a compelling argument for prohibiting child abuse *in addition* to an argument from the defense of the child's rights? It is commonly accepted that there is a social interest of this kind in education, and that does not mean the interest of some abstraction, called "Society," but the interest of other individuals who constitute society.

Unlike the child-abuse situation, however, individuals will certainly differ in their evaluation of the social effects of reproductive decisions. Whether they are viewed as good or bad, important or unimportant, is a function of deeply held values, about which people disagree. Any social policy will necessarily favor some values over others, and thus engender potentially bitter social conflict. Such conflict has largely been avoided through the privatization of reproductive decisions. But when the scope of politics is reduced, that of the market is usually expanded, thus replacing one form of social power with another.

The issues raised by contemporary developments in biomedicine are enormously difficult. There is, alas, no algorithm for their solution. An ethic of radical individualism might insulate reproductive decisions from racist and reactionary forces that dominated the eugenics movement, and thus permit potentially bitter social conflicts to be suppressed. But it also leaves society, as John Dunn has remarked of nineteenth-century liberals, "confronting History in the guise of an ostrich," without any way even of thinking through the issues involved.[46] And this refusal to consider social issues has a consequence even radicals have been reluctant to face: to retreat from politics is ultimately to embrace the market.

Chapter 10

Upside Risks
Social Consequences of Beneficial Biotechnology

GREGORY S. KAVKA

If any one of the millions of Southern Californians fails to install pollution-control devices on his car, the effects seem beneficial: he saves time, effort, and expense, and the extra emissions from his single car are too small to have any perceptible impact on the quality of air in the vast metropolitan Los Angeles air basin. But, of course, if all—or too many—Southern Californians did this, the result would be an environmental and health disaster of significant proportions. This is but one example of a general phenomenon now well known in social theory: the collective effect of a large number of people performing a given type of action may not be simply the sum of the effects of each of those people performing the same type of act in isolation.[1] Indeed, not just the magnitude, but the "moral direction" of the effects— whether they involve human harm or benefit—may differ. Thus, acts that would be beneficial if done alone may be harmful if done together, and acts that would be harmful if done alone (e.g., charging the enemy lines) may be beneficial if done together.

In this chapter, I will use this simple idea from social theory to illuminate some of the ethical issues raised by recent, and possible future, advances in biotechnology. It is readily apparent that such advances carry risks: unanticipated side effects on patients, stemming from new forms of treatment not fully understood; dangers of possibly harmful organisms being accidentally released into the environment; and so on.[2] I call these familiar sorts of risk *downside risks*. They are risks associated with "something going wrong," with biotechnology (or its products) not being applied to the right people, or not having (only) the desired effects on them when it is.

But the idea of collective effects, drawn from social theory, suggests that there may be risks of harmful effects on others, or on society as a whole, even when biotechnology is applied successfully and beneficially to the intended patients. I call these risks of negative social effects stemming from individually beneficial uses of biotechnology *upside risks*.[3] Looked at conceptually, upside risks represent the other side of Adam Smith's invisible hand. Smith observed that, via the mechanism of free markets, unlaudable (because selfish) individual actions are aggregated into socially beneficial outcomes: efficiency and prosperity. The idea behind the notion of upside risks is that acts (such as the effective application of biotechnology) can be individually beneficial but can create serious social problems when aggregated.

My main aim here is to identify various sorts of upside risk associated with advances in biotechnology and to discuss some of the moral and social implications of those problems. My focus will be on diagnostic techniques and therapies arising from recent and projected developments in genetics. For the sake of developing and illustrating my arguments, I take for granted two assumptions that may be controversial. First, I assume the truth of the claims by some of the more ambitious genetic researchers that we will be able to develop genetic techniques to manipulate such traits as intelligence, longevity, and competitiveness. Second, if such techniques become available, and are not prohibited or inhibited by social and legal norms, a significant and growing number of people will over time be inclined to use them to enhance their own—or their offspring's—genetic endowments.

Given these assumptions, I consider, in turn, four categories of upside risk that are likely to eventuate:

1. *Collective imbalance* occurs when a desirable distribution of characteristics in the general population is eliminated by the cumulative effects of individual decisions about the traits of offspring.
2. Biotechnology may supply its recipients with *competitive goods* that enable them to compete more effectively than other members of society for such social goods as power, wealth, and status.
3. If some benefits of biotechnology are scarce, expensive,

or hard to understand and to access, their availability may exacerbate existing patterns of *social inequality*.

4. If our capacity to manipulate genes develops so that we determine the identity of our offspring in a biological as well as a social sense, this may influence—in ways that are not benign—our *collective consciousness*, including our conception of who we are and what our place is in the overall scheme of things.

Each of these categories of upside risk poses a distinct set of moral problems that must be addressed if we are to understand the collective, as well as individual, implications of recent developments in biotechnology.

The "collective effects" idea implies that, in addition to upside risks, there can be *downside benefits* of biotechnology: uses of biotechnology that harm those whom the technology is applied to but that benefit society as a whole. And there are familiar phenomena that clearly qualify as downside benefits. The scientifically useful results of medical experiments that are more dangerous than helpful to their subjects are one clear example.[4] Any culture, such as our own, that takes seriously the value and dignity of the individual will be reluctant to seek the downside benefits of medical experiments done at the expense of the human subjects of those experiments, at least without receiving the fully free and informed consent of those subjects. But biotechnology can generate potential downside benefits by providing *information* as well as therapies and treatments. When we turn to consideration of the use of such information, as I do in the closing section, the moral waters are muddy enough to merit some discussion.

Collective Imbalance

Society may benefit from having certain distributions of genetically determined (or influenced) characteristics among its members. But if parents can select some of the genetic features of their offspring via the application of biotechnology, over time their choices may significantly change the existing distribution. Allowing them to do so can thereby have a harmful impact on society, even if the results of their choices are beneficial in individual cases.

The clearest example concerns sex selection. It is already technologically possible for parents to choose the sex of their children, either by prenatal gender diagnosis and selective abortion or by artificial insemination after preconception separation of sperm cells into son and daughter groups by centrifugation.[5] Given a decided preference in some cultures for male babies (especially for first-born male babies), widespread access to this technology could quite conceivably result in the birth of very many more boys than girls, a trend that may already have begun in some Asian countries.

Of course, general parental access to sex selection would not necessarily lead to gross imbalances in the proportions of men and women in society. As the economist Thomas Schelling points out, a lot would depend upon the form that gender preference takes among prospective parents. At current U.S. family sizes, the resulting imbalance would be small if parents waited until the last child and selected the "preferred" sex only if they had not yet had a child of that sex. On the other hand, if parents selected the (same) preferred sex for their *first* child, the resulting sex ratio would be 70:30![6] Unfortunately, there are two reasons for thinking that the latter behavior might be common. First, parents often do not know, at the time they have their first child, whether they will want (or be able to have) more children; hence, they will have to exercise selection on the first child if they are to maximize their prospects of exercising it at all. Second, many preferences are for a *first* boy (not simply some boy). Thus, current parental gender-preference patterns could produce large gender imbalances if universally implemented through available biotechnologies.

But would they be so implemented, even if these technologies were readily available to all? Schelling observes that parents might alter their preferences in order to correct perceived imbalances. If there are too many men, they will perceive that daughters would have their pick of many good mates while sons would have a hard time finding any mates (and vice versa). So parents will tend to act to "correct" social gender imbalances, and they may be successfully encouraged to do so by social policies that reward them for producing children of the less frequent gender.[7]

I doubt, however, that we could confidently rely on these processes to rectify gender imbalances. As Schelling acknowledges, there would be serious political objections to government policies favoring the selection of a certain gender: they would seem to imply that members of the other gender are less important or less valuable.[8] Nor will parents necessarily be swayed by their potential offspring's mating prospects: some would prefer to remain at the center of their unmarried children's lives, and many will fall prey to wishful thinking in the form of an expectation that *their* offspring will be so special as to find worthy mates no matter how competitive the marriage market might be.[9]

Further, even if most parents tried to produce children of the "less frequent" gender in their children's generation, they would face serious information problems in doing so. For if children are expected to marry in their own age cohort, which gender will yield the best mating prospects for your child will depend upon the outcomes of decisions being made by millions of other potential parents at roughly the same time you are making your decision. If you expect most others to choose "boy," then you should choose "girl" (and vice versa). But others face a similar choice with the same information and can therefore be expected to choose as you do. Indeed, given the situational symmetry of the prospective parents aiming to produce children of the "less frequent" gender, two strategies seem to make the most sense. One could reason that the choices of parents, making similar choices as yours at the same time as yours, are unpredictable. Therefore, one should choose the gender that is less frequent in the previous cohorts (since your offspring might marry into them). But if enough parents in a cohort follow this strategy, it will be self-defeating for them, since they will be producing children of the same gender with their fellows. Alternatively, one could reason that since the simultaneous choices of others are unpredictable, one should randomize. Following this strategy, however, amounts to not employing sex selection at all and will not produce the counterbalancing effect that Schelling hypothesizes.

If I am right that significant gender imbalances represent a real future possibility for some societies, we must ask whether they are a bad thing. The Glover Commission report indicates that they are, but the only reason given is that the current 50:50 ratio "seems likely to make everyone's sex life easier."[10] Schelling, by contrast, points out that significant local imbalances between the genders in numbers of potential marriage partners already exist (e.g., in elderly populations, in Alaska),[11] presumably without producing social catastrophe. In view of this, while I am as ready as the next person to favor Pareto improvements (i.e., everyone's being made better off), especially as regards our sex lives, I think more must be said in order to vindicate the Glover Commission's view that gender imbalances are harmful.

And there is more to say. Let us imagine the likely characteristics of a society very much like ours but having an overall gender ratio of two males per female. Males, we know, are much more prone to commit violent crimes than are women. Further, many violent crimes are committed by young men, who later marry, have families, and settle down to a more law-abiding life.[12] If there were a higher proportion of men in society, then, other things being equal, we could expect the per capita rate of violent crime to rise substantially for at least three reasons:

1. A higher percentage of the population are members of a group that is more inclined to commit violent crimes.
2. Fewer men will marry, or marry as early, thus prolonging the portion of their life cycle most likely to be devoted to criminal activity.
3. With more men competing for fewer mates, the frequency of "crimes of passion" is likely to increase.

There is an international analogue to this potential domestic crime spree. In recent years, a significant political gender gap has developed in the United States on foreign policy issues, with the political views of men tending to be significantly more nationalistic and militaristic than those of women.[13] Together with the easier availability of more front-line soldiers in a society that is two-thirds male, this might lead to a more aggressive and dangerous foreign policy being pursued by such a country. Indeed, wars brought on by, and fought between, nations that are even more male-dominated than today's nations, are one distinctly possible unhappy outcome if certain gender imbalances were to occur as a result of sex selection.

Besides these potential problems, there are the mating problems alluded to by the Glover Commission, problems that could be quite serious in the absence of unlikely reforms in our mating and marrying customs (e.g., allowing—even encouraging—polyandry). There might be some compensating advantages of having more men in society, such as having more people able to do heavy physical labor; but since technology is continually reducing the proportion of "brute strength" occupations, these advantages are unlikely to outweigh the significant disadvantages.[14] Of course, only the mating-mismatch problem would apply to a society containing a preponderance of *female* members, but I pass over this possibility since actual culturewide gender-preference patterns seem either to be neutral or to favor men.

All of this adds up, in my view, to a strong case that societies should discourage and, if necessary, prohibit sex selection by parents, except in cases of sex-linked genetic disease. Unfortunately, most medical geneticists in the United States have a permissive (though ambivalent) attitude toward sex selection: many apparently believe that the patient's autonomy—in the form of parental freedom to choose—must be respected even here.[15] My observations point to considerations that may override patient autonomy in such cases. And they provide a valid justification that could be offered to parents for not allowing them to select the gender of their children. Namely: like pollution, sex selection—while harmless in the individual case—has potentially dangerous cumulative effects upon society as a whole; hence, society has a legitimate interest in preventing or restricting it.

Future developments in genetic-engineering techniques, along with greater knowledge about which specific (sets of) genes determine or influence various human traits, could combine to create the potential for serious collective imbalances besides an altered gender ratio. Suppose that down the road scientists will be able to identify and manipulate genes (or groups of genes) that influence specific psychological or social traits, in the sense of making them more or less likely to develop in a given social and physical environment. Parental selection of such traits could upset some very delicate social balances. To take but one of many stylized examples, hypercompetitive people may function well and tend to be successful in a society in which they are in a distinct minority. (In addition, they may serve a useful social function by stirring others to greater productivity.) This would seem to give parents an incentive to select for their children genes that promote hypercompetitiveness, if this were possible. But if too many parents did this, the effects on their offspring and on society as a whole would likely be bad. The oversupply of hypercompetitive people would create a "too many generals" problem: most would find their high expectations of success dashed, they would be in constant conflict with their hypercompetitive fellows, and the spectacle of their struggles and conflicts would probably discourage other members of society from putting forth greater productive efforts.

My final example concerns longevity. It has been suggested, by some who are in a position to know, that genetic engineering might eventually be able to delay the effects of human aging and prolong significantly the human life span.[16] Obviously, at the individual level, this would be a great benefit. Indeed, we think of the near doubling of mean life span from primitive times to our own as one of the great social benefits of human progress and modern civilization. But our primitive ancestors lived in a sparsely populated world, and their life-styles placed few demands on their biological and physical environment. In a modern world of billions of people, many of whom are living in ways that significantly pollute the earth and reduce its supply of nonrenewable resources, it is not at all clear that substantial further increases in human longevity would be a collective benefit rather than a burden. It is therefore possible to *imagine* a future world in which population pressures and advanced genetic techniques combine such that society, to protect itself, will offer individuals a harsh choice between (1) extending their own life span, at the price of surrendering the right to reproduce, or (2) retaining the right to reproduce without having an extended life span.[17]

In sum, we can conceive of a variety of ways in which parents' selection of their offspring's genetic traits might harm society by changing the frequency of those traits among society's members. Indeed, technologies are now available for one form of such selection—sex selection—in which the implementation of parents' preferences might well alter substantially the current distribution of the trait in question, with predictable ill effects. In formulating social policies to deal with such cases of potential collective imbalance, we should not be misled by the fact that *individual* acts of parental selection are harmless, and thus fall into the conclusion that such acts should necessarily be free of social and legal restrictions.

Competitive Goods

The seventeenth-century political philosopher Thomas Hobbes compared "the life of man to a race." He wrote: "But this *race* we must suppose to have no other *goal,* nor other *garland,* but being foremost, and in it: . . . Continually to be out-gone, is *misery.* Continually to out-go, the next before, is *felicity.* And to forsake the course, is to *die.*"[18] In the spirit of Hobbes, modern social theorists have observed that people seek not only to have, consume, attain, and achieve things; they also seek to be "foremost" in their pursuits, to have, consume, attain, and achieve *more than other people.* In the language of economists, people desire *positional goods* such as status, honor, and victory, which consist in ranking above others along some significant comparative dimension.[19] But positional goods have a drawback: they are inherently scarce. Not everyone can be first in line; for every winner in a meaningful competition, there is at least one loser; and so on. And the pursuit of positional goods tends to be a ceaseless and never-completed one, as Hobbes observes in equating felicity, or happiness, with "continually to out-go, the next before." For as soon as you have surpassed the person ahead of you in some ranking, a new person immediately becomes the person ahead of you, and you may not rest until you have surpassed him or her. And even should you reach the top position in a particular hierarchy, you can hardly rest easy on your laurels, since others seeking your perch will be continually seeking to "out-go" you.

For some people, as Hobbes suggests, positional goods are intrinsic goods: the aim in seeking them is simply to surpass and outdo others. But positional goods are typically valuable as instruments as well, so that they would be sought by rational people who do not care a wit, for its own sake, how they rank with respect to others. Thus, even if it did not matter to M. J. whether or not he was the world's greatest basketball player, he might still reasonably seek to *be* the best (or at least appear to be), for he would then be in a position to earn millions of dollars playing basketball and endorsing commercial products. But wealth is not the only nonpositional good that a high ranking in various hierarchies may make available to those possessing it.[20] Another is *access* (of various sorts) to other persons of high rank in one or another hierarchy. If you want to meet, do business with, become friends with, or even marry people of high rank in a given hierarchy, there is often no better way to do so than to achieve such rank yourself in that or a closely connected hierarchy.

My concern here is with a special class of positional goods that I call *competitive goods*. These are physical or psychological dimensions, like beauty, sociability, and intelligence, along which people are ranked and whose possession in higher degrees is (or is thought to be) positively related to one's chances of obtaining such important social goods as wealth, power, status, and a wider choice of careers, friends, and mates. Suppose that future developments in genetic engineering enabled parents to increase the genetic endowments of their offspring along one or more of these dimensions if they so chose. Would such an increase in the supply of these competitive goods be a good thing?

Looked at from the point of view of the individual parent (or child), the answer is an obvious yes. If parents want a smarter, friendlier, or lovelier child, and if greater intelligence, friendliness, or beauty tend to make a person's life go better, it seems that the results of such genetic manipulation should be regarded as good without qualification. But, of course, if we look at the collective social effects of large numbers of parents indulging in this practice, the issue is seen to be decidedly more complex.

Consider intelligence. On the benefit side, if many parents have more intelligent children, this will raise the average level of intelligence in the population and should, other things being equal, increase productivity. On the other hand, as a competitive good, greater intelligence is valued partly for its own sake as a positional good (i.e., for moving up on the intelligence ladder compared to one's fellows) and as an instrument for competing for other goods such as wealth and career opportunities. But if very many parents were to exercise the option of increasing their offspring's intelligence genetically, it would not have this effect for most. For these children will be competing for intelligence rankings, and for the jobs and wealth made possible by high intelligence, against many others who have been given similar "intelligence boosts." Just as a college degree, now that most other people also have one, buys less vocational advantage, higher intelligence would buy less vocational advantage if, owing to genetic enhancement, most others had it too.

This is not to say there would be *no* competitive advantage gained by supplying your child with a genetic intelligence boost if that were possible. Your child would have an advantage over those whose parents refrained from applying the genetic technology. And at least he or she would not be *dis*advantaged relative to other children who received the genetic treatments. But these last observations raise, in turn, moral concerns about fairness and social welfare.

The fairness issue is a straightforward one: if some parents choose not to boost genetically the intelligence of their offspring—for moral, religious, cultural, or personal reasons—their offspring would be at a competitive disadvantage compared to the offspring of parents without such qualms. This might be unfair to the children in question (who would have to compete in the face of a technologically created disadvantage), and it could put intolerable pressure on parents to choose between their own moral or religious commitments and the future success of their children.

The social welfare or efficiency issue emerges most clearly if we imagine the intelligence-boosting procedure to be imperfect, carrying a slight risk of significant physical or mental damage to the offspring.[21] Then we could have a situation in which both of the following conditions hold:

1. The individual risk of damage is small enough, and the competitive advantage of the intelligence boost is large enough, so that couples will have a net incentive to use the procedure despite its risks.
2. Since most of the competitive advantages of the intelligence boost cancel one another out if enough parents use it, the net social advantage for most people using the technique is outweighed by the social cost of the damaged children that result.

In such a situation, each couple acting in a manner that is individually rational (i.e., using the intelligence boost) would lead to a bad social outcome (i.e., too many damaged children and too little benefit from the increased average intelligence of the population to compensate for that). People would be better off, as a whole, if the individually beneficial intelligence-boost technique were not used, but the structure of the incentives in the situation would likely prevent this from happening.[22]

The classic solution for social problems having this structure, where individual incentives lead to less-than-optimal social outcomes, is to change the incentives by enforcing a ban on certain alternatives.[23] In the case being considered here, that would mean forbidding genetic enhancement of intelligence, or any other competitive good, and thereby attempting to ensure a collective outcome that is both more efficient and more fair. Would such a ban on providing competitive goods to one's offspring by genetic engineering be justified?

One way of arguing contra is to make a distinction between correcting deficiencies and enhancing normal capacities. The genetic enhancement of normal capabilities, so the argument goes, should be banned because of the efficiency and fairness issues just noted. But correcting deficiencies by genetic means must be allowable, for that merely removes an undeserved competitive disadvantage that individuals would otherwise have.

The problem with this argument is that typical competitive goods, like intelligence and beauty, are continuous goods. They come in various degrees—not just "normal" and "deficient"—with the amount of competitive advantage they provide related to the degree to which they are exemplified in a given case. Because of the competitive role of these goods, moreover, what counts as a deficit of them depends upon the degree to which most others have them. (Thus, in a population full of "Einsteins," your average workaday physicist might count as deficient in intelligence.) From our current population, then, suppose we were to designate the lowest 10 percent in level-of-possession of a given competitive good as "deficient" and therefore eligible for enhancement by genetic engineering. Suppose further a procedure (involving preconception—or prenatal—screening followed by genetic engineering) that, on average, could raise to the median level those who otherwise would likely be in the bottom decile. If we were to eliminate the bottom 10 percent in this way, the next-lowest decile would eventually become the bottom 10 percent (and become eligible for enhancement), and so on. The results would be the same as for genetic engineering to enhance the desired trait under no restrictions, except that things would proceed more slowly. The competitive advantages would cancel one another out across the population, and the net social advantage gained by increasing the mean level of the trait in the society might well be outweighed by any risks associated with the genetic procedure. In sum, so long as "normality" and "deficiency" in competitive goods are characterized relative to social averages, the main arguments against genetic enhancement of the normal also apply to genetic enhancement of the deficient.

There is a better strategy, however, for forestalling the conclusion that genetic enhancement of competitive goods should be prohibited. This strategy rests on the analogy between environmental and genetic enhancement of an offspring's possession of competitive goods. An individual's possession of competitive goods is thought to be the result of complex interactions between that individual's genetic endowment and his or her physical and social environment. Parents typically have great influence on a child's environment and thus, particularly as more becomes known about which environments tend to facilitate the development of competitive goods, can affect the level of competitive goods their offspring possess. Despite our awareness that some environments facilitate a child's possession of competitive goods more than others, we do not think we should prohibit parents from providing better *environments* for their children. Even though this may give some children a competitive advantage over others with less favorable environments, our attitude toward parents providing their children with the best possible environment is one of encouragement rather than discouragement. And this is so despite the fact that (1) some of the advantages so gained by individuals are competitive ones that will cancel one another out (on a societywide basis), and (2) environments that promote competitive goods may harm children in other ways (e.g., by depriving them of the joys of a relatively carefree childhood).[24] Thus, we care enough about individual liberty to allow couples to practice positive euthenics (i.e., beneficial environmental manipulation) on their children.[25] For example, we allow parents who can afford it to send their children to superior private schools, despite the competitive damage this may inflict on poorer children. At the same time, we wish to promote overall equality of opportunity. Therefore, we collectively fund not only public schools, but also negative euthenics projects (e.g., Head Start) which try to provide a more favorable environment for some of those we expect to be most environmentally disadvantaged. The analogues of such attitudes at the genetic level would be expressed in allowing genetic enhancement of competitive goods by parents, but assuring availability (and affordability) of the technology to all who wish to take advantage of it.

If we accept the above analogy between genetic enhancement and euthenics with respect to competitive goods,[26] there are two different conclusions we might draw. The more radical conclusion is that we have been much too permissive about euthenics: we should not allow parents to competitively advantage their children to the extent we do. And if this error is too socially entrenched to correct, we should at least not repeat it at the genetic level, where it has not yet become entrenched. An alternative conclusion is that genetic enhancement might be allowable, if provisions are made to deal sufficiently with concerns about fairness and equality. Let us turn to the distributive issues raised in this latter conclusion.

Social Inequality

New medical technologies are typically scarce and expensive when introduced, and they often remain so. Currently, for example, organ transplants are still very expensive, and there is a considerable shortage of organs, relative to the number of needy recipients, available for transplant. When important goods—like needed medical treatments—are scarce and expensive, there is a tendency for them to be obtained by the rich and powerful, and forgone by the poor and powerless. Thus, expensive high-tech medicine tends to advantage those members of society, in disproportion to their numbers, who are already most advantaged. It therefore exacerbates, rather than mitigates, existing patterns of social inequality—unless, that is, public measures are taken to curtail such distributive effects.

Of course, it is seriously controversial whether social inequality, in itself, is a bad thing. Philosophical views on this matter range from egalitarian endorsements of equality as the preeminent social value to the libertarian view that social equality—in itself—has no positive value at all. Nor is this fundamental dispute an easy one to settle. Imagine that you and I initially have equal levels of wealth and well-being. But now your wealth and well-being are doubled, while I remain where I was. Is the resulting social state better or worse than the original? Strict egalitarians might count it worse, solely on the grounds that we have traded equality for inequality. Libertarians, though, would regard this scenario as a paradigm of social improvement, since someone has gained and no one has lost.

However we stand on this theoretical dispute over the intrinsic merits of social equality, the *instrumental* benefits of social equality are clear if we accept the truth of two empirical assumptions. The first is an interpersonal version of the economic principle of "declining marginal utility of income." On average, says this principle, a given increment of income (or some other good) will produce more utility for a poorer person than for a richer one. (This is a generalization of the intuitive idea that five more dollars may mean food and shelter for someone living on the street, but will not improve the life of a millionaire at all.) The second assumption, the "keeping up with the Joneses" principle, is a restatement of some of our earlier observations about positional goods. It says that people care about how they are faring in comparison to people around them, so that their overall level of well-being depends not just on their level of consumption, but on how that level compares with consumption by others. Taken together, these assumptions imply that, other things being equal,[27] a more equal distribution of utility-producing goods—such as income, employment, or health-care services—will produce a higher level of overall social benefit. Since I believe these two assumptions are plausible, at least for the sort of modern societies we live in, I will henceforth assume that it is reasonable to concern ourselves with promoting equality in the distribution of important goods like health-care services.

If we are concerned about social equality, we should worry that as developments in biomedical technology offer greater and greater benefits to individual recipients, the result will be more and more inequality, unless society makes institutional reforms. One obvious reform, already instituted in many countries, is some sort of comprehensive national health-care or health insurance system. However, such systems are now facing serious budgetary and scarcity problems, which are likely to worsen as even more exotic and expensive technological devices for diagnosis and therapy arrive on the scene. The fact is, society may not be able to afford "the best medical care" for everyone, if "best care" means the use of all the expensive technologies that would likely be beneficial in each particular case. Facing up to this reality will require hard allocation decisions that accept some trade-offs among efficiency, social equality, citizen health, and longevity.

In addition to these familiar conundrums, there are two further equality-related issues that merit attention. Even providing affordable access to medical treatment and technology may not equalize the effective use of these services among different social groups and classes. If there are cognitive, emotional, or cultural interferences with the consumption of such services, different social groups may be differentially affected even when they formally have equal access. Thus, for example, information about the health benefits of exercise and not smoking has apparently less effect, in the United States, on the behavior of poor people and minorities than on other citizens. This suggests that if we aspire to anything like equality in the actual *use* of biotechnology, a special effort (beyond financial subsidies) may have to be made to encourage certain groups in society to take advantage of the benefits of biotechnology.[28]

The other issue concerns the possible future effects of widespread genetic engineering. Genetic enhancement has conflicting implications for social equality. If restricted to socially favored groups, of course, genetic enhancement would simply produce greater inequality. But suppose it were equally available to, and used by, members of all social groups. Then it would have the potential to decrease overall social inequality by providing offspring with competitive goods in patterns that are uncorrelated with previous group membership. In other words, the new "genetically improved" human would come in all colors, genders, ethnicities, and so on, and the possible negative social effects of one's membership in historically disparaged groups might well be overshadowed by one's membership in this new favored group. But there, in the term "favored group," lies the rub. Any such move toward genetic enhancement has the potential of reestablishing social inequality, though along new lines. Old aristocracies of birth, color, or gender may dissipate, only to be replaced by a new genetic aristocracy, or "genetocracy." But our worries about such a new aristocracy are not so much about inequality, per se, as they are about the nature of a society that would place so much emphasis on the genes of its members. The character, and validity, of these worries will be touched upon next.

Our Collective Consciousness

Advances in biotechnology have the capacity to influence not only what we do, individually and collectively, but how we think. The most significant social effects of genetic engineering, in particular, may have to do with how we conceive of ourselves and our place in the overall scheme of things. That is because, with the waning of the religious idea that our identities reside in a living soul infused into us by God, we have come to think of our genes as determining our identity as individuals and as a species—as determining who we are. Manipulating our genes, and having the perceived capacity to do so, thus takes on the appearance of "playing God." And it creates, at least in some, a fear of the monstrous consequences of mere mortal beings fooling with the foundations of their own existence and essence—the "Frankenstein factor."[29]

In large part, these are fears about something going wrong in the use of biotechnology—the creation of nonhuman or partly human monsters, the shaping of a docile citizenry for political purposes, and so on. Such risks, to the extent they are real, are among the familiar downside risks of biotechnology and, as such, fall outside the scope of the present chapter. Yet there are also upside risks lurking here—risks that the very successes of biotechnology will change our thinking, and our corresponding social practices, in ways that are not benign. In seeking to identify some of these risks, I am engaging in speculation. But speculation need not be groundless or fruitless, and no alternative procedure seems to be at hand for anticipating future trends in collective thought patterns.

Here, then, are a few possible ways that future successes in genetic engineering might affect our ways of thinking about the world, ourselves, and society. First of all, we might come to view parents as being more responsible for how their children turn out than we now view them. For parents will have had the chance to shape their offspring's genes as well as their environment. Correspondingly, with reproduction mediated by deliberate scientific manipulation, parents might come to see their children more as products or achievements than as pieces or parts of themselves. Among the possible social outcomes that could result from such changes in attitude are parental criminal responsibility for the conduct of their offspring and an increase in the (already high) level of competitiveness that parents induce in their children.

Social tolerance for diversity and abnormality, never in abundant supply, may diminish further if society reduces the amount of diversity and abnormality by means of genetic manipulation. This will leave those relatively few who remain outside the bounds of normality in even more uncomfortable social straits than at present. It may also lead to shifting criteria of normality, whereby any deviation from the usual pattern, if it could have been prevented or corrected by genetic manipulation, counts as a flaw or error. This, in turn, may result in the deviating individuals being regarded and treated as "mistakes" or "social impurities."[30]

Further successes in biotechnology may also strengthen the modern faith in technology as providing adequate solutions to problems of all kinds. Strengthening this faith may not be a good thing. It could lead to an overemphasis on technical, as opposed to humane, solutions to social problems—drug testing rather than drug treatment, for example. It may even foster the illusion that we can overcome any problem—including overpopulation, pollution, and resource depletion—by purely technical means. If we come to believe this, but turn out to be wrong, humankind will pay a heavy price in later generations.

Our ability to influence our offspring's genetic traits could also have a tendency to undermine individualist normative views. If people's characteristics are chosen by society at the deepest level, then the view that people belong to society, that they are its creatures and creations, takes on added force. When God was universally assumed to be our creator, it was considered proper that we follow divine wishes and commands, that we carry out the divine plan whose fulfillment was the purpose of our creation. Should society, or its members, be seen to have created and shaped us (through genetic engineering) with certain purposes in mind, it will seem natural to many that we must conform to these purposes rigidly, just as earlier cultures cleaved to what they took to be God's laws. This attitude is in conflict with the attractive individualist view that society's purposes are composed from the purposes of its members, that there must be limits to the subordination of the individual to the purposes of the larger society.[31]

Yet another possible effect of genetic engineering on our collective psyche is the vaguest of all, but it is potentially the most important. Having captured the power to shape the biological future of our own species, we may feel an awesome, possibly overwhelming, sense of responsibility. What I have in mind is a feeling akin to the "existential dread" that philosophers have claimed people experience when they realize there is no God and, therefore, no external purpose or set of norms written into the structure of the universe. But in the absence of religious belief, we have nonetheless been able to see our collective destiny as controlled by other all-powerful and inexorable forces: chance and natural selection. If we achieve the vast power to alter deliberately our genetic heritage, however, we will see *ourselves*—not God, not chance, not even nature—as ultimately responsible for the human future. This sort of responsibility has some similarity to that created by nuclear weapons, which give us the power to end the human future once and for all.[32] With biotechnology we also have the potential to improve the human future in many different ways; and it will take sound judgment, not simply technical expertise, to find the right way (or even one of the better ways). This combination of vast power, a lack of clear standards, and inescapable choices is a prescription for a tormented collective soul (and, at the operational level, for intense political conflict).

Having set forth these speculations about the effects on our collective psyche of future progress in genetic engineering, I want to emphasize two things. First, some of the effects mentioned, were they to occur, might also generate good social outcomes. It is possible, for example, that a sense of awesome responsibility for our species' biological destiny might force us to become unusually careful and thoughtful as we develop responsive social policies. Second, the most important effects on our collective consciousness may well be ones that we cannot predict at all until they are nearly full upon us. Needless to say, we can do little about such effects other than to be on the look-out for them, so that we might recognize them (and attempt to deal with them if we can) at the earliest possible time.

Uses of Genetic Information

Thus far, my concern has been with the upside risks that flow from recent and projected advances in biotechnology. I now turn briefly to some of the moral problems concerning the use of genetic information. Numerous treatments of this subject have focused on the harm that may be done to individuals owing to the "misuse" of such information (e.g., discrimination in employment and insurance).[33] While not meaning to minimize these downside risks, I will note that they must be balanced against the potential social benefits from public use of genetic information and that, in at least one context, these "downside benefits" could outweigh the harm to individuals.

Suppose, as is apparently already the case with respect to some serious illnesses, genetic testing were able to identify whether a given individual is likely to develop a specific illness at some later time. The availability of this information could harm potentially affected individuals in at least three ways: direct psychological costs, effects on insurability, and employment limitations. Let us consider each, in turn.

It is clear that there are psychological costs of knowing that you are likely (perhaps even certain) to develop a serious illness. Such knowledge, even if it is not shared with anyone else, is likely to have a negative effect on the quality of one's life prior to the onset of any symptoms. Of course, people could avoid these costs by refraining from being tested, but this might be irrational if there are early treatments that offer some hope of improving one's health,[34] or if one is deciding whether to have children and one does not wish to transmit disease susceptibility. Further, if one already has reason to think one is at risk for the disease, the agonizing decision-costs of whether or not to seek more conclusive genetic information may themselves be quite high. (Such costs are borne by people whose family history already puts them at risk of developing Huntington's disease, since genetic testing is now available that provides a clear diagnosis.)

Whatever an individual's reaction to the news that he or she is at high risk of developing a serious illness, the reactions of the insurance companies are predictable. They will refuse to sell life and health insurance to the high-risk individual, or they will charge extremely high premiums. Nor would this problem be solved by making the genetic information available only to the individual in question and to those he or she chooses to share it with. For the insurance companies could then solicit the information indirectly, offering low-premium policies to anyone who provides a clean "genetic bill of health" and charging very high premiums to anyone who declines (or is unable) to do so.

What about forbidding people from providing insurance companies with their genetic test results? As Robert Wright points out, even this would not necessarily work.[35] Companies could respond by offering only high-cost policies against sickness and death from specific illnesses—"à la carte" policies, Wright calls them. High-risk individuals would have to pay the high premiums, if they could afford it, and other individuals could not economically insure themselves against the disease at all. These other individuals would be caught in a trap analogous to that facing someone who tries to sell a quality used car. Economists have pointed out that, owing to the asymmetry in information between sellers and buyers of used cars, and the known fact that people are more likely to sell used cars that are "lemons" than those which are not, sellers of good used cars will—on average—have to discount the value of the car to compensate the buyer for the high risk of buying a lemon.[36] In particular, the prospective seller of a nonlemon on the used-car market will have to expect a price less than *he knows* the car is really worth, because he cannot credibly convey to buyers the true quality of the car. (This, in turn, is because all sellers of used cars—including those selling lemons—claim that their cars are not lemons, and buyers do not know who is lying and who is telling the truth.) A person *not at special genetic risk* for developing a particular illness, but who wants to be insured against that illness (perhaps because of a high aversion to risk or because of a special distaste for the symptoms of that illness) is like the seller of the quality used car. Forbidden to reveal his genetic test results to insurance companies, he cannot credibly convince them that he is a low-risk customer, and he will either pay a high-risk premium rate or go without the insurance.

Wright's argument and the used-car market analogy indicate

that changes which go beyond forbidding the direct provision of genetic information may be necessary if we want insurability to survive future genetic-testing developments. At a minimum, insurance companies would have to be forbidden from providing "à la carte" health and life policies. At a maximum, government might have to step in and provide comprehensive health and life insurance.

All this, however, rests on the supposition that continued insurability, roughly on the present model, is a good thing. But is it? As new genetic information allows us to segregate people into ever more specific risk-pools, why should we remix the different risk-pools so that I—genetically healthy—have to pay higher premiums to protect you—genetically at high risk? Is this any more desirable than, say, careful drivers having to pay the same auto insurance premiums as reckless drivers?

I think it is, for at least two reasons. First, we do not choose and control our genetic endowment as we do our driving behavior (or misbehavior). Hence, the higher premiums paid by the reckless driver can be justified on grounds of fairness (premiums are proportionate to the degree of risk drivers *choose* to impose on others) as well as deterrence (lower premiums for safe driving will encourage safe driving) in ways that higher premiums for genetic susceptibility to disease cannot be.[37] Second, as I have argued elsewhere, society and its members benefit from the feeling that we are all together in a common enterprise and share one another's fate.[38] Insurance can be a device for forcing us to share one another's fate: through it, uncertainty, self-interest, and risk aversion combine to make us take care of one another to some extent. If too much uncertainty is replaced by knowledge—as in the case of genetic information about illness susceptibility—this useful device may be threatened in the ways suggested above, and will need to be repaired and rescued.

Insurance companies are not the only economic agents interested in people's genetic susceptibilities to disease. Employers prefer workers who are less likely to become seriously ill, because this reduces replacement and retraining costs, interruptions in production, and insurance costs. In addition, some work environments may be known to predispose workers to a high rate of certain illnesses: employers, of course, would prefer to hire workers who are genetically resistant, rather than susceptible, to those environment-related illnesses. This raises fears that workers found to be genetically susceptible to illness will be "discriminated against" in job markets. And, as in the insurance scenario, keeping genetic information under the individual's control will not solve the problem: employers could hire only those who "voluntarily" submit genetic data (or they might offer lower wages and salaries to applicants who do not submit such data).

There are "downside" social benefits to such employment practices. Hiring the genetically "healthier" will reduce production costs and increase efficiency; barring susceptible workers from particular work environments will decrease the overall level of illness in the society. However, I think the balance of benefits comes out quite differently in the two cases. General discrimination in wages or employment opportunities against those who are genetically disposed toward serious illness is likely to be quite harmful overall. These people are not helped; they are simply shunted into less desirable jobs, lower wages, or unemployment. Their bad genetic luck is transformed into a bad social and economic outcome as society adds insult and further injury to the physical injuries they are likely to suffer. And while "efficiency" in the narrow sense may be improved in some job categories, much of this gain will be canceled out by the increased inefficiencies (owing to greater illness among workers) in other job categories where the genetically less desirable workers are redirected.

On the other hand, there might be a point to matching workers to specific work environments according to their non-susceptibility to illnesses common in those environments. Assuming that relatively few job opportunities are eliminated for a given person with genetic susceptibilities to specific illnesses, the costs of marginally limiting people's options may be outweighed by the overall health benefits of substantially fewer work-environment-related illnesses. No individual's options would be severely limited, and if the genetic information were available early in the person's life, they could make their choices about training and careers using this information. Indeed, the really delicate issue is not whether matching less-susceptible workers to disease-causing work environments is desirable, but whether employers would be permitted, by law, to perform such matching. The argument against such license is the liberal one that individual workers should be allowed to choose whether or not to work in a risky environment. If they are willing to risk their health and lives, even in the possession of genetic information that indicates these risks are significant, they ought to be allowed to do so. On the other side is the paternalistic argument that people do not always assess risks rationally, and that they often make job decisions under considerable pressure.[39] If such failures in decisionmaking are systematic and predictable, and society can protect its members from them, it ought to do so. Without attempting to settle the liberal/paternalist debate on this issue (or in general), I will simply note that if paternalist arguments succeed in any context, it is probably in a context like this one in which people's lives and health are at stake, and where there are reasons to question the reliability of their decisions.

While employment and insurance discrimination have been widely discussed in the literature, a third important form of discrimination made possible by genetic testing has gone largely unnoticed: mating discrimination. People are normally concerned about the characteristics of their children, including those characteristics determined or influenced by genes. The availability of genetic information thus has a potential impact on people's prospects not only in the insurance and job markets, but in the "marriage market" as well. In the past, people have sought mates who had desirable characteristics to pass on (socially or genetically) to their offspring: wealth, social class, good looks, intelligence, and so on. If better and more specific information about the individual's genes is made available through advances in biotechnology, it would be naive to assume that many individuals would not, in the absence of laws or other social norms to the contrary, make use of that information in their selection of mates.

Currently there are dating services whose members are certified to have tested negative for exposure to the AIDS virus. Even if genetic data were privately controlled by the individual, then, there is nothing to prevent people from demanding, as a precondition, genetic information from those whom they would date, marry, or mate. Nor is it clear that society has a right to prevent such private informational transactions, even if many of us find the mere idea of them degrading and destructive of positive ideals of love and family. It is one thing to forbid insurance companies or employers from demanding someone's genetic test results, it is another to forbid enamored fiancées from disclosing such information to their prospective spouses as a final condition of marriage. Nor is it *necessarily* unreasonable to ask for such information: if one can reasonably refuse to marry a child abuser for the sake of one's future children, then cannot one refuse to marry someone with a horrible genetic disease for the sake of one's future children? And, if so, might it not be reasonable to inquire whether one's prospective spouse had such a disease if the information were readily available?

What is interesting here is that our liberal and paternalistic instincts get turned around from where they were in the employment case. In that scenario, considerations of social benefit ranged on the side of disclosure of genetic information, while liberal principles favored the individual's freedom of nondisclosure and choice. Here, because marriage is a choice between two individuals, liberalism would seem to permit the prospective spouse who is interested in his or her mate's genes to demand all relevant genetic information as a precondition of entering into the voluntary arrangement of marriage. On the other hand, we feel that people as a whole—and society at large—would be harmed by any large-scale exercise of such individual prerogative. Certain positive aspects of marriage would be undermined, and a tendency toward "genocratic" attitudes—which evaluate people not as people but as beanbags of genetic endowment—would be developed and reinforced. Thus, to protect us against ourselves, and each other, we have good reasons to develop—or retain—social norms (including laws) that limit incursions by genetic information into marriage markets.

This, in a sense, brings us back to where we started. Individual liberty to marry a person with the genes you want, like other options being created by advances in biotechnology, may benefit you. But if enough people exercise that liberty, or pursue some of the other individually beneficial options provided by biotechnology, the overall social consequences may well be bad. Developments in biotechnology carry upside, as well as downside, risks.[40]

Chapter 11

When Science Enters the Courtroom
The DNA-Typing Controversy

WILLIAM C. THOMPSON

Tests capable of identifying criminals by "typing" their DNA are an important technological spin-off of the molecular revolution in human genetics. The development of these tests was greeted with enormous enthusiasm. Heralded as "a prosecutors' dream" and "the greatest advance in crime fighting technology since fingerprints," the new DNA-typing tests were introduced swiftly into the legal system.[1] Recently, however, a serious scientific controversy has erupted over the accuracy and reliability of the new tests. A number of scientific critics have charged that the new technology was rushed to court before it was ready.[2]

The scientific dispute has led to confusion (and conflicting rulings) in the legal system. Although DNA evidence has already been used to obtain convictions in several hundred cases,[3] courts have recently ruled DNA evidence inadmissible on grounds that it is not generally accepted to be reliable by the scientific community.[4] Some critics have called for reexamination of the DNA evidence in closed cases.[5] The dispute has generated such heated exchanges, both inside and outside the courtroom, that some participants have called it a "war."[6]

Responding to a "crescendo of questions concerning DNA typing," the National Research Council (NRC) of the National Academy of Sciences established a committee in 1990 to examine the use of DNA technology in forensic science. In April 1992, the NRC released a report that firmly endorsed the general principles behind forensic DNA testing, but acknowledged that there have been problems with the implementation of the new technology.[7] The NRC Report makes a number of recommendations for improving test procedures.

Not surprisingly, proponents of forensic DNA evidence offer very different accounts of the controversy than do critics. According to proponents, an excellent scientific technique has been unfairly maligned by a small group of scientists who have managed to command attention and garner large fees for expert testimony by making exaggerated criticisms.[8] By this account, the root of the controversy is the powerful incentives offered by the legal system for overstated criticisms and ersatz scientific dissent.

Critics argue that commercial pressures on private laboratories competing for market share, and political pressures on the FBI, led forensic laboratories to rush a promising but poorly validated new technique to court before it was ready.[9] When legitimate criticisms were raised, promoters of DNA testing responded by attacking the critics rather than heeding their message. Meanwhile, hundreds of criminal defendants have been convicted by evidence that may have been considerably less probative than juries were led to believe.[10] By this account, problems arose because the new DNA tests received inadequate scientific scrutiny before being used in court.

The scientific and legal issues involved in the "DNA war" warrant close examination because they can tell us much about the problems surrounding the introduction of new technology into the legal system. DNA typing is the first technical spin-off of the molecular revolution in science to reach the courtroom, but it will not be the last. The response of the legal system to future battles may well turn on which account of the current DNA war is most widely accepted as accurate. My goal in this chapter is to cast light on that question by describing the scientific and legal issues involved in the DNA-typing controversy and to suggest some lessons that might be taken from it.

Scientific Issues

Creating DNA Prints

Of the 3 billion nucleotides in the human genome, about one in a thousand is a site of variation, or polymorphism. Some polymorphisms alter the length of the DNA fragments produced when the DNA is cut by restriction enzymes; therefore, they are called restriction fragment-length polymorphisms (RFLPs).[11] The most widely used forensic DNA tests examine RFLPs that occur in areas of human DNA where short sequences of base pairs tend to be repeated over and over. If the chain of nucleotides in DNA were a phonograph record, these areas, known as VNTRs (variable-number tandem repeats) would be places where the record skipped and repeated a number of times before playing the rest of the tune.[12] The number of repeats in each VNTR tends to vary from individual to individual, thus creating an RFLP.[13]

Forensic DNA tests do not "read" the genetic code itself. They simply measure the length of restriction fragments containing particular VNTRs. The process of creating a DNA print is illustrated in Figure 11.1.[14] DNA is first extracted from biological samples and then exposed to a restriction enzyme, which cuts the long chainlike DNA molecules into "restriction fragments." The restriction fragments are separated and sorted by length, using a process known as electrophoresis, and then bound to a nylon membrane using a process known as Southern transfer.[15] At this point, DNA fragments are arrayed across the membrane according to their length, with the larger fragments at the top and the smaller fragments at the bottom. To determine the length of the fragments containing a particular VNTR, one need only locate their position in the array. This is done through the

---

Figure 11.1. Schematic Representation of the Creation of DNA Prints for RFLP Analysis. In the example shown here, DNA from two suspects is compared to DNA in a biological stain, using a single probe. DNA is extracted from specimens, broken into fragments with restriction enzymes, and sorted by length using agarose gel electrophoresis. The DNA fragments in the agarose gel are then imprinted on a nylon membrane and exposed to a radioactive probe. The probe binds to fragments containing VNTRs (variable-number tandem repeats), which tend to vary in length among individuals. When an X-ray film is exposed to the membrane, the radioactivity creates dark bands, indicating the position (and thus the length) of the variable fragments. Here, Suspect 2 had fragments that differ in length from those of the biological stain, and he is therefore excluded as a possible contributor. Suspect 1 has bands of similar lengths, indicating that he might have been the contributor. Exposing the membrane to additional probes can reduce the likelihood of a coincidental match, thereby increasing confidence that a suspect with a matching pattern of bands is the contributor of the stain.

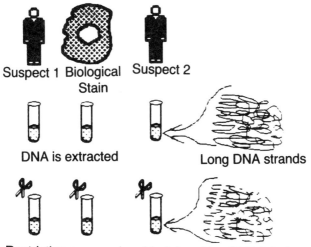

Suspect 1 Biological Suspect 2
Stain

DNA is extracted

Long DNA strands

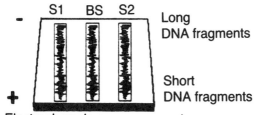

Restriction enzyme is added, breaking DNA into fragments

S1   BS   S2

Long
DNA fragments

Short
DNA fragments

Electrophoresis on agarose gel
separates and sorts DNA fragments
by length

S1   BS   S2

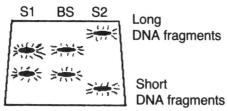

Long
DNA fragments

Short
DNA fragments

DNA fragments are transferred to a nylon membrane.
A radioactive probe binds to "target" fragments, which
vary in length among individuals.

S1   BS   S2

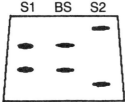

The radioactivity exposes an X-ray film over the
membrane, producing dark bands.

use of radioactive probes that bind selectively to fragments of interest. When X-ray film is placed on the membrane, the radioactive probes expose the film (known as an autorad), producing dark bands. The position of the bands on the autorad reveals the length of the fragments containing a particular VNTR.

Because humans have two copies of most chromosomes, one from the mother and the other from the father, each DNA sample exposed to a single probe will ordinarily show two bands.[16] In Figure 11.1, Suspect 2 and the biological stain have bands in different locations, which indicates that the samples have VNTRs of different lengths and must therefore have come from different individuals. Suspect 1 and the stain have bands in the same position, indicating that they *could* have come from the same individual.

To reduce the chances of a coincidental match, the laboratories use three or four different probes, each of which detects a different VNTR.

Determining Whether DNA Prints Match

To determine whether two DNA prints match, forensic analysts compare the positions of the bands, often using computer-assisted imaging devices to help make the measurements. When faced with DNA prints that are similar, but not identical, the laboratory must decide whether the discrepancies reflect true genetic differences between the samples or are simply the result of variability, or "slop," in the procedure.[17]

To make these determinations, laboratory analysts rely in part on the interpretation of various indicators and controls designed to detect problems that could cause samples from the same source not to match (or vice versa). Additionally, the laboratories have invented "matching rules," which specify how close two bands must be in measured size in order to be declared a match.[18]

Problems of interpretation are sometimes difficult to spot. In the widely publicized case of *People v. Castro*,[19] for example, two experts who initially testified for the prosecution that the results were reliable later recanted their testimony when experts retained by the defense pointed out problems. In an unusual move, the two prosecution experts and two defense experts met privately and issued a statement saying that the results in the case "are not scientifically reliable enough" to support the conclusion that two key samples matched.[20]

Supporters of current testing procedures argue that interpretation problems have been rare and represent, at worst, a misuse of DNA technology rather than a problem in the technology per se. The solution to the problem, they argue, is better training of the technicians. Misinterpretation of DNA tests, if and when it occurs, is a case-specific problem that can be dealt with appropriately in the adversarial process by allowing criminal defendants to hire their own experts to give a second opinion.[21]

In contrast, some critics believe the problems of interpretation are more fundamental. It is not always possible to distinguish matching and nonmatching patterns reliably, they argue, because there is an inadequate base of knowledge about the operating characteristics of the current analytic systems to make such judgments.[22] To determine reliably whether two DNA patterns match or do not match, one must know how often, and under what circumstances, any discrepancies in the patterns could arise if the two patterns are from the same source. We lack an adequate empirical base of research to answer such questions.[23] To call such determinations "matters for expert judgment," critics argue, is to ignore the problem: the experts themselves have an inadequate basis for making such judgments. Worse yet, the experts are rarely blind to the consequences of these subjective judgments. For example, forensic scientists typically know the police theory of the case and may even have been informed of other evidence against the suspect before making such judgments, creating a serious danger of examiner bias.[24]

The recent NRC Report resoundingly endorsed a key tenet of the critics' position: that each DNA-typing method must be rigorously characterized through empirical research to determine the conditions under which DNA patterns from the same source will differ in appearance.[25] Whether the validation research performed to date is adequate continues to be debated.[26]

Determining the Likelihood of a Coincidental Match

To evaluate evidence that two DNA prints "match," one must know how rare the matching pattern is and thus how often such a match would be found by chance. Forensic DNA laboratories estimate the frequency of DNA prints by first determining the frequency of each band (by referring to a data base), and then combining these individual frequencies using a formula that assumes they are statistically independent.[27]

Whether the bands in DNA prints are, in fact, statistically independent is one of the major issues under dispute in the scientific community. Critics fear that there may be "structuring" of human populations such that certain DNA patterns are more frequent in some ethnic, religious, and geographic subgroups than in others. If there is such structuring, the multiplication of band frequencies could produce severe errors. By analogy, if a population survey showed that 10 percent of Europeans have blond hair, 10 percent have blue eyes, and 10 percent have fair skin, it would be a mistake to multiply these frequencies to conclude that the frequency of Europeans with all three traits is 1 in 1,000. Because these traits tend to co-occur in Nordics, the actual frequency is much higher, particularly if one happens to be in Scandanavia.[28]

Critics and supporters of current procedures split over how much "structure" exists in human populations.[29] The supporters claim that there is little if any structure within the large racial and ethnic groups for which the laboratories maintain data (Caucasians, Hispanics, blacks, Asians) and that the computational procedures are sufficiently "conservative" to compensate for any structure that exists.[30] Critics claim that there might well be enough structure to invalidate the laboratory's computations.[31] And they are not persuaded by claims that the computational procedures are "conservative."[32]

The procedures used by some laboratories have also been criticized for underestimating the frequency of particular bands in DNA prints. Because the statistical procedure multiplies the frequency of up to eight bands, systematic underestimation of the frequency of each band can have a large impact. In one case where the FBI estimated the frequency of the defendant's DNA print to be 1 in 6 million, for example, a statistician retained by the defendant determined that the frequency would have been 1 in 1,000 had the FBI used a different, and in his view preferable, approach to determining the frequency of the individual bands, even if one assumed the bands to be independent.[33]

Finally, critics have challenged forensic statistics on grounds that they fail to take into account factors that have a crucial bearing on the weight of the evidence.[34] Jurors are likely to assume that the statistic reported to them in connection with DNA evidence reflects the likelihood that the test could be wrong. If the test incriminates the defendant and the jury is given a number of 1 in 1 million, for example, they might quite reasonably assume there is 1 chance in 1 million that the defendant is not guilty. But this is highly misleading, say the critics, for several reasons. First, the figure of 1 in 1 million fails to take into account any problems with the interpretation of the test. The jury is given the same number when the "match" is highly problematic as when the "match" is perfect, which may lead them to overvalue questionable DNA evidence.[35] Second, the figure of 1 in 1 million fails to take into account the possibility of a laboratory mix-up or sample-handling error that could falsely incriminate the defendant.[36] In proficiency tests, one forensic DNA laboratory had two false matches when asked to process and compare a hundred samples.[37] Both were found to be caused by accidental cross-contamination of samples in the laboratory. Some experts say that the likelihood of a false incrimination owing to a laboratory error of this sort is so much higher than the likelihood of two different people having the same DNA print that it is misleading to give jurors statistics on the latter but not on the former. Third, a figure of 1 in 1 million is misleading in cases where the true perpetrator, if the defendant is innocent, may be a relative of the defendant. If the defendant's brother was the perpetrator, for example, the likelihood that the defendant would "match" by chance could easily exceed 1 in 100.[38]

The report of the National Research Council sided with the critics on several key points. It discussed the special danger of using general population statistics in cases where alternative suspects are relatives of the defendant and concluded that error-rate statistics must be determined for each laboratory and presented along with DNA evidence.[39]

With regard to the central issue of population structure, the NRC Report acknowledged the existence of the scientific dispute and proposed a compromise.[40] The danger of population structure is sufficiently serious that current approaches should not be used, the NRC concluded. Additional empirical studies of ethnic subgroups are necessary (and should be done immediately) to determine the extent of population structure. In the interim, however, it is not necessary, as some critics suggested, to abandon the use of the product rule altogether. Laboratories may continue making statistical estimates by multiplying allele frequencies, so long as they employ a conservative approach for estimating allele frequencies—an approach which takes into account that undetected population structure may make allele frequencies far higher in some groups than in others.

The National Research Council's approach to estimating the frequency of DNA prints is clearly more conservative than current laboratory practice. In one case, for example, a DNA print estimated by the FBI to have a frequency of 1 in 6.2 million was recomputed, under the NRC approach, to have a frequency of 1 in 84.[41] In most cases the difference between the NRC approach and current practice is not so extreme; nevertheless, the NRC numbers are often one to four orders of magnitude higher than those produced by current techniques.

The NRC's statistical method has itself generated considerable debate. Some scientists have attacked it as unnecessarily conservative,[42] others say it is unclear and subject to conflicting interpretations,[43] some have defended it,[44] and a few have argued it may not be conservative enough.[45] The NRC is currently planning a new study that will make a second attempt to resolve the statistical debate, drawing on new data that have emerged since publication of the NRC Report.

Legal Issues

The legal issues surrounding the introduction of forensic DNA testing may be divided into two broad categories: substance and procedure. The substantive issues concern what standards the courts should apply when evaluating the admissibility of novel scientific techniques. The procedural issues concern how litigation on the substantive issue should be conducted, involving such questions as access to scientific data, the availability of funds to retain expert consultants and witnesses, and the nature of the proceedings used to determine admissibility as well as the question of how DNA evidence should be presented to juries once it is found to be admissible.

At present, there is a great deal of ambiguity in both the substantive and procedural rules under which courts are evaluating the admissibility of DNA evidence. Differences among courts in their rulings on DNA evidence are owing as much to differences in how courts interpret the law as to differences in the expert scientific testimony they have heard. Indeed, the DNA war is as much a disagreement over law as over science. The acrimony that makes this litigation a "war" may arise, in part, from the participants' realization that quite a lot is at stake. The precedents created by the current litigation will shape the way the legal system responds to all subsequent innovations involving the use of genetic tests for criminal identification.

Substantive Issues

Courts have traditionally been reluctant to allow the results of a scientific test to be presented to a trier of fact unless there is some assurance that the test is reliable.[46] A common theme in appellate opinions and commentary on the issue is that lay jurors are likely to be overawed by scientific evidence and to lack the capacity to evaluate it critically.[47] Because unreliable tests are likely to be given more weight than they deserve, such evidence is considered prejudicial. There is also concern that efforts to challenge unreliable scientific evidence through cross-examination and expert testimony will consume inordinate amounts of time, distracting the jury from issues more central to the case.

To determine the admissibility of evidence derived from a novel scientific procedure, the majority of jurisdictions follow a rule established in *Frye v. United States.*[48] Under the *Frye* rule, such evidence may be presented to a jury only if the court first determines that the scientific procedure has "gained general acceptance in the particular field in which it belongs."[49] The principal alternative to *Frye* is the so-called relevancy rule, under which the evidence is admitted if the judge determines that it will be more helpful than misleading to the jury.[50]

Although the majority of courts profess adherence to the *Frye* rule, there is considerable variability in how the rule is applied. A few courts have held that the requirement of "general acceptance" applies only to the theory and principles underlying a technique, and not to the specific procedures developed to implement those principles. Because there has been no dispute whatsoever about the theory underlying forensic DNA testing, nor about the basic principles underlying RFLP analysis, courts adopting this approach have had little difficulty finding forensic DNA testing admissible. More commonly, courts require acceptance not just of the underlying theory, but of the method itself.[51]

A number of courts have concluded that the procedures for producing DNA prints and for determining whether they match are generally accepted, but that procedures for statistical computation are not. These courts face an interesting decision: whether to admit evidence of a DNA test match in the absence of statistical data. A few courts have allowed a forensic expert to testify that two DNA patterns "match," but they have barred the expert from presenting statistics to quantify the rarity of the matching DNA pattern or the likelihood of a coincidental match. Other courts have viewed DNA evidence as meaningless and potentially prejudicial in the absence of such statistics. They therefore exclude the evidence altogether on finding the results of the statistical procedures inadmissible. The chief danger of admitting DNA evidence without statistics is that jurors may mistakenly assume that because each person's DNA is unique, any DNA test match is an infallible identification.

Procedural Issues

The party wishing to present novel scientific evidence bears the burden of showing that it meets the standard of admissibility.[52] Such a showing is typically made through expert testimony at a pretrial hearing. Until an appellate court issues a binding ruling on the admissibility of a particular type of scientific evidence, a pretrial admissibility hearing is necessary in each case in which the admissibility of the novel evidence is contested. After an appellate court rules on the question of admissibility, the issue can be raised again at the trial court level only on the basis of new evidence.

Access to Funding. In criminal cases, forensic DNA evidence is most commonly offered by the prosecution. Funds to pay for prosecution experts typically come from the district attorney's budget. DNA evidence is typically opposed by defense attorneys, who must fund expert testimony either out of the client's funds or, in the case of indigent clients, by seeking funding from the court. Because most criminal defendants have limited assets, the willingness and ability of courts to authorize funds for the hiring of expert witnesses determines how seriously the defense can challenge novel evidence.

The variability of funding for expert witnesses is striking: in some states, defense lawyers have difficulty obtaining funds even to have an expert give a second opinion on whether the results of a DNA test are incriminating; in other states, defense lawyers have been able to hire experts to spend considerable time doing research and evaluation of laboratory procedures, including visits to forensic labs to observe procedures and perform independent reviews of validation data. It is not a coincidence that the most thorough hearings on the admissibility of forensic DNA evidence have occurred in jurisdictions that have been relatively generous in funding expert witnesses for the defense (New York, California, Arizona, Minnesota, Massachusetts) and that no serious challenges have occurred in states where such funding is minimal (e.g., Oklahoma). Although there is not yet any case law on the issue, the recent success of challenges to DNA evidence in better-funded jurisdictions may fuel claims by defendants convicted with DNA evidence in other states that they were denied due process, particularly in cases where there was no independent review of the DNA evidence.

Access to Data. Assuming the defense is able to hire experts to help challenge DNA evidence, we must next ask what materials those experts will be allowed to examine. Generally, defense experts have been allowed to see the laboratory reports, lab notes, and autoradiographs in the case in question.[53] But there has been a great deal of controversy, and protracted litigation, over access to laboratory protocols, population databases, and the raw data underlying laboratory validation studies and proficiency tests.

Forensic laboratories have resisted disclosing these materials on a variety of grounds, including claims that the materials are legally irrelevant,[54] constitute trade secrets,[55] and are privileged.[56] The fight against disclosure has been led by prosecutors, with the active assistance of private lawyers hired by the commercial laboratories and FBI staff counsel.

Against this formidable opposition, defense lawyers have fought hard for disclosure, gradually gaining ground. In several early cases, defense lawyers spent more time and money in efforts to obtain information their experts had requested than they did in litigating the substantive issue. A key victory for the defense was a ruling of the Minnesota Supreme Court holding the Cellmark DNA test inadmissible—based, in part, on Cellmark's refusal to disclose information requested by the defense.[57] Another was the ruling of an Iowa district court compelling the FBI to disclose results of its proficiency-testing studies.[58] Efforts to gain access to raw validation data gained impetus when initial examination revealed instances in which conclusions published in scientific journals by employees of forensic laboratories were not supported by the underlying data.[59] But these efforts have met strong resistance and have been only partly successful.

Even when courts have ordered discovery, compliance has been grudging. Internal memorandums obtained through court-ordered discovery from the FBI show that the agency contemplated destroying its own scientific data concerning the performance of its DNA test in proficiency trials rather than turn over the data to defense lawyers.[60] The adversarial nature of the discovery process has engendered game playing by the litigants. Some defense lawyers have made unnecessarily broad discovery requests in the hope of at least obtaining something; the forensic laboratories have stonewalled, provided information in misleading formats, exaggerated the time and expense required to produce materials,[61] and generally released data in a piecemeal manner that made it difficult for experts in any particular case to become fully informed.

The Confidentiality of Discovery. Another controversial issue has been the confidentiality of information obtained by defense lawyers through the discovery process. In cases where courts have ordered extensive disclosure of information by forensic laboratories, prosecutors have often requested that the court also issue a confidentiality order to protect alleged trade secrets and to prevent defense experts from taking unfair advantage of information provided to them in discovery.[62] In some cases, these orders place severe limits on what use defense experts can make of the information, forbidding them from discussing it with anyone who is not involved in the case and specifically barring them from making reference to the information in any publication, lecture, or conversation about forensic DNA testing.[63] Defense lawyers complain that forensic laboratories have used these protective orders to frustrate defendants' preparation of their cases, to prevent necessary consultation among scientific experts, and to keep problems in their techniques secret.

Intertwined with the confidentiality issue is the question of who has the right to comment upon and publish data that are made public in court hearings. Forensic scientists often rely heavily on unpublished data to support their contentions and to respond to critics during courtroom testimony. In such instances, defense counsel may, upon a proper request, obtain copies of the data for their own experts to evaluate. Suppose, however, that the defense experts disagree strongly with the way in which the forensic laboratory has interpreted its unpublished data. Should they be able to say so publicly, in presentations at scientific meetings and publications? Or is this an unfair use of data collected by others? The assumption that it would be unfair for defense experts to comment on others' unpublished data appears to underlie a number of the confidentiality orders that have been issued. However, this assumption acts to prevent public scrutiny and commentary upon data that have been relied upon in litigation but that have not been, and may never be, published.[64]

The recent report of the National Research Council argues powerfully for greater openness and public scrutiny of the techniques used in DNA testing. Noting that some laboratories had used methods that "were not experimentally supported," the NRC Report traced the problem to the absence of "open scientific scrutiny" and to "the failure to publish a detailed explanation and justification of methods."[65]

> Presenting scientific conclusions in a criminal court is at least as serious as presenting scientific conclusions in an academic paper. According to long-standing and wise scientific tradition, the data underlying an important scientific conclusion must be freely available, so that others can evaluate the results and publish their own findings, whether in support or in disagreement. There is no excuse for secrecy concerning the raw data. Protective orders are inappropriate, except for those protecting individuals' names and other identifying information, even for data that have not yet been published or for data claimed to be proprietary. If scientific evidence is not yet ready for both scientific scrutiny and public re-evaluation by others, it is not yet ready for court.[66]

The Proliferation of Hearings. A more fundamental question is whether a running series of scientific confrontations in pretrial admissibility hearings is the best way for the legal system to evaluate novel scientific evidence. Until a binding appellate decision is issued in a particular jurisdiction, an admissibility hearing is necessary in each case where the admissibility of novel evidence is contested. The great majority of these hearings have been poorly organized, poorly funded affairs in which scientists (often recruited at the last minute and placed on the stand after only minimal consultation) were questioned by lawyers having a fuzzy understanding of the scientific issues. Important advances in litigation have come in a relative handful of hearings in which defense counsel managed to retain experts in advance, obtain information through pretrial discovery, and present it in an organized manner. As the inefficiencies of the current approach become more apparent, so will the need for a better approach to evaluating novel scientific evidence.

The Evolution of Courtroom Debate

One reason the DNA war has been difficult to resolve is that the courtroom debate has evolved over time. The evidence before the courts keeps changing as new experts enter the fray, new facts emerge, and new analyses are offered by both sides. The courtroom debate has gone through several stages.

Blind Enthusiasm

When the tests were first introduced in court, beginning in 1987, prosecutors argued that the widespread acceptance of RFLP analysis for research and medical diagnosis demonstrates the reliability and acceptance of forensic DNA tests. The argument was syllogistic: RFLP analysis is accepted; forensic DNA tests use RFLP analysis; therefore, forensic DNA tests are accepted. Prosecutors had no trouble finding academic scientists to support this argument; they drew their experts from lists of academic supporters supplied by the forensic laboratories. Most of the early appellate decisions on forensic DNA evidence adopted the syllogistic argument uncritically, basing a decision to admit the new DNA tests into evidence on the absence of scientific criticism of RFLP analysis.

Defense lawyers were initially handicapped by a lack of information about the new DNA tests. The tests were developed by commercial laboratories whose procedures are proprietary, whose work product is generally not available for examination by outsiders (except when used in a court hearing), who have little incentive to discuss problems, and whose laboratory protocols were, until recently, available only by court order. At first, the only information on forensic DNA tests came from news reports, which were based largely on press releases from the forensic laboratories. Although scientific papers suggesting the feasibility of forensic DNA testing appeared in 1985, there were no articles discussing possible problems of technology until late 1988[67] and, until recently, none that discussed the novel aspects of forensic DNA tests (particularly the matching and statistical procedures) that have become so controversial.[68]

Lacking guidance on what issues to raise, many defense lawyers wasted time in a fruitless search for scientists who would challenge the fundamental principles and theory underlying RFLP analysis. In most of the hearings that occurred before 1989, the defense failed to produce a single witness to challenge the reliability or general acceptance of forensic DNA tests.

The Emergence of Scientific Critics

By 1989, a few defense lawyers, working in collaboration with skeptical scientists, began developing a response to the prosecutors' syllogism. It is dangerous to infer the reliability of forensic DNA tests from the acceptance of RFLP analysis for other purposes, they argued, because problems can arise in the transfer of a proven technology to new applications.[69] Moreover, the forensic tests depend on novel matching rules and statistical procedures that are not used elsewhere in science.

A milestone in the gathering controversy was *People v. Castro*, a *Frye* hearing in New York City that gained national attention because defense lawyers were able to recruit a number of prominent scientists to assist them, and because these experts turned up serious shortcomings in the procedures of a major forensic laboratory called Lifecodes.[70] It was the publicity surrounding the *Castro* case that first brought to the attention of the broader scientific community possible problems in forensic DNA testing, thus making it easier for defense lawyers to recruit experts.

Protracted battles over discovery erupted in 1989 and 1990 as defense lawyers, guided by their new experts, sought more information. As the information emerged, piecemeal, it fueled a running dispute that pitted groups of critics and supporters against one another in one hearing after another.

The Prosecution Counterattack

Prosecutors' chief response to the emergence of critics was to attack them for bias and incompetence. The nasty, personal nature of the exchanges between prosecutors and defense experts, both inside and outside the courtroom, has been widely noted.[71]

The personal nature of the prosecution counterattack was dictated, in part, by the *Frye* rule itself. The "general acceptance" test does not require that scientists unanimously endorse a technique; rather, the test is designed to block the admissibility of evidence about which there is a serious scientific controversy. As the California Supreme Court once put it, "[I]f scientists significant in number or expertise publicly oppose a [scientific] technique on grounds that it is unreliable," a court may safely conclude that it should not be presented to the jury.[72] Consequently, when scientists begin speaking out in opposition to a new scientific technique, the admissibility of the technique in court is threatened.

Proponents of the technique cannot simply argue that the critics are wrong (although they may sincerely believe this). Under the *Frye* rule, courts are not supposed to decide which scientists are right and which are wrong in a scientific dispute; the mere existence of a serious dispute over the fundamental value of a given piece of scientific evidence renders it inadmissible. If proponents debate the critics in a respectful manner, they implicitly admit the existence of the dispute, which is fatal to their cause; in order to win in court, proponents of a new technique must deny the existence of scientific critics, or say that they are ill-informed, or unqualified, or an insignificant minority, or biased, or otherwise unworthy of notice.

The most common charge leveled against scientific critics is that they have exaggerated the problems, or even concocted bogus criticisms, in order to garner the expert witness fees they earn by testifying for the defense in court hearings.[73] In fact, experts on *both* sides of the dispute bill for their time, and nearly all bill at the same rate.[74] However, the defense experts often run up larger bills because they are asked by defense lawyers to review data underlying laboratory validation and proficiency studies, and because they examine databases, looking for problems. Prosecution experts have been more willing to take the work of the forensic laboratory at face value.

Charges of financial bias have been surprisingly successful. A number of trial judges have mentioned the financial motivation of scientific critics as a reason for discounting their criticisms and for ruling DNA tests admissible.[75] The claim that the criticisms are bogus or exaggerated has become less tenable over time with the emergence of more and more scientific critics[76] and with the publication of the NRC's *DNA Technology in Forensic Science*, which acknowledges the importance of the key criticisms.[77] Nevertheless, claims of financial bias continue to offer a convenient justification for ignoring inconvenient critics.[78]

Another common attack on the critics is that they are unaware of certain key facts (often recent, unpublished research findings) that address their concerns. In theory, a court need not consider how well informed the disputing scientific camps are in order to apply the *Frye* rule. The court need only determine whether there is a dispute in the "relevant scientific community." A number of courts, however, have considered scientific knowledge a factor in defining the relevant community and have looked for general acceptance only among "knowledgeable scientists."

This application of *Frye* can rapidly enmesh the court in complex technical disputes about whether particular scientific findings do or do not resolve scientific concerns raised by critics. Moreover, carried to its logical extreme, it can lead to ludicrously narrow requirements for general acceptance.[79] But courts have found it difficult to resist the invitation to ignore ignorant voices, and have been all too willing to undertake the assessment task that follows from accepting such an invitation.

The success of lawyers (on both sides) at discrediting opposition experts by exposing gaps in their knowledge provides an incentive for lawyers to rely on seasoned experts—repeat players who stay on top of every new development. It also places a premium on the strategic use of discovery proceedings, as each side tries during the discovery phase to hold back information that can be used to ambush opposing experts in court, while trying to force disclosure of information that might be used in similar fashion by the the other side.

Another way to neutralize scientific critics, under the *Frye* standard, is to define the "relevant scientific community" in a manner that excludes them. Prosecutors have often argued that the relevant community for evaluating forensic DNA tests is the area of forensic science devoted to genetic testing. This position would guarantee the admissibility of DNA evidence under *Frye* because none of the scientific critics is a forensic scientist; all have come from the academic community. Defense lawyers have generally been successful in convincing courts that the relevant scientific community is broader, encompassing molecular biology, population genetics, and statistics as well as forensic science.[80]

In some cases, however, prosecutors have convinced judges that troublesome scientific critics fall outside the "relevant scientific community." A number of the experts who have been called by the defense to testify about theoretical issues in population genetics, such as the implications of population structure for the independence of alleles, are evolutionary biologists who do experimental work with fruit flies.[81] Prosecutors have argued, with some success, that these experts are not qualified to comment on the frequency of DNA prints, because their expertise concerns flies rather than humans. As one prosecutor put it, discussing the expertise of Professor Laurence Mueller, "[H]e is a guy who studies bugs and things. . . . [T]his case is about people."[82] A few experts have testified in support of this boundary-drawing maneuver,[83] but it has recently been disavowed by several prominent scientists, including some who have testified for the prosecution.[84]

Defense lawyers have less incentive, under *Frye*, to engage in personal attacks on scientific proponents of DNA testing. The defense lawyers need only prove the existence of a scientific dispute; they do not need to discredit scientists on the other side. Nevertheless, some of the most prominent and persistent prosecution witnesses have recently come under attack in court for allegedly hiding conflicts of interest and for intervening improperly in the editorial review process in order to prevent publication of articles by litigation opponents.

The Battle Outside the Courtroom

Recently, proponents of DNA testing have been accused of harassing scientific critics outside the courtroom in an effort to intimidate and silence them.[85] Prosecutors and FBI personnel have been accused of making threatening comments and spreading false rumors about scientists who have testified for the defense. Perhaps the most disturbing allegations, however, are that proponents of DNA testing have attempted to corrupt the peer-review process in order to prevent publication of articles critical of the forensic tests.

In one episode, a federal prosecutor twice called Professor Daniel Hartl and allegedly pressured him to withdraw an article that had already been accepted for publication by *Science*.[86] According to Hartl, who found the calls "chilling," the prosecutor cited the "political consequences" of publishing the article and "possible disastrous consequences for future DNA fingerprint-based prosecutions."[87] After Hartl refused to withdraw the paper, a prominent scientific supporter of DNA testing, Dr. Thomas Caskey, who has been a frequent prosecution witness, persuaded the editor of *Science* to reconsider publication of the article.[88] It was eventually published, but only after Hartl and his coauthor, Richard Lewontin, agreed to "tone down" their criticisms.[89] Furthermore, at Caskey's recommendation, the editor took the unusual step of soliciting from two proponents of DNA testing a rebuttal article, which was published in the same issue. Caskey told *Nature* that he had intervened in the editorial process of *Science* because "he was concerned that 'publishing defence testimony in a scientific journal' gives it such weight that courts might reopen, perhaps to overturn convictions obtained on the basis of DNA evidence."[90] Another defense witness, Professor Laurence Mueller, has been the target of numerous public attacks by a California prosecutor.[91] That prosecutor has sent a series of letters criticizing Mueller to editors considering publication of Mueller's scientific papers and to Mueller's department chair and university chancellor. The letters make disparaging statements about the quality of Mueller's scientific testimony and suggest that he is an unethical individual whose work warrants special scrutiny. The prosecutor characterizes Mueller's ideas as "knuckle-headed" and claims that they "could conceivably result in a vicious, violent criminal being freed to continue to prey on society."[92]

In yet another episode, a Minneapolis prosecutor was tipped off that a defense witness, Professor Seymour Geisser, had submitted an article to *Genetics* and that the article had been rejected based on negative reviews.[93] The prosecutor had apparently learned about the bad reviews before Geisser himself. Fifteen minutes before Geisser received, by fax, the comments of the editor and reviewers on his article, he received a fax from the prosecutor requesting that he bring the reviews with him to court when he came to testify the following week. Subsequent inquiry revealed that the author of the most negative review was Dr. Ranajit Chakraborty, a frequent prosecution witness, who is often at loggerheads with Geisser in the courtroom. Chakraborty has collaborated with FBI scientists on research designed to validate the FBI's DNA test, of which Geisser has been critical, and was the corecipient of a $300,000 grant from the Department of Justice in support of additional validation research. He did not inform the editor of *Genetics* of any potential conflict of interest when he was asked to review Geisser's article.[94]

Lessons to be Taken from the DNA War

While debate has raged over RFLP-based DNA identification tests, new procedures are already being developed. Molecular biology is advancing rapidly, and forensic scientists have been eager to adapt the new DNA technology to their purposes. Already, new tests that combine RFLP analysis with DNA amplification (through polymerase chain reaction) are on the horizon. What lessons have we learned from the "war" over the first round of DNA technology that will help in evaluating the new tests?

It is hard to disagree with a comment Eric Lander has made: "When you try to manage the quality of scientific evidence, the legal system is a very, very blunt instrument."[95] The legal debate has polarized the scientific community and created perverse incentives for secrecy, posturing, personal attacks, and other behavior contrary to the ideal norms and values of science. Like most wars, the DNA war evokes a powerful feeling in retrospect that there must have been a better way.

Nevertheless, the courtroom debates have served a useful purpose. Forensic laboratories were forced to open themselves up to scientific scrutiny—scrutiny that was greatly needed. For all of its disadvantages, the adversarial system at least ensured that someone looked at the new techniques with a critical eye and tried to explore their limitations. Whether all of the criticisms raised in court were valid remains to be seen. Only time and additional research will tell us, for example, the extent of population structure or the rate of false positives in forensic DNA testing. Whether the situation turns out to be as good as supporters hope or as bad as critics fear, these concerns needed to be raised and evaluated. Indeed, recent developments have been kind to the critics. Leading scientists have sided with the earliest critics and the report of the National Research Council has acknowledged the seriousness of their concerns. Their concerns are not "counterfeit dissent" that should have been ignored.

Perhaps the real problem is that we rely too heavily on admissibility hearings for screening new scientific innovations. These hearings would be less costly and more manageable if new forensic procedures were to receive broader scrutiny before they came to court. The NRC Report makes a number of helpful suggestions to this end. First, the report condemns the sort of secrecy that has surrounded RFLP-based tests and urges that laboratory protocols, databases, and validation studies be open and available for public scrutiny.[96] Second, the report urges the creation of a National Committee on Forensic DNA Typing, consisting of distinguished independent scientists and legal experts, that would provide advice to forensic laboratories and review new technologies before they go to court.[97] The new committee would have no formal regulatory authority, but would be a body to which courts might look for authoritative guidance when evaluating the admissibility of a new technique. Third, the report suggests that a formal system be developed for accreditation of laboratories doing forensic DNA testing, that admissibility of test results in court be contingent on the laboratory being accredited, and that accreditation depend on complying with rigorous standards for quality assurance, such as participation in externally administered proficiency tests.[98]

These NRC proposals have great merit. They would not eliminate the need for judicial review of future innovations, but would help ensure that future DNA wars are more limited than the first.

Notes

L. L. Deaven,
Mapping and Sequencing the Human Genome

1. U.S. Congress, Office of Technology Assessment, *Mapping Our Genes. The Genome Project: How Big, How Fast?* OTA-BA-373 (Washington, D.C.: GPO, 1988). The terms "Human Genome Initiative" and "Human Genome Project" are used interchangeably in this chapter. Although the Human Genome Project is not a single project, it is the title most commonly used to refer to a large collection of genome programs and projects throughout the world.

2. H. O. Smith and K. W. Wilcox, "A Restriction Enzyme from *Haemophilus influenzae*: I. Purification and General Properties," *Journal of Molecular Biology* 51 (1970): 379–391.

3. David Botstein, Raymond L. White, Mark Skolnick, and Ronald W. Davis, "Construction of a Genetic Linkage Map in Man Using Restriction Fragment Length Polymorphisms," *American Journal of Human Genetics* 32 (1980): 314.

4. "Paris Conference (1971): Standardization in Human Cytogenetics," *Birth Defects: Original Article Series* 8 (1972): 7.

C. Weiner,
Consequences of Genetic Engineering

1. *NOVA*: "DeCoding the Book of Life," WGBH-TV/Boston, aired October 31, 1989.

2. Quoted in Leon Jasoff, "The Gene Hunt," *Time*, March 20, 1989, 67.

3. See, for example, the papers, by supporters as well as critics of the project, in *Issues in Science and Technology* 4 (1987).

4. U.S. Atomic Energy Commission, *In the Matter of J. Robert Oppenheimer: Transcript of Hearing before Personnel Security Board* (Washington, D.C.: GPO, 1954), 251.

5. "Probing Heredity's Secrets" (editorial), *New York Times*, September 12, 1963.

6. In T. M. Sonneborn, ed., *The Control of Human Heredity and Evolution* (New York: Macmillan, 1965), 47.

7. "Rockefeller University Meeting on Genetic Intervention in Hu-

mans, 1966," Alexander Hollaender Papers, American Philosophical Society Library, Philadelphia.

8. "Summary of a Meeting Held on October 1, 1966 at the Rockefeller University," Recombinant DNA History Collection, MIT Institute Archives, Cambridge, Mass., 1–7.

9. Ibid., 8.

10. Ibid., 10–11.

11. Marshall Nirenberg, "Will Society Be Prepared?" (editorial), *Science* 157 (1967): 633.

12. Leon R. Kass, "Genetic Tampering" (letter), *Washington Post*, November 3, 1967. Kass was responding to Joshua Lederberg's column, "Unpredictable Variety Still Rules Human Reproduction," *Washington Post*, September 30, 1967. See also Joshua Lederberg, "Genetic Intervention Is a Way of Improving Our Species," *Washington Post*, November 4, 1967.

13. Guido Pontecorvo, in Watson Fuller, ed., *The Biological Revolution: Social Good or Social Evil?* (New York: Anchor Books, Doubleday & Co., 1971), 119–120.

14. Senate Committee on Government Operations, *Hearings before the Subcommittee on Government Research of the Committee on Government Operations on S. J. Res. 145*, 90th Cong., 2nd sess., 1968, 5. These hearings concerned a joint resolution for the establishment of the National Commission on Health, Science, and Society.

15. "Scientist Doubts Genetic Abuse, Calls Research the Best Defense," *New York Times*, March 9, 1968.

16. Senate Committee, *Hearings*, 50–52.

17. *Special Study: Implications of Advances in Biomedical and Behavioral Research*, Report and Recommendations of the National Commission for the Protection of Human Subjects of Biomedical and Behavioral Research (1974), 112–113. Human genetic engineering was not included in the study. The staff director of the commission was Michael Yesley, who is currently coordinator of the ELSI (Ethical, Legal, and Social Implications) program of the U.S. Department of Energy's genome project. See Michael S. Yesley, "The Use of an Advisory Commission," *Southern California Law Review* 51 (1978): 1451–1469. The President's Commission for the Study of Ethical Problems in Medicine and Biomedical and Behavioral Research was set up in 1978; it issued a report on human genetic engineering in 1982 and one on genetic screening in 1983, the year it went out of existence.

18. House Committee on Science and Astronautics, *Technology: Processes of Assessment and Choice*, Report of the National Academy of Sciences (1969), 32, 34–35. See Langdon Winner, "On Criticizing Technology," *Public Policy* 20 (1972): 35–39, for a perceptive critique of the

assumptions embedded in the philosophy of technology assessment during the period.

19. For a discussion of the slow start and early political conflicts of the OTA, see Bruce Bimber, "Institutions and Information: The Politics of Expertise in Congress" (Ph.D. diss., MIT, 1992).

20. Herman Lewis, "Science and Societal Problems: The NSF Role in Dealing with the Moral Implications of Scientific and Technological Advances," November 15, 1971, Recombinant DNA History Collection, MIT Institute Archives, Cambridge, Mass., 1, 4, 5.

21. Portions of this and the next section draw on my previously published articles, including "Relations of Science, Government and Industry: The Case of Recombinant DNA," in Albert H. Teich and Ray Thornton, eds., *Science, Technology and the Issues of the Eighties: Policy Outlook* (Boulder, Colo.: Westview, 1982), and "Universities, Professors, and Patents: A Continuing Controversy," *Technology Review* 89 (1986): 33–43.

22. "Audiotape of the International Conference on Recombinant DNA Molecules (Asilomar Conference)," February 24, 1975, Recombinant DNA History Collection, MIT Institute Archives, Cambridge, Mass.

23. One important exception was Marc Lappé's analysis of the ethical issues involved in the "ends and purposes" of the recombinant-DNA techniques. See Lappé, "The Human Uses of Molecular Genetics," *Federation Proceedings* 34 (1975): 1425–1427.

24. "Senator Edward Kennedy, Address to Harvard School of Public Health," May 9, 1975, Recombinant DNA History Collection, MIT Institute Archives, Cambridge, Mass.

25. For historical studies of these antiregulatory efforts, see Sheldon Krimsky, *Genetic Alchemy: The Social History of the Recombinant DNA Controversy* (Cambridge: MIT Press, 1982); Susan Wright, "Recombinant DNA Technology and Its Social Transformation, 1972–1982," *Osiris*, 2nd ser., 2 (1986): 303–360; Charles Weiner, "Relations of Science, Government and Industry: The Case of Recombinant DNA," in Albert H. Teich and Ray Thornton, eds., *Science, Technology and the Issues of the Eighties: Policy Outlook* (Boulder, Colo.: Westview, 1982), 71–97; and Susan Wright, *Molecular Politics: The Formation of Regulatory Policy for Genetic Engineering in the United States and Britain* (Chicago: University of Chicago Press, forthcoming). Accounts of several leading participants are included in Raymond A. Zilinskas and Burke K. Zimmerman, eds., *The Gene-Splicing Wars: Reflections on the Recombinant DNA Controversy* (New York: Macmillan, 1986).

26. Charles Weiner, "Universities, Professors, and Patents: A Continuing Controversy," *Technology Review* 89 (1986): 33–43; Christopher

Anderson, "Conflict Concerns Disrupt Panels, Cloud Testimony," *Nature* 355 (1992): 753–754; Sheldon Krimsky, *Biotechnics and Society: The Rise of Industrial Genetics* (New York: Praeger, 1991), chap. 4; Elizabeth Culotta, "New Startups Move in as Gene Therapy Goes Commercial," *Science* 260 (1993): 914–915. See also "Conflicts of Interest," a special section in *Science* 257 (1992): 616–625, focusing on contemporary biology.

27. For a critique of these claims, see Abby Lippman, "Led (Astray) by Genetic Maps: The Cartography of the Human Genome and Health Care," *Social Science and Medicine* 35 (1992): 1469–1476; R. C. Lewontin, "The Dream of the Human Genome," *New York Review of Books*, May 28, 1992; Robert N. Proctor, "Genomics and Eugenics: How Fair Is the Comparison?" 57–93, and Evelyne Shuster, "Determinism and Reductionism: A Greater Threat because of the Human Genome Project?" 115–127, in George J. Annas and Sherman Elias, eds., *Gene Mapping: Using Law and Ethics as Guides* (New York: Oxford University Press, 1992); Evelyn Fox Keller, "Nature, Nurture, and the Human Genome Project," in Daniel J. Kevles and Leroy Hood, eds., *The Code of Codes: Scientific and Social Issues in the Human Genome Project* (Cambridge: Harvard University Press, 1992), 281–299; and Council for Responsible Genetics, *Position Paper on Human Genome Initiative* (Boston: Committee for Responsible Genetics, 1990).

28. Eric S. Lander, testimony in House Committee on Appropriations, Departments of Labor, Health and Human Services, Education, and Related Agencies, *Hearings before the Subcommittee on National Center for Human Genome Research*, 101st Cong., 2nd sess., 1990, pt. 8A, 876.

29. Ibid.

30. James D. Watson, "The Human Genome Project: Past, Present, and Future," *Science* 248 (1990): 46.

31. George J. Annas, "Who's Afraid of the Human Genome?" *Hastings Center Report* (1989): 21.

32. Senate Committee, *Hearings*, 51.

33. Interview, March 1984. Permission to identify respondent has not been requested.

34. Recent efforts to relate the ELSI program's findings to public policy are focused on the expected results of the genome project. See House Committee on Government Operations, *Designing Genetic Information Policy: The Need for an Independent Policy Review of the Ethical, Legal, and Social Implications of the Human Genome Project*, 102nd Cong., 2nd sess., H. Rept. 102-478; and "Future Directions of Human Genome Project Considered," *Human Genome News* 5 (1993): 5–6.

35. Leslie Biesecker, B. Bowles-Biesecker, F. Collins, and M. Kaback, "General Population Screening for Cystic Fibrosis Is Premature" (let-

ter), *American Journal of Human Genetics* 50 (1992): 438–439; Sherman Elias, George J. Annas, and Joe Leigh Simpson, "Carrier Screening for Cystic Fibrosis: A Case Study in Setting of Medical Practice," in Annas and Elias, eds., *Gene Mapping*, 186–202; David A. Asch, J. P. Patton, J. C. Hershey, and M. T. Mennuti, "Reporting the Results of Cystic Fibrosis Carrier Screening," *American Journal of Obstetrics and Gynecology* 168, pt. 1 (1993): 1–6.

R. Doyle, Vital Language

1. See Michael Fortun, "Making and Mapping Genes and Histories: The Genomics Project in the United States, 1980–1990" (Ph.D. diss., Harvard University, 1993).

2. Jacques Derrida, *Of Grammatology*, trans. Gayatri Chakravorky Spivak (Baltimore: Johns Hopkins University Press, 1976), 15.

3. Aristotle, *Poetics* 21.7.

4. "Synecdoche" refers to the substitution of a part for the whole, as in Erwin Schrödinger's substitution of "code-script" for "organism," below. "Metonymy" refers to the substitution of a word for a related word.

5. Erwin Schrödinger, *What Is Life? The Physical Aspect of the Living Cell* (Cambridge: Cambridge University Press, 1944), 21.

6. Ibid., 22.

7. Sigmund Freud, *The Interpretation of Dreams*, trans. and ed. James Strachey (New York: Avon, 1965), 463.

8. Paul de Man, *The Resistance to Theory* (Minneapolis: University of Minnesota Press, 1986), 11.

9. Schrödinger, *What Is Life?* 22.

10. Ibid., 23.

11. James Watson, *The Double Helix: A Personal Account of the Discovery of the Structure of DNA* (New York: Atheneum, 1980), 13.

12. For an extended account of the notion of causation in contemporary biology, see Richard Lewontin's *Biology as Ideology: The Doctrine of DNA* (New York: Harper Perennial, 1991), 40–44. See also Cranor's essay in the present book (Chapter 8).

13. J. D. Watson and F.H.C. Crick, "Genetical Implications of the Structure of Deoxyribonucleic Acid," *Nature* 171 (1953): 964–967.

14. A. L. Dounce, "Duplication Mechanism for Peptide Chain and Nucleic Acid Synthesis," *Enzymologia* 15 (1952): 251.

15. G. Gamow, "Possible Relation between Deoxyribonucleic Acid and Protein Structures," *Nature* 173 (1954): 318.

16. Ibid.

17. Ernst Robert Curtius, *European Literature and the Latin Middle Ages*, trans. Williard R. Trask (London: Routledge & Kegan Paul, 1953), 324.

18. Gamow, "Possible Relation," 318.

19. Ibid.

20. Ibid.

21. Freud, *The Interpretation of Dreams*, 10. I have alluded to similarities between Freud's project of interpreting dreams and Gamow's goal of interpreting genes, a subject beyond the scope of the present essay but nonetheless implicated in it. Both projects are, in a sense, a hermeneutic attempt "to understand what life is" in the tradition of the identification of life with the Word, logocentrism. The off ramp that leads from the royal road of the unconscious to the royal road of disease will be followed in a future essay. This could take months or years, depending on the traffic. See *The Interpretation of Dreams*, 129–130.

22. Gamow, "Possible Relation," 318.

23. Francis Crick, *Of Molecules and Men* (Seattle: University of Washington Press, 1966), 10, emphasis in original.

24. U.S. Congress, Office of Technology Assessment, *Mapping Our Genes. The Genome Project: How Big, How Fast?* OTA-BA-373 (Washington, D.C., GPO, 1988), 85. This document also contains some murmurs of a "better" eugenics: "The problem with positive eugenics has more to do with means than with ends" (85).

25. Michel Foucault, *The Order of Things: An Archeology of the Human Sciences* (London: Tavistock Publications, 1974), 161.

J. R. Griesemer,
Tools for Talking

1. Ernst Mayr, "Cause and Effect in Biology." *Science* 134 (1961): 1501–1506.

2. Alexander M. Capron, Marc Lappé, Robert F. Murray, Tabitha M. Powledge, Summer B. Twiss, and Daniel Bergsma, "Appraising the Legitimacy of Genetic Concepts: Introduction," in Alexander M. Capron, Marc Lappé, Robert F. Murray, Tabitha M. Powledge, Summer B. Twiss et al., eds., *Genetic Counseling: Facts, Values, and Norms* (New York: Alan R. Liss, 1979), 17.

3. In the sociology of science, reduction is considered to *be* a social process. See, for example, Bruno Latour and Steve Woolgar, *Laboratory Life: The Construction of Scientific Facts*, 2nd ed. (Princeton: Princeton University Press, 1986). My point here is that one cannot question the biotechnological approach to social problems implicit in the HGI without first distinguishing between the biological and the social and only

then challenging the distinction in the way sociologists of science have. See Bruno Latour, *The Pasteurization of France* (Cambridge: Harvard University Press, 1990).

4. See, for example, U.S. Congress, Office of Technology Assessment, *Mapping Our Genes. The Genome Project: How Big, How Fast?* (Baltimore: Johns Hopkins University Press, 1988); National Research Council, *Mapping and Sequencing the Human Genome* (Washington, D.C.: National Academy Press, 1988); U.S. Department of Health and Human Services and U.S. Department of Energy, *Understanding Our Genetic Inheritance. The U.S. Human Genome Project: The First Five Years, FY 1991–1995* (Springfield, Va.: National Technical Information Service, U.S. Department of Commerce, 1990); "The Randolph W. Thrower Symposium: Genetics and the Law," special issue of *Emory Law Journal* 39 (1990).

5. William C. Wimsatt, "Developmental Constraints, Generative Entrenchment, and the Innate-Acquired Distinction," in William Bechtel, ed., *Integrating Scientific Disciplines* (Dordrecht: Martinus Nijhoff, 1986), 185–208.

6. Ernst Mayr, *Animal Species and Evolution* (Cambridge: Harvard University Press, 1963). See also Michael Ghiselin, "A Radical Solution to the Species Problem," *Systematic Zoology* 23 (1974): 536–544; David L. Hull, "Central Subjects and Historical Narratives," *History and Theory* 14 (1975): 253–274; David L. Hull, "On Human Nature," in *PSA 1986*, vol. 2, ed. Arthur Fine and Peter Machamer (East Lansing, Mich.: Philosophy of Science Association, 1987), 3–13; and David L. Hull, *Science as a Process: An Evolutionary Account of the Social and Conceptual Development of Science* (Chicago: University of Chicago Press, 1988).

7. John Beatty, "The Insights and Oversights of Molecular Genetics: The Place of the Evolutionary Perspective," in *PSA 1982*, vol. 1, ed. Peter Asquith and Thomas Nickles (East Lansing, Mich.: Philosophy of Science Association, 1982), 341–355.

8. Quoted ibid., 341.

9. See references in note 4, above. Also see Lori B. Andrews's introduction to "The Randolph W. Thrower Symposium," 619–628; and James D. Watson, "The Human Genome Project: Past, Present, and Future," *Science* 248 (1990): 44–49.

10. Jan Sapp, *Beyond the Gene: The Struggle for Authority in Genetics* (New York: Oxford University Press, 1987).

11. See Frederick Churchill, "Weismann's Continuity of the Germ-Plasm in Historical Perspective," *Freiburger Universitätsblätter* 24 (1985): 107–124; Frederick Churchill, "From Heredity Theory to *Vererbung*: The Transmission Problem, 1850–1915," *Isis* 78 (1987): 337–364. James R. Griesemer, "The Informational Gene and the Substantial Body: On the Generalization of Evolutionary Theory by Abstraction," in Nancy

Cartwright and Martin Jones, eds., *Varieties of Idealization* (Amsterdam: Rodopi, forthcoming); Ernst Mayr, "Weismann and Evolution," *Journal of the History of Biology* 18 (1985): 295–329; and Gloria Robinson, *A Prelude to Genetics. Theories of a Material Substance of Heredity: Darwin to Weismann* (Lawrence, Kans.: Coronado Press, 1979).

12. C. Boone, "Bad Axioms in Genetic Engineering," *Hastings Center Report* 18 (1988): 9; Capron et al., "Appraising."

13. For recent work on visual representation in science, see Gordon Fyfe and John Law, eds., *Picturing Power: Visual Depiction and Social Relations* (New York: Routledge, 1988); Michael Lynch and Steve Woolgar, eds., *Representation in Scientific Practice* (Cambridge: MIT Press, 1990); and Peter J. Taylor and Ann S. Blum, eds., "Pictorial Representation in Biology," special issue of *Biology & Philosophy* 6 (1991).

14. See Latour, *Pasteurization*.

15. See, for example, Leo Buss, *The Evolution of Individuality* (Princeton: Princeton University Press, 1987); Griesemer, "The Informational Gene"; Eva Jablonka and Marion J. Lamb, "The Inheritance of Acquired Epigenetic Variations," *Journal of Theoretical Biology* 139 (1989): 69–83.

16. Churchill, "Heredity Theory"; Griesemer, "The Informational Gene." See also Jane Maienschein, "Heredity/Development in the United States, circa 1900," *History and Philosophy of the Life Sciences* 9 (1987): 79–83.

17. August Weismann, *The Germ-Plasm: A Theory of Heredity*, trans. W. Newton Parker and Harriet Ronnfeldt (New York: Scribner's, 1893).

18. Edmund B. Wilson, *The Cell in Development and Inheritance* (London: Macmillan, 1896), fig. 5 at 13.

19. The first description appears in Francis Crick, "On Protein Synthesis," *Symposia of the Society for Experimental Biology* 12 (1958): 138–163. A diagram appears in Francis Crick, "Central Dogma of Molecular Biology," *Nature* 227 (1970): 561–563.

20. See John Maynard Smith, *The Theory of Evolution*, 2nd ed. (Middlesex: Penguin, 1965).

21. But see Griesemer, "The Informational Gene," on molecular continuity.

22. See Churchill, "Heredity Theory."

23. Weismann, *The Germ-Plasma*, fig. 16 at 193.

24. See Buss, *Evolution of Individuality*.

25. Steve Jones, *The Language of the Genes: Biology, History and the Evolutionary Future* (London: HarperCollins, 1993), 225–238.

26. Ibid., 229.

E. F. Keller,
Master Molecules

This essay was written as a "talk piece" for the conference "Genes R Us," sponsored by the Humanities Research Institute at the University of California–Irvine, June 1991. Its intended function was to stimulate discussion. Although I still hold by the main arguments presented here, I would write a rather different essay today—one more clearly reflecting the work I have been doing since then on the history of developmental biology and reflecting the ways in which my thinking has been influenced by that work. I have accordingly borrowed extensively from my recent Tanner Lecture, "Rethinking the Meaning of Genetic Determinism," delivered at the University of Utah, February 1993, and to be published by The Tanner Lectures on Human Values.

1. In most of these early discussions, the cytoplasm was taken to stand for the organism, and the nucleus for its genes. Debate thus tended to focus on the relative importance of nucleus and cytoplasm. L. C. Dunn spoke for his entire discipline when he wrote in 1917: "The whole case of the supporters of any theory which views the cytoplasm as determinative rests on either their refusal to go back and inquire the source of the cytoplasm, or on their refusal to give due emphasis to the source, even though they recognize it" ("Nucleus and Cytoplasm as Vehicles of Heredity," *American Naturalist* 51 [1917]: 286–300).

2. A common observation by molecular biologists is that "genetics is blind to genes for essential traits" (e.g., Stuart Kim, "Frontiers in Developmental Biology," seminar, Stanford University, March 4, 1992).

3. The term "environment" is intended to include animate constituents (e.g., the presence and actions of other organisms) as well as inanimate ones. Translated into human terms, this means that the term "environment" must be understood as including the social context along with the physical and material context.

4. See Monod's assertion that "what was true for *E. coli* would be true for the elephant" (Horace Judson, *The Eighth Day of Creation* [New York: Simon & Schuster, 1979], 613).

5. F. Jacob and J. Monod, "Genetic Regulatory Mechanisms in the Synthesis of Proteins," *Journal of Molecular Biology* 3 (1961): 354. See Richard Doyle's extended and insightful discussion of Monod and Jacob's rhetorical elision of the gap between "instruction" and "construction"—a gap that can be filled only by the material dynamics of cytoplasm; that is, by the cell's body (Richard Doyle, "On Beyond Living: Rhetorics of Vitality and Post Vitality in Molecular Biology" [Ph.D. diss., University of California–Berkeley, 1993]).

6. Joseph Needham, "Organizer Phenomena after Four Decades,"

in K. R. Dronamraju, ed., *Haldane and Modern Biology* (Baltimore: Johns Hopkins University Press, 1968), 289.

7. Ross G. Harrison, "Embryology and Its Relations," *Science* 85 (1937): 369–374.

8. Ian Hacking, *The Taming of Chance* (Cambridge: Cambridge University Press, 1990), 168.

9. Sir Peter Medawar's remarks in his 1965 presidential address to the British Association for the Advancement of Science ("A Biological Retrospect," *Nature* 207 [1966]: 1327–1330) are to the point, and worth quoting at length: "Wise after the event, we can now see the embryology simply did not have, and could not have created, the background of genetical reasoning which would have made it possible to formulate a theory of development. It is not now generally believed that a stimulus external to the system on which it acts can specify the primary structure of a protein, that is, convey instructions that amino-acids shall be assembled in a given order. The 'instructive' stimulus has gone the way of the philosopher's stone, an agent dimly akin to it in certain ways. Embryonic development . . . must therefore be an unfolding of pre-existing capabilities, an acting-out of genetically encoded instructions" (1328–1329). In much the same spirit, Joshua Lederberg observed a year later, in his inaugural remarks for the first issue of *Current Topics in Developmental Biology*, that "embryology has historically had more than its share of mysticism, with some mysterious property of 'organization' always in the background to inhibit field experiments" ("Introductory Remarks," *Current Topics in Developmental Biology* 1 [1966]: ix–x).

10. Tim Beardsley, "Smart Genes," *Scientific American*, August 1991, 86–95, emphasis added.

11. Perhaps a better case would be alcoholism. Precisely because the role of genetics is here more ambiguous, the dangers and difficulties of our excessive focus on genes can be seen more clearly. In response to repeated failures to find an "alcoholism gene," the National Institute on Alcohol Abuse and Alcoholism has now budgeted $25 million, not for the study of usually relevant factors that may be nongenetic but, rather, for casting an even wider genetic net—for what has been described as "a kind of Manhattan Project on the genetics of alcoholism" (Constance Holden, *Psychology Today* 19 [1985]: 38–44).

12. By a similar logic, it is also not possible to infer the meaning of health or normality from the characterization of one or more abnormalities, whether or not they are seen as genetically based.

13. See Evelyn Fox Keller, "Nature, Nurture, and the Human Genome Project," in D. J. Kevles and L. Hood, eds., *The Code of Codes: Scientific and Social Issues in the Human Genome Project* (Cambridge: Harvard University Press, 1992).

14. For a more extended discussion of this issue, see ibid.

15. Hacking, *The Taming of Chance*, 168.

E. A. Lloyd,
Normality and Variation

1. Renato Dulbecco, "A Turning Point in Cancer Research: Sequencing the Human Genome," *Science* 231 (1986): 1055–1056. Cf. J. Fujimara, "The Molecular Biological Bandwagon in Cancer Research: Where Social Worlds Meet," *Social Problems* 35 (1988): 261.

2. Shari Roan, "Check It Out," *Oakland Tribune*, April 18, 1991.

3. James D. Watson, "The Human Genome Project: Past, Present, and Future," *Science* 248 (1990): 44.

4. T. Friedmann, "Progress toward Human Gene Therapy," *Science* 244 (1989): 1275.

5. B. J. Culliton, "Mapping Terra Incognita (Humani Corporis)," *Science* 250 (1990): 211. See also T. H. Jukes, "The Human Genome Project: Labeling Genes," *California Monthly*, December 1988, 15–17.

6. Another misleading aspect of the typical genetic presentations of disease concerns implicit assumptions of genetic determinism and disease. See the following for relevant discussion: D. S. Karjala, "A Legal Research Agenda for the Human Genome Initiative," *Jurimetrics* 32 (1992): 121–219; E. S. Gollin, G. Stahl, and E. Morgan, "On the Uses of the Concept of Normality in Developmental Biology and Psychology," *Advances in Child Development and Behavior* 21 (1989): 49–71.

7. Jukes, "The Human Genome Project," 16. Friedmann describes the goals of molecular genetic explanations also: "Predicting the exact structure and regulated expression of any gene, the tertiary and quaternary structures of its products, their interactions with other molecules, and finally, their exact functions, constitutes a problem of the highest priority in molecular genetics" (T. Friedmann, "The Human Genome Project—Some Implications of Extensive 'Reverse Genetic' Medicine" [opinion], *American Journal of Human Genetics* 46 [1990]: 409).

8. James Watson speaks ambiguously of "the genetic diseases that result from *variations* in our genetic messages" ("The Human Genome Project," 46, emphasis added). Not all variations result in genetic diseases.

9. Ibid., 48.

10. O. Temkin, *The Double Face of Janus* (Baltimore: Johns Hopkins University Press, 1977), 444.

11. Ibid.

12. Gollin et al., "On the Uses of the Concept of Normality," include in their list of uses "an index of acceptable physiological function or

behavior" (50). Such views derive ultimately from Herman Boerhaave, who defined diseases as occurring when a person could not exercise a function.

13. Theodore Friedmann admits that a great deal of sequence information and "comparison" is needed in order to distinguish between "polymorphisms" and "disease-related mutations" ("The Human Genome Project," 409).

14. See Friedmann's discussion of "normal, functional" genes in "Progress toward Human Gene Therapy," 1275.

15. See Cranor, "Genetic Causation," Chapter 8 in the present volume.

16. Temkin, *The Double Face of Janus*, 447. Cf. A. L. Caplan, "The Concepts of Health and Disease," in R. M. Veatch, ed., *Medical Ethics* (Boston: Jones & Bartlett, 1989), 49–62.

17. Caplan offers a useful summary of the debates about the extent of values in definitions of health and disease ("Concepts of Health and Disease," 55–59).

18. R. Bayer, *Homosexuality and American Psychology: The Politics of Diagnosis* (New York: Basic Books, 1981).

19. P. Sedgwick, "Illness—Mental and Otherwise," *Hastings Center Report* 1 (1973): 19–40.

20. Simon Levay, "A Difference in Hypothalamic Structure between Homosexual and Heterosexual Men," *Science* 253 (1991): 1034–1037.

21. See the discussion in Cranor (Chapter 8, below) and in R. Hubbard, *The Politics of Women's Biology* (New Brunswick: Rutgers University Press, 1990).

22. Gollin et al. describe this unjustified shift from developmental theory to the physiological level as follows: "The observed regularities [in development] are mistaken for universals and the construed universals are regarded as indicators of health and developmental adequacy" ("On the Uses of the Concept of Normality," 51).

23. Even Theodore Friedmann, who is committed to the medical benefits of the Human Genome Project, discusses the distance between a DNA-level characterization of an "abnormal" gene and a medical and physiological understanding of the disease. "Most successes of medical genetics have begun with an understanding of an aberrant metabolic pathway; the genes responsible were identified and isolated through this physiological knowledge" ("The Human Genome Project," 407).

24. E.g., Council for Responsible Genetics, *Position Paper on Human Genome Initiative* (Boston: Committee for Responsible Genetics, 1990).

25. M. Vicedo, "The History, Scientific Value, and Social Implications of the Human Genome Project" (MS, 1991).

26. The distinction between "congenital" and "genetic" birth disorders has long been recognized: "congenital" refers only to disturbances

from the normal pattern of development that are not believed to be genetically caused.

27. D. C. Gajdusek, "Physiological and Psychological Characteristics of Stone Age Man," *Engineering and Science* 22 (1970): 56–62.

28. See the discussion in Gollin et al., "On the Uses of the Concept of Normality."

29. P. A. Baird, "Genetics and Health Care: A Paradigm Shift," *Perspectives in Biology and Medicine* 33 (1990): 203–213.

30. See Cranor, Chapter 8, below.

31. V. A. McKusick, "Mapping and Sequencing the Human Genome," *New England Journal of Medicine* 320 (1989): 910–915, quoted in Culliton, "Mapping Terra Incognita," 212.

32. N. Angier, "Molecular 'Hot Spot' Hits at a Cause of Liver Cancer," *New York Times*, April 14, 1991.

33. Friedmann, "Progress toward Human Gene Therapy," 1279.

34. This supports Cranor's point against Hubbard that in cases where disease occurs, a single gene can be picked out as a cause (see Chapter 8, below).

35. C. Holden, "Probing the Complex Genetics of Alcoholism," *Science* 251 (1991): 163–164.

36. Vicedo, "History, Scientific Value, and Social Implications," 19.

37. A misleading overreliance on biochemical causal models can lead to the complete disappearance of the influence of environment on phenotype. For example, Watson, in arguing for the sequencing of the complete *Caenorhabditis elegans* genome, says: "If we are to integrate and understand all the events that lead, for example, to the differentiation of a nervous system, we have to work from the whole set of genetic instructions" ("The Human Genome Project," 48).

38. See Roan, "Check It Out."

39. B. D. Davis, "The Human Genome and Other Initiatives," *Science* 249 (1990): 342.

40. See the discussion in Hubbard, *Politics*, and Cranor (Chapter 8, below). I believe that Hubbard's view can be interpreted as a rejection of the medical appropriateness of the biochemical causal model owing to the fact that it omits environment as a causal factor.

41. Another problem with this model of genetic disease is that "diseases caused by a malfunction in one gene tend to be rare," according to molecular geneticists at Harvard Medical School (Davis et al., 343).

42. N. D. Zinder, "The Genome Initiative: How to Spell Human," *Scientific American*, July 1990, 96; L. Smith and L. Hood, "Mapping and Sequencing the Human Genome: How to Proceed," *BioTechnology* 5 (1987): 933–939. Cf. Watson, "The Human Genome Project"; and Vicedo, "History, Scientific Value, and Social Implications."

C. Limoges,
Do Genetic Errors Have a Future?

1. Renato Dulbecco, "A Turning Point in Cancer Research: Sequencing the Human Genome," *Science* 231 (1986): 1055–1056; James D. Watson and Elke Jordan, "The Human Genome Program at the National Institutes of Health," *Genomics* 5 (1989): 654–656.

2. James D. Watson, "The Human Genome Initiative: A Statement of Need," *Hospital Practice* 26 (1991): 69. See also James D. Watson and Robert M. Cook-Deegan, "Origins of the Human Genome Project," *FASEB Journal* 5 (1991): 8–11. Medical applications have also been used to justify the program in economic terms: "The cost of finding individual genes, one at a time, is often staggering. The ultimate benefits of finding even one major disease gene that might not have been observed by methods less systematic than the genome project could well recoup the entire cost of that project" (Charles S. Cantor, "Orchestrating the Human Genome Project," *Science* 248 [1990]: 51).

3. Linus Pauling, Harvey A. Itano, S. J. Singer, and Ibert C. Wells, "Sickle Cell Anemia, a Molecular Disease," *Science* 110 (1949): 543–548.

4. George W. Beadle, "Biochemical Genetics," *Chemical Reviews* 37 (1945): 25.

5. George W. Beadle, "Genes and Chemical Reactions in Neurospora" (1958), in David Baltimore, comp., *Nobel Lectures in Molecular Biology* (New York: Elsevier, 1976), 52–53.

6. Erwin Schrödinger, *What Is Life? & Mind and Matter* (New York: Cambridge University Press, 1967), 21–22. *What Is Life?* was first published in 1944, from lectures given in 1943.

7. Ibid., 38–39.

8. Ibid., 44.

9. Francis Crick, "On Protein Synthesis," in *Symposium of the Society for Experimental Biology* (Cambridge: Cambridge University Press, 1957), 153. Crick had already, in a privately circulated paper, used the phrase "mistakes in sequences" ("On Degenerate Templates and the Adaptor Hypothesis: A Note for the RNA Tie Club" [1955]; see Horace F. Judson, *The Eighth Day of Creation* [New York: Simon & Schuster, 1979], 291).

10. Ernst Freese, "The Specific Mutagenic Effects of Base Analogues on Phage T4," *Journal of Molecular Biology* 1 (1959): 102.

11. R. B. Lotfield, "The Frequency of Errors in Protein Biosynthesis," *Biochemical Journal* 89 (1963): 81.

12. Vernon M. Ingram, "Abnormal Human Haemoglobin," *Biochemica and Biophysica Acta* 28 (1958): 539–545.

13. Arthur Kornberg, "Biologic Synthesis of Deoxyribonucleic Acid," *Science* 131 (1960): 1503.

14. François Jacob and Jacques Monod, "Genetic Regulatory Mechanisms in the Synthesis of Proteins," *Journal of Molecular Biology* 3 (1961): 318–356.

15. James D. Watson, Nancy H. Hopkins, Jeffrey W. Roberts, Joan Argetsinger Steitz, and Alan M. Winer, *Molecular Biology of the Gene*, 4th ed. (Menlo Park, Calif.: The Benjamin/Cummings Publishing Co., 1987), 339–357.

16. Maxine Singer and Paul Berg, *Genes and Genomes: A Changing Perspective* (Mill Valley, Calif.: University Science Books, 1991), 107, emphasis added.

17. Charles Scriver has suggested that gene mapping provides a "neo-Vesalian" basis for medicine. According to Victor McKusick, "The anatomic metaphor prompts one to think in terms of the morbid anatomy . . . of the human genome" ("Current Trends in Mapping Human Genes," *FASEB Journal* 5 [1991]: 17).

18. Belinda J. Rossiter and C. Thomas Caskey, "Molecular Studies of Human Genetic Disease," *FASEB Journal* 5 (1991): 21. McKusick also uses the expression "genetic lesion" ("Current Trends," 18).

19. Even strong proponents of gene therapy recognize that "despite the obvious certainty that a great deal of important basic scientific information will flow from undertaking a thorough characterization of the entire human genome and other genomes, the likelihood and timing of the anticipated medical benefits is somewhat less clear" and "there remains a serious gap between disease characterization and treatment" (Theodore Friedmann, "The Human Genome Project—Some Implications of Extensive 'Reverse Genetic' Medicine"—[opinion], *American Journal of Human Genetics* 46 (1990): 407, 411. See also Christopher Joyce, "Physician, Heal Thy Gene," *New Scientist*, September 15, 1990, 53–56; and D. J. Weatherall, "Gene Therapy in Perspective," *Nature* 349 (1991): 275–276.

20. Evelyn Fox Keller, "Nature, Nurture and the Human Genome" (MS, 1990).

21. P. A. Baird, "Genetics and Health Care: A Paradigm Shift," *Perspectives in Biology and Medicine* 33 (1990): 203–213.

22. Jan Sapp, *Where the Truth Lies: Franz Moewus and the Origins of Molecular Biology* (New York: Cambridge University Press, 1990), chap. 2.

23. Joshua Lederberg, "Edward Lawrie Tatum: December 14, 1909–November 7, 1975," *Biographical Memoirs, National Academy of Sciences* 59 (1989): 366–367.

24. Joshua Lederberg, "Foreword," in Charles R. Scriver and Barton

Childs, eds., *Garrod's Inborn Factors in Disease* (Oxford: Oxford University Press, 1989), v, vi.

25. Scriver and Childs, eds., *Garrod's Inborn Factors in Disease*, 17–20.

26. See Barton Childs, "Sir Archibald Garrod's Conception of Chemical Individuality: A Modern Appreciation," *New England Journal of Medicine* 282 (1970): 71–77; also, Alexander D. Bairn and Elizabeth D. Miller, "Archibald Garrod and the Development of the Concept of Inborn Errors of Metabolism," *Bulletin of the History of Medicine* 53 (1979): 315–328.

27. Barton Childs, "Implications for Disease of Sir Archibald Garrod's Views on Chemical Individuality," in Raul A. Wapnir, ed., *Congenital Metabolic Diseases: Diagnosis and Treatment* (New York: Marcel Dekker, 1985), 3–10; G. Roberto Burgio, " 'Inborn Errors of Metabolism' and 'Chemical Individuality', Two Ideas of Sir Archibald Garrod Briefly Revisited 50 Years after His Death," *European Journal of Pediatrics* 145 (1986): 2–5; Charles R. Scriver, "Inborn Errors of Metabolic Homeostasis: Garrod's Message Revisited," in Wapnir, ed., *Congenital Metabolic Diseases*, 11–40; Charles R. Scriver, "The Salience of Garrod's 'Molecular Groupings' and 'Inborn Factors in Disease,' " *Journal of Inherited Metabolic Disease* 12, supp. 1 (1989): 9–24.

28. Archibald Garrod, "The Incidence of Alkaptonuria: A Study in Chemical Individuality," *Lancet* 2 (1902): 1620.

29. Archibald Garrod, *The Inborn Factors in Disease: An Essay* (1931), reprinted in Scriver and Childs, eds., *Garrod's Inborn Factors*.

30. Scriver and Childs, eds., *Garrod's Inborn Factors*, 189.

31. Ibid., 185.

32. Ibid., 209.

33. Ibid., 222.

34. Ibid.

35. Edward L. Tatum, "A Case History in Biological Research," *Science* 129 (1959): 1711–1715.

36. Arthur L. Beaudet, "Genetics and Biochemistry of Variant Human Phenotypes," in Charles R. Scriver, Arthur L. Beaudet, William S. Sly, and David Valle, eds., *The Metabolic Basis of Inherited Disease*, 6th ed. (New York: McGraw-Hill, 1989), 1: 4–5, 9–10.

37. Singer and Berg, *Genes and Genomes*, 504–505, 519–520, 532, 595–596, 878.

38. David Hull, *Science as a Process* (Chicago: University of Chicago Press, 1988), 405–406.

39. Paul Berg, "All Our Collective Ingenuity Is Needed," *FASEB Journal* 5 (1991): 75. In contrast, one has to recall that it has been commonly asserted that some 90 percent, or even 95 percent, of the genome is "junk DNA."

40. Stephen J. Gould, *An Urchin in the Storm* (New York: W. W. Norton & Co., 1987), 238.

41. John B. Stanbury, James B. Wyngaarden, Donald S. Fredrickson, Joseph L. Goldstein, and Michael S. Brown, eds., *The Metabolic Basis of Inherited Disease*, 5th ed. (New York: McGraw-Hill, 1983), xv.

42. Ibid., 3.

43. Scriver et al., eds., *The Metabolic Basis of Inherited Disease*, xxvii.

44. "While there is often a tendency in medicine to regard patient populations as a homogeneous group of 'wild-type individuals' or normal humans with 'normal values' for all determinants, this is an erroneous conception" (Beaudet et al., "Genetics and Biochemistry of Variant Human Phenotypes," 12–13, 18–19.

45. Scriver, "The Salience of Garrod's 'Molecular Groupings' and 'Inborn Factors in Disease,' " 11.

46. Ibid., 19.

47. Charles R. Scriver, "The Hartnup Phenotype: Mendelian Transport Disorder, Multifactorial Disease," *American Journal of Genetics* 40 (1987): 401–412.

48. National Committee for the Protection of Human Subjects of Biomedical and Behavioral Research, *The Belmont Report* (Washington, D.C.: DHEW, 1978).

49. Robert B. Scott and P. Robert, "Genetic Diversity in Hemoglobins: Disease and Nondisease," *Journal of the American Medical Association* 239 (1978): 2681–2684, emphasis added.

50. The locus classicus for a discussion of this notion remains Georges Canguilhem's *The Normal and the Pathological* (New York: Zone Books, 1989), first published in 1943. See also Ian Hacking, *The Taming of Chance* (New York: Cambridge University Press, 1990), esp. chap. 19.

51. Schrödinger, *What Is Life? & Mind and Matter*, 38–39.

C. F. Cranor,
Genetic Causation

1. Victor A. McKusick, *Mendelian Inheritance in Man: Catalogs of Autosomal Dominant, Autosomal Recessive and X-linked Phenotypes* (Baltimore: Johns Hopkins University Press, 1992).

2. P. A. Baird, "Genetics and Health Care: A Paradigm Shift," *Perspectives in Biology and Medicine* 33 (1990): 203.

3. Theodore Friedmann, "Progress toward Human Gene Therapy," *Science* 244 (1989): 1275.

4. See Ruth Hubbard, "Genes as Causes," in *The Politics of Women's Biology* (New Brunswick: Rutgers University Press, 1990), 76; Robert Moyzis, presentation at Human Genome Initiative seminar, Los Alamos National Laboratory, January 18, 1991; and Baird, "Genetics and Health Care," 203–213.

5. Hubbard, "Genes as Causes," 72–76.

6. H.L.A. Hart and A. M. Honoré, "Causation in the Law," in *Punishment and Responsibility* (Stanford: Stanford University Press, 1961), 325–342. "A" or "the" cause must also be a *functioning* member, not an irrelevant one" of that set of conditions; that is, it must "be a nonredundant member of some set of conditions which is jointly sufficient for the effect" (Michael Scriven, "The Logic of Cause," *Theory and Decision* 2 [1971]: 52). Scriven represents this statement symbolically by $C_1 + C_2 + \ldots C_n \to E$, where the C's are causes or conditions and E is the effect; the arrow stands for inference according to known laws.

7. Hart and Honoré, "Causation in the Law," 330.

8. Joel Feinberg, "Sua Culpa," in *Doing and Deserving* (Princeton: Princeton University Press, 1990), 203, 204. One can get a sense of this by reading some good science writing, such as John McPhee's *The Control of Nature* (New York: Farrar, Straus & Giroux, Noonday Press, 1989).

9. Hart and Honoré, "Causation in the Law," 334.

10. Ibid., 329. But the explanation need not involve "known general laws." As philosophers of science have pointed out, in many circumstances one can frequently "establish beyond reasonable doubt that A caused X in the circumstances (C) surrounding the experiment, but [one] cannot specify what elements of cause are 'essential'; nor can [one] provide a reliable description of all the components in C" (Michael Scriven, "Causation as Explanation," *Nous* 9 [1975]: 9).

11. Feinberg, "Sua Culpa," 204.

12. Ibid., 204, 205.

13. Walter G. Vincenti, *What Engineers Know and How They Know It: Analytical Studies from Aeronautical History* (Baltimore: Johns Hopkins University Press, 1990), 167.

14. Hart and Honoré, "Causation in the Law," 329, emphasis added.

15. Feinberg, "Sua Culpa," 205; Hart and Honoré, "Causation in the Law," 329.

16. See Hubbard, "Genes as Causes."

17. Ibid., 79; Ruth Hubbard and Elijah Wald, *Exploding the Gene Myth: How Genetic Information Is Produced and Manipulated by Scientists, Physicians, Employers, Insurance Companies, Educators and Law Enforcers* (Boston: Beacon Press, 1993).

18. Hubbard, "Genes as Causes," 82.

19. Ibid., 82–83.

20. Ibid., 73.

21. Ibid., 77; Hubbard and Wald, *Exploding the Gene Myth*, 63–65, 75–78.

22. Hubbard and Wald, *Exploding the Gene Myth*, 64.

23. The notion of a malfunctioning or "defective" gene could be quite

troublesome; for, as Elisabeth Lloyd points out elsewhere in the present volume (see Chapter 6), some may be too quick to label a genetic difference from a statistical norm as a "defective gene." Genetic variation is not necessarily genetic deficiency. We should therefore be careful about labeling genes as defective or abnormal, for these normatively laden terms can easily be abused.

24. Hubbard and Wald, *Exploding the Gene Myth*, 64.

25. Ian Hacking, "Philosophers of Experiment," *PSA* 2 (1988): 152.

26. Ibid., 152.

27. Hubbard and Wald, *Exploding the Gene Myth*, 65.

28. C. Holden, "Probing the Complex Genetics of Alcoholism," *Science* 251 (1991): 163–164. There are additional problems in focusing on *behavior* as the outcome of a particular genetic condition; Hubbard and Wald (*Exploding the Gene Myth*, 93–100) discuss some of these issues.

29. Hubbard and Wald (*Exploding the Gene Myth*, 78) make this point about type I diabetes, a disease that appears initially to have a significant genetic component.

30. Hubbard and Wald (ibid., 77) point out that even when some people with a disease appear to have a genetically caused disease, the vast majority with that disease do not have an identifiable genetic anomaly.

31. Baird, "Genetics and Health Care: A Paradigm Shift," 203, 205, 206, 207.

32. Ibid., 208.

33. T. Friedmann, "Progress toward Human Gene Therapy," 1275.

34. Ibid., 1279.

35. T. Friedmann, presentation at the University of California Humanities Research Institute, Irvine, April 19, 1991.

36. Charles R. Scriver and Barton Childs, eds., *Garrod's Inborn Factors in Disease* (Oxford: Oxford University Press, 1989), 194.

37. Ibid., 205; Evelyn Fox Keller, "Master Molecules," and Camille Limoges, "*Errare Humanum Est*" (Chapters 5 and 7 in the present volume) make similar points.

38. Scriver and Childs, eds., *Garrod's Inborn Factors*, 209.

39. David Hull, *Science as Process: An Evolutionary Account of the Social and Conceptual Development of Science* (Chicago: University of Chicago Press, 1988).

40. Thomas Kuhn, *The Structure of Scientific Revolutions* (Chicago: University of Chicago Press, 1970).

41. Leon Jasoff, "Crisis in the Labs," *Time*, August 26, 1991, 26–49.

D. B. Paul,
Eugenic Anxieties

A slightly different version of this chapter appeared under the same title in *Social Research* 59.3 (1992): 663–683.

1. Robert Wright, "Achilles' Helix," *New Republic*, July 9, 1990, 27.

2. Michael Lockwood, "The Improvement Movement," *Nature* 317 (1985): 481.

3. Charles Rosenberg notes: "Eugenics has become a familiar term to historians and informed readers, but debate has on the whole stimulated more posturing and self-congratulatory moralizing than serious scholarship" (review of Daniel J. Kevles, *In the Name of Eugenics*, in *Journal of American History* 73 [1986]: 232). A number of more nuanced accounts have appeared since Rosenberg's review. See particularly the collection of essays edited by Mark Adams, *The Wellborn Science: Eugenics in Germany, France, Brazil, and Russia* (New York: Oxford University Press, 1990); Pauline M. H. Mazumdar, *Eugenics, Human Genetics and Human Failings: The Eugenics Society, Its Sources and Critics in Britain* (London: Routledge, 1992); and Richard A. Soloway's *Demography and Degeneration: Eugenics and the Declining Birthrate in Twentieth-Century Britain* (Chapel Hill: University of North Carolina Press, 1990).

4. Daniel E. Koshland, Jr., dismisses the issue in his editorial, "Sequences and Consequences of the Human Genome," in *Science* 246 (1989): 189; and in his reply to Salvador Luria in *Science* 247 (1989): 270. Nancy Wexler suggests that "it's critical that people appreciate the limits of what can be done, so that their fears don't intrude on the benefits that could come out of genetic research" (quoted in William Saletan, "Genes 'R Us," *New Republic*, July 16, 1989, 18).

5. James D. Watson, "The Human Genome Project: Past, Present, and Future," *Science* 248 (1990): 44–49, is typical.

6. See, for example, Joel Davis, *Mapping the Code* (New York: Wiley, 1991); Lois Wingerson, *Mapping Our Genes* (New York: Dutton, 1990); and Jerry E. Bishop and Michael Waldholz, *Genome* (New York: Simon & Schuster, 1990).

7. "Modified Proposal for a Council Decision Adopting a Specific Research and Technological Development in the Field of Health: Human Genome Analysis (1990 to 1991)," *Official Journal of the European Communities*, CB-CO-89-485-EN-C (Brussels: November 13, 1989): 3.

8. This double meaning of eugenics is discussed by Elof Axel Carlson in "Ramifications of Genetics," *Science* 232 (1986): 531–532.

9. The term comes from the Greek for "well-born." See Galton's *Inquiries into the Human Faculty and Its Development*, 2nd ed. (New York: E. P. Dutton & Co., 1907), 17.

10. Mark H. Haller, *Eugenics: Hereditarian Attitudes in American Thought*, 2nd ed. (New Brunswick: Rutgers University Press, 1984), ix.

11. Wingerson, *Mapping Our Genes*, 304.

12. Elof Axel Carlson, *Human Genetics* (Lexington, Mass.: D. C. Heath & Co., 1984), glossary.

13. Davis, *Mapping the Code*, 283.

14. Carlson, "Ramifications of Genetics," 531.

15. Wright, "Achilles' Helix," 27. See also Troy Duster, *Backdoor to Eugenics* (New York: Routledge, 1990).

16. Neil Holtzman, *Proceed with Caution: Predicting Genetic Risks in the Recombinant DNA Era* (Baltimore: Johns Hopkins University Press, 1989), 223.

17. Thus the authors of an Office of Technology Assessment analysis of the Human Genome Project write: "It may well be that the problem with positive eugenics has more to do with the means than with the ends. The basic objective of improving the human condition is generally supported, although debates about just what constitutes such improvement continue. Many concerns about eugenic policies in the past focused on the methods used to obtain them, such as sterilization, rather than on the ends themselves" (*Mapping Our Genes. The Genome Project: How Big, How Fast?* OTA-BA-373 [Washington, D.C.: GPO, 1988], 85).

18. Havelock Ellis, *The Task of Social Hygiene* (London: Constable, 1912), 45–46.

19. For a related discussion of the ways in which the discourse of choice functions to disguise social reality, see Abby Lippman, "Prenatal Genetic Testing and Screening: Constructing Needs and Reinforcing Inequities," *American Journal of Law & Medicine* 17 (1991): 15–50.

20. See, for example, David Suzuki and Peter Knudtson, *Genethics: The Clash between the New Genetics and Human Values* (Cambridge: Harvard University Press, 1989), 160, 346.

21. See Daniel J. Kevles, *In the Name of Eugenics: Genetics and the Uses of Human Heredity* (New York: Knopf, 1985).

22. Ibid., 301.

23. Madison Grant, *The Passing of the Great Race* (New York: Scribner, 1916), 44–45.

24. Lancelot Hogben, *Genetic Principles in Medicine and Social Science* (London: Williams & Norgate, 1931), 207.

25. Shaw wrote: "[T]here is now no reasonable excuse for refusing to face the fact that nothing but a eugenic religion can save our civilization." See his *Sociological Papers* (London: Constable, 1905), 74–75.

26. Bertrand Russell, "Eugenics," in *Marriage and Morals* (London: 1924), 272–273.

27. Jane Clapperton, *Scientific Meliorism* (London, 1885), quoted in Soloway, *Demography and Degeneration*, 102.

28. Dorothy C. Wertz and John C. Fletcher, eds., *Ethics and Human Genetics: A Cross-Cultural Perspective* (New York: Springer-Verlag, 1989), 26–31.

29. Dorothy C. Wertz, John C. Fletcher, and John J. Mulvihill, "Medical Geneticists Confront Ethical Dilemmas: Cross-Cultural Comparisons among 18 Nations," *American Journal of Human Genetics* 46 (1990): 1209–1210.

30. Deborah Pencarinha, "Study of the Attitudes and Reasoning of M.S. Genetic Counselors Regarding Ethical Issues in Medical Genetics," poster no. 1821, Eighth International Congress of Human Genetics, Washington, D.C., October 6–11, 1991.

31. R. J. Cynkar, "*Buck v. Bell*: 'Felt Necessities' v. 'Fundamental Values'?" *Columbia Law Review* 81 (1981): 1419.

32. Philip R. Reilly, *The Surgical Solution: A History of Involuntary Sterilization in the United States* (Baltimore: Johns Hopkins University Press, 1991), 155.

33. *Eisenstadt v. Baird*, 405 U.S. 438, 453 (1972).

34. For an excellent discussion of this development, see Ronald Bayer, *Private Acts, Social Consequences: AIDS and the Politics of Public Health* (New Brunswick: Rutgers University Press, 1989), esp. chap. 1.

35. See, for example, Maura A. Ryan, "The Argument for Unlimited Procreative Liberty: A Feminist Critique," *Hastings Center Report* 19 (1990): 6–12; and Caroline Whitbeck, "Ethical Issues Raised by the New Medical Technologies," in Judith Rodin and Aila Collins, eds., *Women and New Reproductive Technologies: Medical, Psychosocial, Legal, and Ethical Dilemmas* (Hillsdale, N.J.: Lawrence Erlbaum Associates, 1991), 49–64.

36. Elizabeth Fox-Genovese, *Feminism without Illusions* (Chapel Hill: University of North Carolina Press, 1991), esp. chaps. 2 and 3.

37. Dorothy C. Wertz and John C. Fletcher, "Fatal Knowledge? Prenatal Diagnosis and Sex Selection," *Hastings Center Report* 18 (1989): 24. For an opposed view, see Ruth Schwartz Cowan, "Genetic Technology and Reproductive Choice: An Ethics for Autonomy," in Daniel J. Kevles and Leroy Hood, eds., *The Code of Codes: Scientific and Social Issues in the Human Genome Project* (Cambridge: Harvard University Press, 1992), 318–352.

38. Beth A. Fine, "The Evolution of Nondirectiveness in Genetic Counseling and Implications of the Human Genome Project," in Dianne M. Bartels, Bonnie S. LeRoy, and Arthur L. Caplan, eds., *Prescribing our Future: Ethical Challenges in Genetic Counseling* (Hawthorne, N.Y.: Aldine de Gruyter, 1993), 101–117.

39. Carl R. Rogers, *Client-Centered Therapy: Its Current Practice, Impli-*

cations, and Theory (Boston: Houghton Mifflin, 1951), discussed in Fine, "The Evolution of Nondirectiveness," 108.

40. Robert Nozick, *Anarchy, State, and Utopia* (New York: Basic Books, 1974), 315.

41. Wright, "Achilles' Helix," 27.

42. There is no direct evidence that children with genetic disabilities are being born unequally to the poor; however, access to genetic services (like other medical services) is strongly class-based. Thus, nearly a quarter of all children are born to women who received no prenatal health care at all. Specific studies of amniocentesis utilization rates demonstrate large geographic, racial, and socioeconomic differentials. David Sokal and colleagues found substantial geographic and racial variation among Georgia women aged forty and older, ranging from a 60 percent use rate among whites in the Atlanta and Augusta health districts to 0.5 percent among rural blacks. See David C. Sokal, J. Rogers Byrd, Andrew T. L. Chan, Marshall F. Goldberg, and Godfrey P. Oakley, Jr., "Prenatal Chromosomal Diagnosis: Racial and Geographic Variation for Older Women in Georgia," *Journal of the American Medical Association* 244 (1980): 1355–1357. Abby Lippman summarizes the literature on socioeconomic differentials in "Prenatal Genetic Testing and Screening."

43. John Stuart Mill, "On Liberty" (1855), in *Essential Works of John Stuart Mill* (New York: Bantam, 1961), 263.

44. Ibid., 353–354.

45. Mill also wrote that "every one has a right to live . . . [b]ut no one has a right to bring creatures into life, to be supported by other people. . . . There are abundance of writers and public speakers, including many of most ostentatious pretensions to high feeling, whose views of life are so truly brutish, that they see hardship in preventing paupers from breeding hereditary paupers in the workhouse itself. Posterity will one day ask, with astonishment, what sort of people it could be among whom such preachers could find proselytes" (John Stuart Mill, *Principles of Political Economy* [1st ed. 1848] [1909; reprint, New York: Augustus M. Kelley, 1969], 364).

46. John Dunn, *Western Political Theory in the Face of the Future* (Cambridge: Cambridge University Press, 1979), 51.

G. S. Kavka,
Upside Risks

For their helpful comments on an earlier version of this essay, I am grateful to the other participants in the University of California Humanities Research Institute seminar, "Bioethics: Anticipating Ethical Issues of New Developments in Genetics and Genetic Technology," held in early 1991.

1. See, for example, Russell Hardin, *Collective Action* (Baltimore: Johns Hopkins University Press, 1982). For application to environmental issues like the pollution example, see Carl F. Cranor, "Collective and Individual Duties to Protect the Environment," *Journal of Applied Philosophy* 2 (1985): 243–259.

2. Some of these issues are discussed in Stephen P. Stich, "The Recombinant DNA Debate," *Philosophy and Public Affairs* 7 (1983): 187–205.

3. In her contribution to the present volume (see Chapter 9), Diane B. Paul observes that individual reproductive decisions can have social consequences. The idea of upside risks explains, and illustrates, one way in which they can.

4. One well-known experiment that may have generated useful knowledge at the expense of subjects' interests is the Willowbrook hepatitis study. For discussion, see Stephen Golby, Saul Krugman, M. H. Pappworth, and Geoffrey Edsell, "The Willowbrook Letters: Criticism and Defense," in Ronald Munson, ed., *Intervention and Reflection* (Belmont, Calif.: Wadsworth, 1988), 314–316.

5. Jonathan Glover, *Ethics of New Reproductive Technologies: The Glover Commission Report to the European Commission* (DeKalb: Northern Illinois University Press, 1989), 141.

6. Thomas C. Schelling, *Micromotives and Macrobehavior* (New York: W. W. Norton, 1978), 201.

7. Ibid., 202.

8. Ibid., 202–203.

9. On the prevalence and adaptiveness of wishful thinking, see Shelley E. Taylor, *Positive Illusions* (New York: Basic Books, 1989).

10. Glover et al., *Ethics of New Reproductive Technologies*, 142.

11. Schelling, *Micromotives and Macrobehavior*, 201–202.

12. Charles E. Silberman, *Criminal Violence, Criminal Justice* (New York: Random House, 1978), 49, 67–68.

13. Louis Harris, "The Gender Gulf," *New York Times*, December 7, 1990.

14. Having a smaller proportion of women in the population might, however, somewhat alleviate one pressing world problem: overpopulation and rapid population growth. I do not know how to balance this potential advantage against the disadvantages cited in the text.

15. See Dorothy C. Wertz, John C. Fletcher, and John J. Mulvihill, "Medical Geneticists Confront Ethical Dilemmas: Cross-Cultural Comparisons among 18 Nations," *American Journal of Human Genetics* 46 (1990): 1209–1210.

16. See Caleb E. Finch, *Longevity, Senescence, and the Genome* (Chicago: University of Chicago Press, 1990), where the author writes that "many aspects of senescence should be strongly modifiable by interventions at the level of gene expression" (xv).

17. If longevity can be genetically induced only prenatally, then parents might have to make this choice for each of their children. That is, each time they reproduce, they might have to choose between having a sterile, long-lived child or having a fecund, shorter-lived one.

18. Thomas Hobbes, *Human Nature: Body, Man, and Citizen* (1650), ed. Richard Peters (New York: Collier, 1962), 224–225.

19. See Fred Hirsch, *The Social Limits to Growth* (Cambridge: Harvard University Press, 1976); and Robert Frank, *Choosing the Right Pond* (New York: Oxford University Press, 1985).

20. I use the term "wealth" here to refer to absolute amounts of material resources. In ordinary usage, terms like "wealthy" or "rich" have a positional component: they refer to someone who has many more financial resources than most other people.

21. In the terminology introduced earlier, then, we are imagining that there are downside risks associated with this procedure.

22. In the language of game theorists, the couples are in a many-party *prisoner's dilemma* in regard to boosting their offspring's intelligence by genetic means. See Frank, *Choosing*, chap. 7, on how prisoner's dilemmas often arise when competitive goods are at stake.

23. Gregory S. Kavka, *Hobbesian Moral and Political Theory* (Princeton: Princeton University Press, 1986), 139–140, 245–246, 451.

24. One such harmful environment is described in John Stuart Mill's 1873 *Autobiography* (New York: Columbia University Press, 1924). Another must have been created by the Texas woman who recently tried to improve her teenage daughter's prospects of making the cheerleading squad by hiring someone to murder the mother of the daughter's chief rival. See Michael Jaffe, "For the Record," *Sports Illustrated*, February 11, 1991, 208.

25. I am grateful to Diane Paul for informing me of the existence of the term "euthenics." Prior to receiving this information, I had been forced to coin the awkward term "envirogenics" to express this idea perspicuously.

26. There remain some disanalogies that might be morally significant. For example, individuals typically *participate* in the environmental enhancement of their capacities in ways that would not be possible in the genetic enhancement of their capacities.

27. One thing that typically is *not* equal is the overall supply of the good in question: too much equality in the distribution of the good may sap production incentives and thereby reduce the supply.

28. Doing this without stigmatizing the groups in question may be a

politically delicate task. A similar problem concerning genetic screening is mentioned in George J. Annas, "Mapping the Human Genome and the Meaning of Monster Mythology," *Emory Law Journal* 39 (1990): 641.

29. See ibid.; and President's Commission for the Study of Ethical Problems in Medicine and Biomedical and Behavioral Research, *Splicing Life: A Report on the Social and Ethical Issues of Genetic Engineering with Human Beings* (Washington, D.C.: The Commission, 1982), 14–17, 53–60.

30. On the dangers of "blaming the victims" when defects come to be seen as more controllable by genetic means, see Neil A. Holtzman, *Proceed with Caution: Predicting Genetic Risks in the Recombinant DNA Era* (Baltimore: Johns Hopkins University Press, 1989), 227.

31. In this vein, a prominent philosopher writes that, "the emergence of the sense that man is an artifact, constructed through an increasingly known and alterable process of genetic engineering . . . may [not be] compatible with our ideas of individuality and autonomy" (David Gauthier, *Morals by Agreement* [Oxford: Clarendon Press, 1986], 354).

32. On the psychological effects of nuclear weapons, see Ralph K. White, ed., *Psychology and the Prevention of Nuclear War* (New York: New York University Press, 1986), 7–33.

33. See, for example, Alexander Morgan Capron, "Which Ills to Bear? Reevaluating the 'Threat' of Modern Genetics," *Emory Law Journal* 39 (1990): 689–693; and Robert Wright, "The End of Insurance," *New Republic*, July 9, 1990, 26.

34. The drug AZT apparently offers such hope to those testing positive for AIDS. The development of AZT and other drugs has altered the nature of the decision about whether to be tested for this disease.

35. Wright, "The End of Insurance," 26.

36. Schelling, *Micromotives and Macrobehavior*, 99–101.

37. To the extent that parents may come to control their children's genetic endowments through selective abortion or genetic engineering, they might perhaps be further deterred from having children genetically prone to illness if they knew such children would have no access to insurance.

38. Gregory S. Kavka, "Some Social Benefits of Uncertainty," *Midwest Studies in Philosophy* 15 (1990): 311–326.

39. On risk assessment, see Daniel Kahneman, Paul Slovic, and Amos Tversky, *Judgment under Uncertainty: Heuristics and Biases* (Cambridge: Cambridge University Press, 1982). On the issue of whether people are free to refuse jobs and low wages, see David Zimmerman, "Coercive Wage Offers," *Philosophy and Public Affairs* 10 (1981): 121–145.

W. C. Thompson,
The DNA-Typing Controversy

1. A number of journalistic accounts heralded DNA typing as a "breakthrough" that "could revolutionize law enforcement." See, for example, Ricki Lewis, "DNA Fingerprints: Witness for the Prosecution," *Discover*, June 1988, 44.

2. See generally William Thompson, "Evaluating the Admissibility of New Genetic Identification Tests: Lessons from the DNA War," *Journal of Criminal Law and Criminology* (forthcoming); William Thompson and Simon Ford, "DNA Testing: Debate Update," *Trial* 28 (1992): 52; Leslie Roberts, "Fight Erupts over DNA Fingerprinting," *Science* 254 (1991): 1721; Peter Neufeld and Neville Colman, "When Science Takes the Witness Stand," *Scientific American*, May 1990, 46; William Thompson and Simon Ford, "Is DNA Fingerprinting Ready for the Courts?" *New Scientist*, March 31, 1990, 38; and Eric Lander, "DNA Fingerprinting on Trial," *Nature* 339 (1989): 501.

3. Shannon Brownlee, "Courtroom Genetics," *U.S. News and World Report*, January, 27, 1992, 60; U.S. Congress, Office of Technology Assessment, *Genetic Witness: Forensic Uses of DNA Tests* (Washington, D.C.: GPO, 1990).

4. Appellate decisions holding DNA evidence inadmissible include *State v. Schwartz*, 447 N.W.2d 422 (Minn. 1989); *Commonwealth v. Curnin* (1991) 409 Mass. 218 (565 N.E.2d 440); *Commonwealth v. Lanigan* (1992) 413 Mass. 154 (596 N.E.2d 311); and *People v. Barney and People v. Howard* (1992) 8 Cal.App.4th 798. Trial court decisions holding DNA tests inadmissible include *People v. Castro*, 545 N.Y.S.2d 985 (1989); *State of Oregon v. Wheeler* (Washington County District Court, Case no. C89-0901CR, March 8, 1990); *State of Arizona v. Despain* (Yuma County Superior Court, no. 15589, February 12, 1991); *State of Illinois v. Michael Fleming and Vernon Watson* (Circuit Court of Cook County, nos. 90-CR-2716 and 90-CR-5546, March 12, 1991); *State of Vermont v. Arthur Passino* (District Court of Vermont, Unit no. 2, Franklin Circuit, Docket no. 185-1-90, May 13, 1991); *People v. Halik* (Superior Court of Los Angeles County, Calif., no. VA00843, September 26, 1991); and *U.S. v. Porter et al.* (Superior Court of District Columbia, September 20, 1991).

5. Neufeld and Colman, "When Science Takes the Witness Stand," Thompson and Ford, "DNA Testing," 60.

6. "This is no [longer] a search for the truth, it is a war, the way people are behaving" (John Hicks, head of the FBI Laboratory Division, quoted in Leslie Roberts, "Science in Court: A Culture Clash," *Science* 257 [1992]: 736). For other accounts of the heated nature of the dispute,

see Roberts, "Fight Erupts over DNA Fingerprinting"; Christopher Anderson, "DNA Fingerprinting Discord," *Nature* 354 (1991): 500.

7. National Research Council, *DNA Technology in Forensic Science* (Washington, D.C.: National Academy Press, 1992); hereafter, NRC Report.

8. André Moenssens, "DNA Evidence and Its Critics—How Valid Are the Challenges?" *Jurimetrics* 31 (1990): 87; George Clarke, "DNA Fingerprinting Critics Have Run Afoul of Science," *Los Angeles Daily Journal*, January 28, 1992 (editorial comment of a prominent California prosecutor, arguing that scientific criticism of forensic DNA testing is "counterfeit dissent").

9. See Neufeld and Colman, "When Science Takes the Witness Stand"; Lander, "DNA Fingerprinting on Trial."

10. Richard Lewontin, "The Dream of the Human Genome," *New York Review of Books*, May 28, 1992, 39.

11. About three thousand RFLPs have been identified. Since the early 1980s, geneticists have relied heavily on RFLPs as genetic markers for studying heredity. Most of the major advances in detecting disease genes that have occurred during the past decade have resulted from this application of RFLP analysis. For general background on the development of RFLP analysis, see Jan Witkowski, "Milestones in the Development of DNA Technology," in Mark A. Farley and James J. Harrington, eds., *Forensic DNA Technology* (Chelsea, Mich.: Lewis Publishers, 1991), 1; also see NRC Report, chap. 1.

12. The function of VNTRs is not understood. They do not code for protein, but they are thought to be areas where mutations are common; hence, there is speculation that they may be fountainheads of evolutionary change.

13. The VNTRs examined by forensic DNA tests are "hypervariable"—that is to say, there is a great deal of variation among individuals in the number of repeats and, thus, a great deal of variation among individuals in the length of restriction fragments containing those VNTRs. The notion that analysis of hypervariable VNTRs could be useful in criminal identification was first voiced by Alec Jeffreys. See A. Jeffreys, V. Wilson, and S. L. Thein, "Individual-Specific 'Fingerprints' of Human DNA," *Nature* 316 (1985): 76.

14. A good general discussion of test procedures may be found in the NRC Report, chap. 1.

15. In electrophoresis, the DNA samples are placed at one end of an agarose gel, an electric current is applied, and the DNA, which carries a negative charge, is drawn through the gel. The shorter restriction fragments move more quickly than the longer fragments so that, after a time, the fragments are arrayed across the gel according to their length.

Typically, several DNA samples are run together in separate lanes on the same gel.

16. A person who inherits an identical fragment of DNA from both parents, however, will show only one band. Individuals who have two bands are called heterozygotes; those with one band are called homozygotes.

17. For a general discussion of problems that may arise in interpreting DNA test results, see William Thompson and Simon Ford, "The Meaning of a Match: Sources of Ambiguity in the Interpretation of DNA Prints," in Farley and Harrington, eds., *Forensic DNA Technology*, 93; Lander, "DNA Fingerprinting on Trial"; NRC Report, chap. 2.

18. The matching rules developed by the forensic laboratories are novel. Scientists who use RFLP analysis for scientific research and genetic diagnosis do not need these sorts of matching rules because they do not attempt to make the fine grade distinctions among DNA prints that are necessary for criminal identification. See Lander, "DNA Fingerprinting on Trial."

In designing matching rules, a forensic laboratory must strike a balance between two potential errors: if the rules are too strict, the laboratory may fail to call a match between samples that really are from the same person, but if the rules are too lenient the laboratory may call a match between samples from different people.

19. 545 N.Y.S.2d 985 (supp. 1989).

20. Lander, "DNA Fingerprinting on Trial."

21. Moenssens, "DNA Evidence."

22. Lander, "DNA Fingerprinting on Trial"; Eric Lander, "Research on DNA Typing Catching Up with Courtroom Application" (invited editorial), *American Journal of Human Genetics* 48 (1991): 819; Thompson and Ford, "The Meaning of a Match."

23. Thompson, "Evaluating the Admissibility of New Genetic Identification Tests."

24. Thompson and Ford, "The Meaning of a Match," 141.

25. NRC Report, chap. 2, esp. 54–56.

26. For example, several scientists have attacked the FBI's validation research: "I find no scientific basis for [the FBI's] conclusions. Many of the key experiments were badly designed and poorly executed, and many interpretations of data appear to be arbitrary, often because key controls failed or were omitted entirely. . . . Thus, instead of concluding that the FBI has developed and validated a reliable, sensitive procedure for identification of forensic specimens, I conclude they have not, and that the validation procedures themselves are badly flawed" (Peter D'Eustachio, "Expert's Report" [submitted on behalf of defendants in *U.S. v. Yee*, 134 F.R.D. 161, 1991], 5–7; D'Eustachio is a professor of

molecular genetics at New York University). Others, however, take a more charitable view; see Lander, "Research on DNA Typing."

27. R. C. Lewontin and D. L. Hartl, "Population Genetics in Forensic DNA Typing," *Science* 254 (1991): 1745; Laurence Mueller, "Population Genetics of Hypervariable Human DNA," in Farley and Harrington, eds., *Forensic DNA Technology*, 51.

28. NRC Report, 76.

29. Roberts, "Fight Erupts over DNA Fingerprinting."

30. Ranajit Chakraborty and Kenneth Kidd, "The Utility of DNA Typing in Forensic Work, *Science* 254 (1991): 1735.

31. Some isolated populations have been identified in which the frequency of matching DNA prints is quite high. One DNA profile, predicted by forensic statistical-estimation methods to occur in 1 person in 96 million, was observed to occur with a frequency of 1 in 37 among Central American and South American Indian groups. See Laurence Mueller, "The Use of DNA Typing in Forensic Science," *Accountability in Research* 3 (1993): 1, 5.

32. Lewontin and Hartl, "Population Genetics."

33. Thompson and Ford, "DNA Testing," 57.

34. Thompson, "Evaluating the Admissibility of New Genetic Identification Tests."

35. Thompson and Ford, "The Meaning of a Match," 97.

36. Paul Hagerman, letter, *American Journal of Human Genetics* 47 (1990): 876; R. Lempert, "Docket Data and Local Knowledge: Studying the Court and Society Link over Time," *Law and Sociology Review* 24 (1990): 323–328; Michael Saks and Jonathan Koehler, "What DNA 'Fingerprinting' Can Teach the Law about the Rest of Forensic Science," *Cardozo Law Review* 13 (1991): 361.

37. See Thompson and Ford, "The Meaning of a Match," 142–145.

38. NRC Report, 87.

39. Ibid., 86–89.

40. Ibid., chap. 3.

41. Affidavit of Laurence Mueller concerning DNA prints used as evidence in *State of New Mexico v. Anderson* (Bernalillo County, no. CR-46255).

42. See Peter Aldous, "Geneticists Attack NRC Report as Scientifically Flawed," *Science* 259 (1993): 755.

43. Bruce Weir, "Population Genetics in the Forensic DNA Debate," *Proceedings of the National Academy of Science* 89 (1993): 11,654.

44. Eric Lander, "DNA Fingerprinting: The NRC Report" (letter), *Science* 260 (1993): 1221.

45. Jennifer Slimowitz and Joel Cohen, "Violations of the Ceiling Principle: Exact Conditions and Statistical Evidence," *American Journal of Human Genetics* 53 (1993): 314.

46. A distinction is usually drawn between the results of scientific tests and mere "expert opinion." A person who qualifies as an expert is generally free to state an opinion on a scientific issue without having to demonstrate that the opinion is derived from reliable assumptions or procedures. In order to present the results of a "test" or "procedure," however, there must be a preliminary showing that it is reliable.

The term "reliable" is generally used in legal writings as if it were synonymous with "valid" or "accurate." For the sake of clarity in discussing legal materials, I will follow that usage here, although it is arguably incorrect. For a discussion of the distinctions between validity, reliability, and accuracy, see any good text on social science methodology.

47. "Because 'science' is often accepted in our society as synonymous with truth, there is a substantial risk of overweighting by the jury. The rules concerning scientific evidence are aimed at that risk" (M. Udall and J. Livermore, *Law of Evidence* [Minneapolis: West Publishing, 1982], sec. 102).

48. 293 F. 1013 (D.C. Cir. 1923).

49. 293 F. 1014. For a general discussion of the application of the *Frye* rule to forensic DNA testing, see William Thompson and Simon Ford, "DNA Typing: Acceptance and Weight of the New Genetic Identification Tests," *Virginia Law Review* 75 (1989): 45.

50. In relevancy jurisdictions, judges bear the burden of making a correct assessment of the reliability of a scientific technique, and this may be a difficult task. For a general discussion of the evaluation of DNA evidence under relevancy rules, see Janet Hoeffel, "The Dark Side of DNA Profiling: Unreliable Scientific Evidence Meets the Criminal Defendant," *Stanford Law Review* 42 (1990): 465.

51. For example, California's version of the *Frye* test states that "the reliability of the *method* must be established" (*People v. Kelly* [1976] 17 Cal.3d 24, 30, emphasis in original).

52. The proponent of novel scientific evidence generally must show that it meets the standard for admissibility by a preponderance of the evidence. However, some courts have argued that a higher standard is appropriate for DNA evidence because it is "likely to have an enormous effect in resolving completely a matter in controversy" (opinion of Judge Keddie in *Arizona v. Despain*, Superior Court of Yuma County, Ariz., no. 15589, February 12, 1991, holding the FBI DNA test inadmissible under the *Frye* standard).

53. This has not always been the case, however. In one capital case in Texas, a case I have studied, the prosecutor provided to the defense in advance of trial only his own expurgated (and incorrect) summary of what the laboratory report had said.

54. A summary of some of the legal arguments may be found in the

order of a federal magistrate, granting discovery to the defense in *United States v. Yee,* 129 Federal Rules Decisions 629 (N.D. Ohio, 1990).

55. The "trade secret" argument lost its force after commentators pointed out the fundamental incompatibility of the claim that the protocol is a trade secret with the claim that it is generally accepted by the scientific community within the meaning of the *Frye* standard. See Thompson and Ford, "DNA Typing," 60.

56. Information is "privileged" when the law makes it inadmissible in legal proceedings in order to further some important public policy. For example, communications between spouses are privileged, presumably to protect marital harmony. The FBI claimed that some of the scientific studies it had conducted to check the accuracy of its DNA tests were privileged, arguing that forced disclosure of the results of such research would deter the agency from doing similar research in the future and would therefore be a bad policy.

57. "The fair trial and due process rights are implicated when data relied upon by a laboratory in performing tests are not available to the opposing party for review and cross examination. . . . The defense request for . . . specific information regarding its methodology and population data base was denied by Cellmark" (*State v. Schwartz,* 447 N.W.2d 422, 427 [Minn. 1989]).

58. *Iowa v. Smith* (District Court of Polk County, no. 41733, vol. II, TR 57, December 18, 1989). When the judge in *Smith* held a hearing on a defense request for discovery of the results of the FBI's internal proficiency tests in late 1989, FBI administrator James Kearney, section chief of the FBI's Forensic Science Research and Training Center, flew to Des Moines, along with FBI Legal Counsel L. W. McFarland, to argue against such an order. In his testimony during a pretrial hearing, Kearney suggested that a court order compelling disclosure could spell the end of meaningful internal proficiency testing in forensic laboratories; labs would be reluctant to do such work because the results could be used in court "to pistol-whip us" (vol. II, p. 64). The court nevertheless granted the discovery request, becoming the first court in the United States to do so.

59. For example, employees of the FBI laboratory published a study which reported that its DNA-typing procedures are largely unaffected by "environmental insults" to the DNA samples. See B. Budowle, S. Baechtel, and D. Adams, "Validation with Regard to Environmental Insult of the RFLP Procedures for Forensic Purposes," in Farley and Harrington, eds., *Forensic DNA Technology,* 83. When New York University molecular biologist Peter D'Eustachio examined the underlying data at the request of defense counsel in *U.S. v. Yee,* however, he concluded that the FBI's conclusions were not supported by its raw data (*U.S. v. Yee,* 134 F.R.D. at 177–179).

60. "Memorandum from FBI Legal Counsel to Assistant Director, FBI Laboratory Division," April 20, 1990 (introduced in evidence in *U.S. v. Yee*).

61. In a recent civil paternity action, for example, one commercial laboratory estimated the cost of complying with a request for information about studies validating its procedures to be $684,925. After a lengthy hearing on the issue, the court found that the laboratory's response to discovery "lacked credibility" and that the laboratory had wanted "to charge defendant money to produce . . . information that did not exist" (*Rodick v. Cazale* [24th Judicial District Court, Jefferson Parish, La., December 5, 1991]).

62. Forensic scientists have expressed fears that their unpublished data may be "stolen" by defense experts or used in a manner or for purposes they disapprove of. Fear of disclosure is also said to hinder efforts of forensic scientists to establish collaborations, because "[o]ther scientists . . . are afraid we will be forced to turn [their data] over in discovery before they have had a chance to finish their studies, formulate valid and substantiated interpretations, and personally present the results" (affidavit of FBI employee Bruce Budowle in support of the federal government's motion opposing the defendant's discovery request in *U.S. v. Yee*, 8).

63. E.g., "Order Relating to Discovery of DNA Typing Material," issued in *State v. Ferguson* (St. Louis County, Mo., no. 591717, June 25, 1991).

64. See Christopher Anderson, "FBI Attaches Strings to Its DNA Database," *Nature* 358 (1992): 618.

65. NRC Report, 56.

66. Ibid., 93–94.

67. The first articles to raise these issues were William Thompson and Simon Ford, "DNA Typing: Promising Technique Needs Additional Validation," *Trial* 24 (1988): 56; and Lander, "DNA Fingerprinting on Trial."

68. E.g., Lander, "Research on DNA Typing"; Thompson and Ford, "The Meaning of a Match"; Lewontin and Hartl, "Population Genetics."

69. Lander, for example, writes: "[T]rial judges have raced to admit DNA fingerprinting as evidence on the grounds that the methods are 'generally accepted in the scientific community', citing the application of RFLPs in DNA diagnostics and accepting claims that false positives are virtually impossible.

"With due respect, the courts have been too hasty. Although DNA fingerprinting clearly offers tremendous potential as a forensic tool, the rush to court has obscured two critical points: first, DNA fingerprinting is far more technically demanding than DNA diagnostics; and second, the scientific community has not yet agreed on standards that ensure the reliability of the evidence" (Lander, "DNA Fingerprinting on Trial," 501).

70. The best account of the problems uncovered in the *Castro* case is Lander, "DNA Fingerprinting on Trial."

71. Roberts, "Science in Court"; Roberts, "Fight Erupts over DNA Fingerprinting"; Anderson, "DNA Fingerprinting Discord"; Gina Kolata, "Critic of 'Genetic Fingerprint' Tests Tells of Pressure to Withdraw Paper," *New York Times*, December 20, 1991.

72. *People v. Shirley* (1984): 31 Cal.3d 18, 56.

73. Leslie Roberts, "Hired Guns or True Believers?" *Science* 257 (1992): 735; Leslie Roberts, "Prosecutor v. Scientist: A Cat and Mouse Relationship," *Science* 257 (1992): 733.

74. The standard rate of pay for experts who testify in this legal area is $150 per hour (Roberts, "Hired Guns or True Believers?").

75. One judge dismissed the testimony of Professor Laurence Mueller, a population geneticist who has been a key scientific critic, saying that Mueller "appeared to be part of a welfare system for academics" (*People v. Howard* [Superior Court of Alameda County, Calif., no. 99217, March 1990]).

76. The testimony of the scientists most frequently condemned as "hired guns" is very similar to that of other critics who have testified without fee. For example, relying on courtroom transcripts, I have compared the testimony of Professor Mueller, who has been called a "hired gun," with the testimony of Eric Lander, Jerry Coyne, and Richard Lewontin, all of whom testified without fee. The positions of these scientists seem indistinguishable either in substance or in fervor.

77. Chapter 3 of the NRC Report presents an analysis of the problem of population structure that parallels the analyses of Lewontin and Hartl, "Population Genetics"; Mueller, "Population Genetics of Hypervariable Human DNA." Chapter 2 of the NRC Report makes recommendations similar to those of a number of molecular biologists who have testified for the defense.

78. It is perhaps telling that Eric Lander's decision to testify without fee has not shielded him from charges of venality. In briefs filed with the Texas Court of Criminal Appeal, a prosecutor characterized Lander as "a defense hired gun" (state's brief in *Hicks v. Texas*, 860 S.W.2d 419 [Tex. Cr. App. 1993]). The defendant's attorney made no effort to contest this characterization.

79. One population geneticist testified that the FBI's statistical technique was "universally accepted" among knowledgeable scientists. During cross-examination, when confronted with criticisms of the FBI's methods made by other population geneticists (Hartl, Lewontin, Lander, Mueller), he acknowledged their expertise but discounted their

opinions because they were unfamiliar with an important set of data. Further cross-examination revealed that the data in question had not been published, were not publicly available, and had been analyzed only by the witness himself. Under the witness's narrow definition of the relevant community, "universal acceptance" was tantamount to acceptance by a single individual: himself (testimony of Bruce Weir in *People v. Halik*, Superior Court of Los Angeles County, no. VA-000843, July 23, 1991, 99–120).

80. Experts in these academic disciplines understand the fundamentals of the tests, defense lawyers argue, while forensic scientists are merely users of a technology created outside their field. Moreover, the forensic scientists, whose business it is to help law enforcement, have a professional and, in some instances, a financial stake in the success of DNA testing, and therefore are not disinterested and impartial. Courts are often reluctant to conclude that a technique is "generally accepted" under *Frye* when the only experts vouching for its reliability are those whose "livelihood was intimately connected with the new technique" (*People v. Young*, 425 Mich. 470, 483, 391 N.W.2d 270, 275–276 [1986]).

81. Because it breeds profusely, using diploid sexual reproduction, with a very short time between generations, the fruit fly is an ideal organism for studying the transfer and distribution of genetic characteristics through large populations over multiple generations.

82. Carol Nelson, Ventura County Deputy District Attorney. Thus, for example, in two *Frye* hearings in California, a judge issued written findings indicating that "human population genetics" and "non-human population genetics" are distinct fields and that "non-human Population Genetics is not within this relevant scientific community. Drosophila experts in the field of Evolutionary Biology are not within the relevant scientific community" (findings of Judge Theodore Millard in *People v. Martinez*, Orange County, Calif., no. C-82183, June 18, 1991 [a case concerning the admissibility of a DNA test performed by the Orange County, Calif., Sheriff's Crime Laboratory]; the same findings were issued by this judge in *People v. Gross*, Orange County, Calif., no. C-75486, April 4, 1991 [a case concerning the admissibility of the FBI DNA test]). Indeed, Judge Millard initially refused the defendant's request to have Professor Mueller appointed to examine the Orange County DNA Laboratory's statistical computations, on grounds that Mueller "is not qualified in a relevant scientific community. . . . [H]e is a non-human population geneticist—it takes a human population geneticist to qualify" (ruling of Judge Millard on defendant's request to appoint Mueller as an expert, May 29, 1991).

It is perhaps noteworthy that Judge Millard also expressed skepticism about the theory of evolution. In explaining his concerns about Professor Mueller's expertise, the judge noted with obvious disapproval that Mueller had "testified in this courtroom that we all come from a common DNA somewhere and we are all related to fruit flies." When the defense lawyer asked whether the judge argued with this position, Millard responded: "I don't think there is any scientific basis that we are related to fruit flies" (ruling of Judge Millard on defendant's request to appoint Mueller as an expert, May 29, 1991).

83. The main supporters of this position are forensic scientists and medical geneticists whose primary research involves the mapping of disease-related genes in humans.

84. For example, Bruce Weir, who is perhaps the most distinguished population geneticist to testify in favor of current statistical procedures, has adamantly denied that there is any distinction between human and nonhuman population genetics (testimony of Bruce Weir in *People v. Halik*, Superior Court of Los Angeles County, no. VA-000843, July 23, 1991, 90). Weir stated that the techniques used for evaluating the presence of population structure are the same for all diploid sexual organisms, and that it would be wrong to conclude that a population geneticist who studies fruit flies is not part of the relevant scientific community for evaluating the assumptions underlying forensic DNA statistics. Weir testified that about half of the experimental work he has published is based on studies of fruit flies. Eric Lander has gone even further, asserting that "there's a funny sense in which a drosophila population geneticist is better qualified to talk about theory than a human population geneticist can talk about theory" (testimony of Eric Lander in *U.S. v. Yee*, vol. XVII, p. 191).

85. See Kolata, "Critic of 'Genetic Fingerprint' Tests"; Roberts, "Prosecutor v. Scientist"; Anderson, "Conflict Concerns Disrupt Panels, Cloud Testimony."

86. See Kolata, "Critic of 'Genetic Fingerprint' Tests"; Roberts, "Science in Court"; Anderson, "DNA Fingerprinting Discord."

87. Anderson, "DNA Fingerprinting Discord."

88. Roberts, "Science in Court," 735.

89. Anderson, "DNA Fingerprinting Discord."

90. Ibid.

91. See Roberts, "Prosecutor v. Scientist."

92. Ibid., 733.

93. Christopher Anderson, "Coincidence or Conspiracy?" *Nature* 355 (1992): 753.

94. Ibid.

95. Quoted in Roberts, "Science in Court."

96. NRC Report, 56, 93–94.

97. Ibid., 70–72.

98. Ibid., chap. 4.

A Selective Bibliography on Ethical, Legal, and Social Implications of the Human Genome Project

Compiled by MICHAEL S. YESLEY
With the support of the U.S. Department of Energy

Adams, Mark B., ed. *The Wellborn Science: Eugenics in Germany, France, Brazil, and Russia.* New York: Oxford University Press, 1990.

Adler, Reid G. "Genome Research: Fulfilling the Public's Expectations for Knowledge and Commercialization." *Science* 257 (1992): 908–914.

Allen, G. "The Misuse of Biological Hierarchies: The American Eugenics Movement, 1900–1940." *History & Philosophy of the Life Sciences* 5 (1983): 105–128.

Alper, Joseph S., and Marvin R. Natowicz. "Genetic Discrimination and the Public Entities and Public Accommodations Titles of the Americans with Disabilities Act." *American Journal of Human Genetics* 53 (1993): 26–32.

Alpern, Kenneth D., ed. *The Ethics of Reproductive Technology.* New York: Oxford University Press, 1992.

American Association for the Advancement of Science. *The Genome, Ethics and the Law: Issues in Genetic Testing.* Washington, D.C.: AAAS, 1991.

Anderson, W. French. "Human Gene Therapy: Scientific and Ethical Considerations." *Journal of Medicine and Philosophy* 10 (1985): 275–291.

——. "Human Gene Therapy: Why Draw a Line?" *Journal of Medicine and Philosophy* 14 (1989): 681–693.

Andrews, Lori B. *Medical Genetics: A Legal Frontier.* Chicago: American Bar Foundation, 1987.

——. "DNA Testing, Banking and Individual Rights." In Knoppers and Laberge, eds., *Genetic Screening: From Newborns to DNA Typing* (1990), 217–242.

——. "Torts and the Double Helix: Malpractice Liability for Failure to Warn of Genetic Risks." *Houston Law Review* 29 (1992): 149–184.

Andrews, Lori B., and Ami S. Jaeger. "Confidentiality of Genetic Information in the Workplace." *American Journal of Law & Medicine* 17 (1991): 75–108.

Annas, George J. "Who's Afraid of the Human Genome?" *Hastings Center Report* 19 (1989): 19–21.

———. "Mapping the Human Genome and the Meaning of Monster Mythology." *Emory Law Journal* 39 (1990): 629–664.

———. "The Human Genome Project in Perspective: Confronting Our Past to Protect Our Future." In Caplan, ed., *When Medicine Went Mad: Bioethics and the Holocaust* (1992), 301–319.

Annas, George J., and Sherman Elias, eds. *Gene Mapping: Using Law and Ethics as Guides.* New York: Oxford University Press, 1992.

Atkinson, Gary M., and Albert S. Moraczewski. *Genetic Counseling, the Church, and the Law.* St. Louis: Pope John XXIII Medical-Moral Research and Education Center, 1980.

Baird, P. A. "Genetics and Health Care: A Paradigm Shift." *Perspectives in Biology and Medicine* 33 (1990): 203–213.

Ballantyne, Jack, George Sensabaugh, and Jan Witkowski, eds. *DNA Technology and Forensic Science.* Cold Spring Harbor, N.Y.: Cold Spring Harbor Laboratory Press, 1989.

Bankowski, Z., and A. M. Capron, eds. *Genetics, Ethics and Human Values: Human Genome Mapping, Genetic Screening and Gene Therapy.* Geneva: Council for International Organizations of Medical Sciences, 1991.

Bartels, Dianne M., Bonnie S. LeRoy, and Arthur L. Caplan, eds. *Prescribing Our Future: Ethical Challenges in Genetic Counseling.* Hawthorne, N.Y.: Aldine de Gruyter, 1993.

Bartels, Dianne M., Reinhard Priester, Dorothy E. Vawter, and Arthur L. Caplan, eds. *Beyond Baby M: Ethical Issues in New Reproductive Techniques.* Clifton, N.J.: Humana Press, 1990.

Baruch, Elain Hoffman, Amadeo F. D'Adamo, Jr., and Joni Seager, eds. *Embryos, Ethics, and Women's Rights: Exploring the New Reproductive Technologies.* New York: Haworth Press, 1988.

Bayles, Michael D. *Reproductive Ethics.* Englewood Cliffs, N.J.: Prentice Hall, 1984.

Beckwith, Jon. "Thinking of Biology: A Historical View of Social Responsibility in Genetics." *BioScience* 43 (1993): 327–333.

Berger, Edward M., and Bernard M. Gert. "Genetic Disorders and the Ethical Status of Germ-Line Gene Therapy." *Journal of Medicine and Philosophy* 16 (1991): 667–683.

Bergsma, Daniel, Marc Lappé, Richard O. Roblin, and James M. Gustafson, eds. *Ethical, Social and Legal Dimensions of Screening for Human Genetic Disease.* New York: Stratton Intercontinental Medical Books, 1974.

Biesecker, Barbara, Patricia Magyari, and Natalie W. Paul. "Strategies in Genetic Counseling: II. Religious, Cultural and Ethnic Influences on the Counseling Process." *Birth Defects* 23 (1987): 115–281.

Billings, Paul R., ed. *DNA on Trial: Genetic Identification and Criminal Justice*. Cold Spring Harbor, N.Y.: Cold Spring Harbor Laboratory Press, 1992.

Billings, Paul R., Jonathan Beckwith, and Joseph S. Alper. "The Genetic Analysis of Human Behavior: A New Era?" *Social Science and Medicine* 35 (1992): 227–238.

Billings, Paul R., Mel A. Kohn, Margaret de Cuevas, Jonathan Beckwith, Joseph S. Alper et al. "Discrimination as a Consequence of Genetic Screening." *American Journal of Human Genetics* 50 (1992): 476–482.

Bishop, Jerry E., and Michael Waldholz. *Genome*. New York: Simon & Schuster, 1990.

Blank, Robert H. *Regulating Reproduction*. New York: Columbia University Press, 1990.

Bonnicksen, Andrea. "Genetic Diagnosis of Human Embryos." *Hastings Center Report* 22 (1992): S5–S11.

Bowman, James E. "Genetic Screening Programs and Public Policy." *Phylon* 38 (1977): 117–142.

Brock, Dan W. "The Human Genome Project and Human Identity." *Houston Law Review* 29 (1992): 7–22.

Brown, R. Steven, and Karen Marshall, eds. *Advances in Genetic Information: A Guide for State Policy Makers*. Lexington, Ky.: Council of State Governments, 1992.

Butzel, Henry M. *Genetics in the Courts*. Lewiston, N.Y.: Edwin Mellen Press, 1987.

Byk, Christian. "The Human Genome Project and the Social Contract: A Law Policy Approach." *Journal of Medicine and Philosophy* 17 (1992): 371–380.

Caplan, Arthur L. "Mapping Morality: Ethics and the Human Genome Project." In Caplan, *If I Were a Rich Man, Could I Buy a Pancreas? And Other Essays on the Ethics of Health Care*. Bloomington: Indiana University Press, 1992, 118–142.

———, ed. *When Medicine Went Mad: Bioethics and the Holocaust*. Totowa, N.J.: Humana Press, 1992.

Capron, Alexander Morgan. "Which Ills to Bear? Reevaluating the 'Threat' of Modern Genetics." *Emory Law Journal* 39 (1990): 665–696.

———, ed. "Symposium on Biomedical Technology and Health Care: Social and Conceptual Transformations." *Southern California Law Review* 65 (1991).

Capron, Alexander M., Marc Lappé, Robert F. Murray, Tabitha M. Powledge, Sumner B. Twiss et al., eds. *Genetic Counseling: Facts, Values, and Norms*. New York: Alan R. Liss, 1979.

Carlson, Elof Axel. *The Gene: A Critical History*. Ames: Iowa State University Press, 1989.

Chadwick, Derek, Greg Bock, and Julie Whelan, eds. *Human Genetic Information: Science, Law and Ethics*. Chichester, U.K.: John Wiley, 1990.

Chadwick, Ruth F., ed. *Ethics, Reproduction and Genetic Control*. London: Routledge, 1987.

Charo, R. Alta. "And Baby Makes Three—or Four, or Five, or Six: Defining the Family after the Genetic Revolution." In Frankel and Teich, eds., *Ethics, Law and Policy at the Genetic Frontier* (1993): 37–71.

Clayton, Ellen Wright. "Screening and Treatment of Newborns." *Houston Law Review* 29 (1992): 85–148.

Cohen, Bernice H., Abraham M. Lilienfeld, and P. C. Huang, eds. *Genetic Issues in Public Health and Medicine*. Springfield, Ill.: Charles C Thomas, 1978.

Cohen, Sherrill, and Nadine Taub, eds. *Reproductive Laws for the 1990s*. Clifton, N.J.: Humana Press, 1989.

Cole-Turner, Ronald. *The New Genesis: Theology and the Genetic Revolution*. Louisville, Ky.: Westminster/John Knox Press, 1993.

Conneally, P. Michael. "The Genome Project and Confidentiality in the Clinical Setting." In Rothstein, ed., *Legal and Ethical Issues Raised by the Human Genome Project* (1991), 184–196.

Cook-Deegan, Robert M. *The Gene Wars: Science, Politics, and the Human Genome*. New York: Norton, forthcoming 1994.

Council of Europe. *Recommendations on Genetic Tests and Screening for Medical Purposes and on the Use of DNA Analysis within the Penal Justice System*. Strasbourg: The Council, 1992.

Council for Responsible Genetics. *Genetic Engineering: Unresolved Issues—A Biotechnology Reader*. Cambridge, Mass.: Council for Responsible Genetics, 1993.

Cowan, Ruth S. "Genetic Technology and Reproductive Choice: An Ethics for Autonomy." In Kevles and Hood, eds., *The Code of Codes* (1992), 244–263.

Czeizel, Andrew. *The Right to be Born Healthy: The Ethical Problems of Human Genetics in Hungary*. New York: Alan R. Liss, 1988.

Daniels, Norman. "The Genome Project: Individual Differences and Just Health Care." In Murphy and Lappé, eds., *Justice and the Human Genome Project*, forthcoming 1994.·

Danish Council of Ethics. *Ethics and Mapping of the Human Genome: Protection of Sensitive Personal Information—Genetic Screening—Genetic Testing in Appointments, etc.* Copenhagen: The Council, 1993.

Davis, Bernard D., ed. *The Genetic Revolution: Scientific Prospects and Public Perceptions*. Baltimore: Johns Hopkins University Press, 1991.

De Wit, G. W. "Genetic Technology, Insurance and the Future." In Fundación BBV, *Human Genome Project: Ethics 2* (1992): 297–314.

Dobzhansky, Theodosius Grigorievich. *Genetic Diversity and Human Equality*. New York: Basic Books, 1973.

Draper, Elaine. *Risky Business: Genetic Testing and Exclusionary Practices in the Hazardous Workplace*. New York: Cambridge University Press, 1991.

Dreyfuss, Rochelle Cooper, and Dorothy Nelkin. "The Jurisprudence of Genetics." *Vanderbilt Law Review* 45 (1992): 313–348.

Duster, Troy. *Backdoor to Eugenics*. New York: Routledge, 1990.

———. "Human Genetics, Evolutionary Theory, and Social Stratification." In Frankel and Teich, eds., *Ethics, Law and Policy at the Genetic Frontier* (1993), 209–247.

Edgar, Harold S. H. "The Genome Project and the Legal Right to Medical Confidentiality." In Rothstein, ed., *Legal and Ethical Issues Raised by the Human Genome Project* (1991), 197–221.

Eisenberg, Rebecca S. "Genes, Patents, and Product Development." *Science* 257 (1992): 903–908.

Elias, Sherman, and George J. Annas. *Reproductive Genetics and the Law*. Chicago: Year Book Medical Publishers, 1987.

Etzioni, Amitai. *Genetic Fix*. New York: Macmillan, 1973.

Evans, Debra. *Without Moral Limits: Women, Reproduction and the New Medical Technology*. Westchester, Ill.: Crossway Books, 1989.

Evans, M. I., ed. "Reproductive Genetic Testing: Impact upon Women" (NIH Workshop, November 21–23, 1991). *Fetal Diagnosis and Therapy* 8, supp. (1993).

Evans, Mark I., Alan O. Dixler, John C. Fletcher, and Joseph D. Schulmann, eds. *Fetal Diagnosis and Therapy: Science, Ethics and the Law*. Philadelphia: Lippincott, 1989.

Evers-Kiebooms, Gerry, ed. *Genetic Risk, Risk Perception, and Decision Making*. New York: Alan R. Liss, 1987.

Fine, Beth. "The Evolution of Nondirectiveness in Genetic Counseling and Implications of the Human Genome Project." In Bartels et al., eds., *Prescribing Our Future: Ethical Challenges in Genetic Counseling* (1993), 101–117.

Fleisher, Lynn D. "The Effect of the Genome Project on Malpractice Litigation." In Rothstein, ed., *Legal and Ethical Issues Raised by the Human Genome Project* (1991), 144–164.

Fletcher, John C. "Evolution of Ethical Debate about Human Gene Therapy." *Human Gene Therapy* 1 (1990): 55–68.

Fletcher, J. C., and M. I. Evans. "Ethics in Reproductive Genetics." *Clinical Obstetrics and Gynecology* 35 (1992): 763–782.

Fletcher, John C., and Dorothy C. Wertz. "Ethics, Law, and Medical Genetics: After the Human Genome Is Mapped." *Emory Law Journal* 39 (1990): 747–791.

———. "Ethics and Prenatal Diagnosis: Problems, Positions, and Proposed Guidelines." In Aubrey Milunsky, ed., *Genetic Disorders and the Fetus*, 3rd ed. Baltimore: Johns Hopkins University Press, 1992, 823–854.

Fletcher, Joseph. *The Ethics of Genetic Control: Ending Reproductive Roulette*. Buffalo: Prometheus Books, 1988.

Fost, Norman. "Ethical Implications of Screening Asymptomatic Individuals." *FASEB Journal* 6 (1992): 2813–2817.

Frankel, Mark S., and Albert H. Teich, eds. *Ethics, Law and Policy at the Genetic Frontier*. Washington, D.C.: AAAS, 1993.

Freedman, Warren. *Legal Issues in Biotechnology and Human Reproduction: Artificial Conception and Modern Genetics*. Westport, Conn.: Quorum Books, 1991.

Friedmann, Theodore. "The Human Genome Project—Some Implications of Extensive 'Reverse Genetic' Medicine." *American Journal of Human Genetics* 46 (1990): 407–414.

———, ed. *Therapy for Genetic Disease*. New York: Oxford University Press, 1991.

Fujiki, N., V. Bulyzhenkov, and Z. Bankowski, eds. *Medical Genetics and Society*. Amsterdam: Kugler Publications, 1991.

Fujiki, Norio, and Darryl Macer, eds. *Human Genome Research and Society*. Christchurch, N.Z.: Eubios Ethics Institute, 1992.

Fundación BBV. *Human Genome Project: Ethics 2*. Madrid: Fundación BBV, 1992.

Garver, Kenneth L., and Bettylee Garver. "Eugenics: Past, Present, and the Future." *American Journal of Human Genetics* 49 (1991): 1109–1118.

Geller, Gail, and Neil A. Holtzman. "Implications of the Human Genome Initiative for the Primary Care Physician." *Bioethics* 5 (1991): 318–325.

Glover, Jonathan. *What Sort of People Should There Be?* Harmondsworth, U.K.: Penguin Books, 1984.

Gore, Al. "Federal Biotechnology Policy: The Perils of Progress and the Risks of Uncertainty." *University of Michigan Journal of Law Reform* 20 (1987): 965–977.

Gostin, Larry. "Genetic Discrimination: The Use of Genetically Based Diagnostic and Prognostic Tests by Employers and Insurers." *American Journal of Law & Medicine* 17 (1991): 109–144.

Graham, Loren R. "Science and Values: The Eugenics Movement in Germany and Russia in the 1920s." *American Historical Review* 82 (1977): 1133–1164.

Greely, Henry T. "Health Insurance, Employment Discrimination, and the Genetics Revolution." In Kevles and Hood, eds., *The Code of Codes* (1992), 264–280.

Gros, François. *The Gene Civilization*. New York: McGraw-Hill, 1989.

Haller, Mark H. *Eugenics: Hereditarian Attitudes in American Thought.* New Brunswick: Rutgers University Press, 1963.

Hamilton, Michael Pollock, ed. *The New Genetics and the Future of Man.* Grand Rapids, Mich.: William B. Eerdmans, 1972.

Harris, John. *Wonderwoman and Superman: The Ethics of Human Biotechnology.* New York: Oxford University Press, 1992.

Harsanyi, Zsolt, and Richard Hutton. *Genetic Prophecy: Beyond the Double Helix.* New York: Rawson, Wade, 1981.

Heyd, David. *Genethics: Moral Issues in the Creation of People.* Berkeley: University of California Press, 1992.

Hicks, E. K., and J. M. Berg, eds. *The Genetics of Mental Retardation: Biomedical, Psychosocial and Ethical Issues.* Boston: Kluwer Academic, 1988.

Hilton, Bruce, Daniel Callahan, Maureen Harris, Peter Condliffe, and Burton Berkley, eds. *Ethical Issues in Human Genetics: Genetic Counseling and the Use of Genetic Knowledge.* New York: Plenum Press, 1973.

Holmes, Helen B., Betty B. Hoskins, and Michael Gross, eds. *The Custom-Made Child? Women-Centered Perspectives.* Clifton, N.J.: Humana Press, 1981.

Holtzman, Neil A. *Proceed with Caution: Predicting Genetic Risks in the Recombinant DNA Era.* Baltimore: Johns Hopkins University Press, 1989.

———. "The Diffusion of New Genetic Tests for Predicting Future Disease." *FASEB Journal* 6 (1992): 2806–2812.

Holtzman, Neil A., and Mark A. Rothstein. "Eugenics and Genetic Discrimination." *American Journal of Human Genetics* 50 (1992): 457–459.

Horgan, John. "Trends in Behavioral Genetics: Eugenics Revisited." *Scientific American* 268 (1993): 123–131.

Hubbard, Ruth. *The Politics of Women's Biology.* New Brunswick: Rutgers University Press, 1990.

Hubbard, Ruth, and Elijah Wald. *Exploding the Gene Myth: How Genetic Information Is Produced and Manipulated by Scientists, Physicians, Employers, Insurance Companies, Educators and Law Enforcers.* Boston: Beacon Press, 1993.

Jonsen, Albert R. *The New Medicine and the Old Ethics.* Cambridge: Harvard University Press, 1990.

Juengst, Eric T. "Germ-Line Gene Therapy: Back to Basics." *Journal of Medicine and Philosophy* 16 (1991): 587–592.

Juengst, Eric T., and James D. Watson. "Human Genome Research and the Responsible Use of New Genetic Knowledge." *International Journal of Bioethics* 2 (1991): 99–102.

Karjala, Dennis S. "A Legal Research Agenda for the Human Genome Initiative." *Jurimetrics* 32 (1992): 121–311.

Kass, Leon R. *Toward a More Natural Science: Biology and Human Affairs.* New York: Free Press, 1985.

Keller, Evelyn F. "Nature, Nurture, and the Human Genome Project." In Kevles and Hood, eds., *The Code of Codes* (1992), 281–299.

Kevles, Daniel J. *In the Name of Eugenics: Genetics and the Uses of Human Heredity.* New York: Knopf, 1985.

Kevles, Daniel J., and Leroy Hood, eds. *The Code of Codes: Scientific and Social Issues in the Human Genome Project.* Cambridge: Harvard University Press, 1992.

King, Patricia A. "The Past as Prologue: Race, Class, and Gene Discrimination." In Annas and Elias, eds., *Gene Mapping: Using Law and Ethics as Guides* (1992), 94–111.

Knoppers, Bartha Maria. *Human Dignity and Genetic Heritage.* Ottawa: Law Reform Commission of Canada, 1991.

Knoppers, Bartha Maria, and Claude Laberge, eds. *Genetic Screening: From Newborns to DNA Typing.* Amsterdam: Elsevier Science Publishers, 1990.

Koshland, Daniel. "Nature, Nurture, and Behavior." *Science* 235 (1987): 1445.

Koshland, Daniel E., Jr. "Sequences and Consequences of the Human Genome." *Science* 246 (1989): 189.

Krimsky, Sheldon. *Biotechnics and Society: The Rise of Industrial Genetics.* New York: Praeger, 1991.

Lander, Eric. "DNA Fingerprinting: Science, Law, and the Ultimate Identifier." In Kevles and Hood, eds., *The Code of Codes* (1992), 191–210.

Lappé, Marc. *Broken Code: The Exploitation of DNA.* San Francisco: Sierra Club Books, 1984.

———. "The Limits of Genetic Inquiry." *Hastings Center Report* 17 (1987): 5–10.

———. "Ethical Issues in Manipulating the Human Germ Line." *Journal of Medicine and Philosophy* 16 (1991): 621–639.

Lappé, Marc, James M. Gustafson, and Richard Roblin. "Ethical and Social Issues in Screening for Genetic Disease." *New England Journal of Medicine* 286 (1972): 1129–1132.

Lappé, Eric, and Robert S. Morison, eds. "Ethical and Scientific Issues Posed by Human Uses of Molecular Genetics." *Annals of the New York Academy of Sciences* 265 (1976).

Lebacqz, Karen. *Genetics, Ethics, and Parenthood.* New York: Pilgrim, 1983.

Lederberg, Joshua. "The Genome Project Holds Promise, but We Must Look Before We Leap." *Scientist* 3 (1989): 10.

Lee, Thomas F. *The Human Genome Project: Cracking the Genetic Code of Life.* New York: Plenum Press, 1991.

Lerner, Richard M. *Final Solutions: Biology, Prejudice, and Genocide.* University Park: Penn State Press, 1992.

Lewontin, Richard C. *Biology as Ideology: The Doctrine of DNA.* New York: Harper Perennial, 1991.

Lewontin, R. C., Steven Rose, and Leon J. Kamin, eds. *Not in Our Genes: Biology, Ideology and Human Nature.* New York: Pantheon, 1984.

Lipkin, Mack, Jr., and Peter T. Rowley, eds. *Genetic Responsibility: On Choosing Our Children's Genes.* New York: Plenum Press, 1974.

Lippman, Abby. "Prenatal Genetic Testing and Screening: Constructing Needs and Reinforcing Inequities." *American Journal of Law & Medicine* 17 (1991): 15–50.

Ludmerer, Kenneth M. *Genetics and American Society: A Historical Appraisal.* Baltimore: Johns Hopkins University Press, 1972.

Macer, Darryl. *Shaping Genes: Ethics, Law and Science of Using Genetic Technology in Medicine and Agriculture.* Tsukuba, Japan: Eubios Ethics Institute, 1990.

McEwen, Jean E., and Philip R. Reilly. "State Legislative Efforts to Regulate Use and Potential Misuse of Genetic Information." *American Journal of Human Genetics* 51 (1992): 637–647.

Macklin, Ruth. "Privacy and Control of Genetic Information." In Annas and Elias, eds., *Gene Mapping: Using Law and Ethics as Guides* (1992), 157–172.

McKusick, Victor A. "The Human Genome Project: Plans, Status, and Applications in Biology and Medicine." In Annas and Elias, eds., *Gene Mapping: Using Law and Ethics as Guides* (1992), 18–42.

McLaren, Angus M. *Our Own Master Race: Eugenics in Canada, 1885–1945.* Toronto: McClelland & Stewart, 1990.

Markl, Hubert. *Genetics and Ethics.* Bonn: Alexander von Humboldt–Stiftung, 1989.

Marsh, Frank H., and Janet Katz, eds. *Biology, Crime, and Ethics: A Study of Biological Explanations for Criminal Behavior.* Cincinnati: Anderson, 1985.

Mazumdar, Pauline M. H. *Eugenics, Human Genetics and Human Failings: The Eugenics Society, Its Sources and Critics in Britain.* London: Routledge, 1992.

Medical Research Council of Canada. *Guidelines for Research on Somatic Cell Gene Therapy in Humans.* Ottawa: Ministry of Supply and Services, 1990.

Milunsky, Aubrey. *Heredity and Your Family's Health.* Baltimore: Johns Hopkins University Press, 1992.

Milunsky, Aubrey, and George J. Annas, eds. *Genetics and the Law.* New York: Plenum Press, 1976.

———, eds. *Genetics and the Law II.* New York: Plenum Press, 1980.

———, eds. *Genetics and the Law III.* New York: Plenum Press, 1985.

Miringoff, Marque-Luisa. *The Social Costs of Genetic Welfare.* New Brunswick: Rutgers University Press, 1991.

Motulsky, Arno G. "Societal Problems in Human and Medical Genetics." *Genome* 31 (1989): 870–875.

Muller, Hermann J. "Means and Aims in Human Genetic Betterment." In Robert Hunt and John Arras, eds., *Ethical Issues in Modern Medicine*. Palo Alto, Calif.: Mayfield, 1977, 57–69.

Muller-Hill, Benno. *Murderous Science. Elimination by Scientific Selection of Jews, Gypsies, and Others: Germany 1933–1945*. New York: Oxford University Press, 1988.

———. "The Shadow of Genetic Injustice." *Nature* 362 (1993): 491–492.

Murashige, Kate. "Intellectual Property and Genetic Testing." In Frankel and Teich, eds., *Ethics, Law and Policy at the Genetic Frontier* (1993), 288–321.

Murphy, Timothy F., and Marc Lappé, eds. *Justice and the Human Genome Project*. Berkeley: University of California Press, forthcoming 1994.

Murray, Robert F. "Genetic Counseling: Boon or Bane?" In Marguerite Neumann, ed., *The Tricentennial People: Human Applications of the New Genetics*. Ames: Iowa State University Press, 1978, 29–47.

Murray, Robert F., Jr. "Problems behind the Promise: Ethical Issues in Mass Genetic Screening." *Hastings Center Report* 2 (1972): 11–13.

Murray, Thomas H. "Ethical Issues in Human Genome Research." *FASEB Journal* 5 (1991): 55–60.

———. "Genetics and the Moral Mission of Health Insurance." *Hastings Center Report* 22 (1992): 12–17.

National Council of Churches of Christ. *Genetic Engineering: Social and Ethical Consequences*. New York: Pilgrim Press, 1984.

National Research Council. *Mapping and Sequencing the Human Genome*. Washington, D.C.: National Academy Press, 1988.

———. *DNA Technology in Forensic Science*. Washington, D.C.: National Academy Press, 1992.

Nelkin, Dorothy, and Laurence Tancredi. *Dangerous Diagnostics: The Social Power of Biological Information*. New York: Basic Books, 1989.

Nelson, J. Robert. *On the Frontiers of Genetics and Religion*. Grand Rapids, Mich.: William B. Eerdmans, forthcoming 1994.

Nishimi, R. Y. "Forensic DNA Analysis: Scientific, Legal, and Social Issues." *Cancer Investigation* 10 (1992): 553–563.

Nolan, Kathleen, and Sara Swenson. "New Tools, New Dilemmas: Genetic Frontiers." *Hastings Center Report* 18 (1988): 40–46.

Ostrer, H., W. Allen, L. A. Crandall, R. E. Moseley, M. A. Dewar et al. "Insurance and Genetic Testing: Where Are We Now?" *American Journal of Human Genetics* 52 (1993): 565–577.

Paul, Diane. "Eugenics and the Left." *Journal of the History of Ideas* 45 (1984): 567–590.

———. " 'Our Load of Mutations' Revisited." *Journal of the History of Biology* 20 (1987): 321–335.

Pelias, Mary Z. "Duty to Disclose in Medical Genetics: A Legal Perspective." *American Journal of Medical Genetics* 39 (1991): 347–354.

Pelias, Mary Z., and Margery W. Shaw. "Medicolegal Aspects of Prenatal Diagnosis." In Aubrey Milunsky, ed., *Genetic Disorders and the Fetus*, 3rd ed. Baltimore: Johns Hopkins University Press, 1992, 799–821.

Perpich, Joseph G., ed. *Biotechnology in Society: Private Initiatives and Public Oversight*. New York: Pergamon Press, 1986.

Peters, Ted, and Robert Russell. "The Human Genome Initiative: What Questions Does It Raise for Theology and Ethics?" *Midwest Medical Ethics* 8 (1992): 12–17.

Pickens, Donald K. *Eugenics and the Progressives*. Nashville: Vanderbilt University Press, 1968.

Piller, Charles, and Keith R. Yamamoto. *Gene Wars: Military Control over the New Genetic Technologies*. New York: William Morrow, 1988.

Plomin, Robert. "Behavioral Genetics." In Paul R. McHugh and Victor A. McKusick, *Genes, Brain, and Behavior*. New York: Raven Press, 1991, 165–180.

Powers, Madison. "Privacy and the Control of Genetic Information." In Frankel and Teich, eds., *Ethics, Law and Policy at the Genetic Frontier* (1993), 120–160.

President's Commission for the Study of Ethical Problems in Medicine and Biomedical and Behavioral Research. *Splicing Life: A Report on the Social and Ethical Issues of Genetic Engineering with Human Beings*. Washington, D.C.: The Commission, 1982.

———. *Screening and Counseling for Genetic Conditions: The Ethical, Social and Legal Implications of Genetic Screening, Counseling, and Education Programs*. Washington, D.C.: The Commission, 1983.

Privacy Commissioner of Canada. *Genetic Testing and Privacy*. Ottawa: Ministry of Supply and Services, 1992.

Proctor, Robert N. *Racial Hygiene: Medicine under the Nazis*. Cambridge: Harvard University Press, 1988.

———. "Genomics and Eugenics: How Fair Is the Comparison?" In Annas and Elias, eds., *Gene Mapping: Using Law and Ethics as Guides* (1992), 57–93.

Rainer, John D., Sylvia P. Rubin, Michael K. Bartalos, Jack E. Maidman, Austin H. Kutscher et al., eds. *Genetic Disease: The Unwanted Inheritance*. New York: Haworth Press, 1989.

Ramsey, Paul. *Fabricated Man: The Ethics of Genetic Control*. New Haven: Yale University Press, 1970.

Rapp, Rayna. "Chromosomes and Communication: The Discourse of Genetic Counseling." In Linda Whiteford and Marilyn Poland, eds., *New Approaches to Human Reproduction: Social and Ethical Dimensions*. Boulder, Colo.: Westview Press, 1989, 25–41.

Reilly, Philip. *Genetics, Law, and Social Policy*. Cambridge: Harvard University Press, 1977.

———. *The Surgical Solution: A History of Involuntary Sterilization in the United States*. Baltimore: Johns Hopkins University Press, 1991.

Rigter, H., J.C.F. Bletz, A. Krijnen, B. Wijnberg, H. D. Banta et al., eds. *The Social Consequences of Genetic Testing*. The Hague: Netherlands Scientific Council for Government Policy, 1990.

Robertson, John A. "Procreative Liberty and Human Genetics." *Emory Law Journal* 39 (1990): 697–719.

Roll-Hansen, Nils. "The Progress of Eugenics: Growth of Knowledge and Change in Ideology." *History of Science* 26 (1988): 295–331.

Roslansky, John D., ed. *Genetics and the Future of Man*. New York: Appleton-Century-Crofts, 1966.

Rothman, Barbara Katz. *The Tentative Pregnancy: Prenatal Diagnosis and the Future of Motherhood*. New York: Viking, 1986.

———. "The Tentative Pregnancy: Then and Now." In *Fetal Diagnosis and Therapy* 8, supp. (1993): 60–63.

Rothstein, Mark A. "Genetic Discrimination in Employment and the Americans with Disabilities Act." *Houston Law Review* 29 (1992): 23–84.

———, ed. *Legal and Ethical Issues Raised by the Human Genome Project*. Houston: University of Houston Law Center, Health Law and Policy Institute, 1991.

Saxton, Marsha. "Prenatal Screening and Discriminatory Attitudes about Disability." In Baruch et al., eds., *Embryos, Ethics, and Women's Rights* (1988), 217–224.

Shaw, Margery W. "Conditional Prospective Rights of the Fetus." *Journal of Legal Medicine* 5 (1984): 63–116.

———. "Testing for the Huntington Gene: A Right to Know, a Right Not to Know, or a Duty to Know." *American Journal of Medical Genetics* 26 (1987): 243–246.

Shinn, Roger L. "Family Relationships and Social Policy: An Ethical Inquiry." In Frankel and Teich, eds., *Ethics, Law and Policy at the Genetic Frontier* (1993), 10–36.

Shuster, Evelyne. "Determinism and Reductionism: A Greater Threat because of the Human Genome Project?" In Annas and Elias, eds., *Gene Mapping: Using Law and Ethics as Guides* (1992), 115–127.

Singer, Eleanor. "Public Attitudes towards Genetic Testing." *Population Research and Policy Review* 10 (1991): 235–255.

———. "Public Attitudes toward Fetal Diagnosis and the Termination of Life." *Social Indicators Research* 28 (1993): 117–136.

Sinsheimer, Robert L. "The Prospect of Designed Genetic Change." In Chadwick, ed., *Ethics, Reproduction and Genetic Control* (1987), 136–146.

————. "Whither the Genome Project?" *Hastings Center Report* (July-August 1990): 5.

Smith, George Patrick II. *The New Biology: Law, Ethics, and Biotechnology.* New York: Plenum Press, 1989.

Soloway, Richard A. *Demography and Degeneration: Eugenics and the Declining Birthrate in Twentieth-Century Britain.* Chapel Hill: University of North Carolina Press, 1990.

Sorenson, James. "What We Still Don't Know about Genetic Screening and Counseling." In Annas and Elias, eds., *Gene Mapping: Using Law and Ethics as Guides* (1992), 203–212.

Sorenson, James R., Judith P. Swazey, and Norman A. Scotch. *Reproductive Pasts and Reproductive Futures: Genetic Counseling and Its Effectiveness.* New York: Alan R. Liss, 1981.

Spallone, Pat. *Generation Games: Genetic Engineering and the Future for Our Lives.* Philadelphia: Temple University Press, 1992.

Spallone, Patricia, and Deborah Lynn Steinberg, eds. *Made to Order: The Myth of Reproductive and Genetic Progress.* Oxford: Pergamon Press, 1987.

Sram, R. J., V. Bulyzhenkov, L. Prilipko, and Y. Christen, eds. *Ethical Issues of Molecular Genetics in Psychiatry.* New York: Springer-Verlag, 1991.

Stanworth, Michelle, ed. *Reproductive Technologies: Gender, Motherhood and Medicine.* Minneapolis: University of Minnesota Press, 1987.

Stepan, Nancy. *The Hour of Eugenics: Race, Gender and Nation in Latin America.* Ithaca: Cornell University Press, 1991.

Suzuki, David, and Peter Knudtson. *Genethics: The Clash between the New Genetics and Human Values.* Cambridge: Harvard University Press, 1989.

Swazey, Judith P. "Those Who Forget Their History: Lessons from the Recent Past for the Human Genome Quest." In Annas and Elias, eds., *Gene Mapping: Using Law and Ethics as Guides* (1992), 45–56.

Thompson, William C., and Simon Ford. "DNA Typing: Acceptance and Weight of the New Genetic Identification Tests." *Virginia Law Review* 75 (1989): 45–108.

U.S. Congress. House Committee on Government Operations. *Designing Genetic Information Policy: The Need for an Independent Policy Review of the Ethical, Legal, and Social Implications of the Human Genome Project.* 102nd Cong., 2nd sess., H. Rept. 102-478. Washington, D.C.: 1992.

————. Office of Technology Assessment. *The Role of Genetic Testing in the Prevention of Occupational Disease.* Washington, D.C.: GPO, 1983.

————. Office of Technology Assessment. *Biology, Medicine, and the Bill of Rights.* Washington, D.C.: GPO, 1988.

————. Office of Technology Assessment. *Mapping Our Genes. The Genome Project: How Big, How Fast?* OTA-BA-373. Washington, D.C.: GPO, 1988.

———. Office of Technology Assessment. *Genetic Monitoring and Screening in the Workplace*. Washington, D.C.: GPO, 1990.

———. Office of Technology Assessment. *Genetic Witness: Forensic Uses of DNA Tests*. Washington, D.C.: GPO, 1990.

———. Office of Technology Assessment. *Cystic Fibrosis and DNA Tests: Implications of Carrier Screening*. Washington, D.C.: GPO, 1992.

Vicedo, M. "The Human Genome Project—Towards an Analysis of the Empirical, Ethical, and Conceptual Issues Involved." *Biology & Philosophy* 7 (1992): 255–278.

Wachbroit, Robert. "Making the Grade: Testing for Human Genetic Orders." *Hofstra Law Review* 16 (1988): 583–599.

Walters, Leroy. "Human Gene Therapy: Ethics and Public Policy." *Human Gene Therapy* 2 (1991): 115–122.

———. "A National Advisory Committee on Genetic Testing and Screening." In Annas and Elias, eds., *Gene Mapping: Using Law and Ethics as Guides* (1992), 255–266.

———. "Ethical Obligations of Genetic Counselors." In Bartels et al., eds., *Prescribing Our Future: Ethical Challenges in Genetic Counseling* (1993), 131–147.

Watson, James D. "The Human Genome Project: Past, Present, and Future." *Science* 248 (1990): 44–49.

———. "A Personal View of the Project." In Kevles and Hood, eds., *The Code of Codes* (1992), 164–173.

Weatherall, D. J. *The New Genetics and Clinical Practice*. New York: Oxford University Press, 1991.

Weatherall, David, and Julian H. Shelley, eds. *Social Consequences of Genetic Engineering*. New York: Elsevier Science Publishers, 1989.

Weindling, Paul. *Health, Race and German Politics between National Unification and Nazism, 1870–1945*. New York: Cambridge University Press, 1989.

Weiss, Sheila Faith. *Race, Hygiene and National Efficiency: The Eugenics of Wilhelm Schallmayer*. Berkeley: University of California Press, 1987.

Wertz, D. C. "Ethical and Legal Implications of the New Genetics: Issues for Discussion." *Social Science and Medicine* 35 (1992): 495–505.

Wertz, Dorothy C., and John C. Fletcher, eds. *Ethics and Human Genetics: A Cross-Cultural Perspective*. New York: Springer-Verlag, 1989.

Westin, Alan F. "Privacy and Genetic Information: A Sociopolitical Analysis." In Frankel and Teich, eds., *Ethics, Law and Policy at the Genetic Frontier* (1993), 81–119.

Wexler, Nancy S. "Genetic 'Russian Roulette': The Experience of Being 'At-Risk' for Huntington's Disease." In Seymour Kessler, ed., *Genetic Counseling: Psychological Dimensions*. New York: Academic Press, 1979, 199–220.

———. " 'Will the Circle Be Unbroken?' Sterilizing the Genetically Impaired." In Milunsky and Annas, eds., *Genetics and the Law II* (1980), 313–329.

———. "Clairvoyance and Caution: Repercussions from the Human Genome Project." In Kevles and Hood, eds., *The Code of Codes* (1992), 211–243.

———. "The Tiresias Complex: Huntington's Disease as a Paradigm of Testing for Late-Onset Disorders." *FASEB Journal* 6 (1992): 2820–2825.

Wikler, Daniel, and Eileen Palmer. "Neo-Eugenics and Disability Rights in Philosophical Perspective." In Fujiki and Macer, eds., *Human Genome Research and Society* (1992), 105–113.

Wilfond, Benjamin S., and Norman Fost. "The Introduction of Cystic Fibrosis Carrier Screening into Clinical Practice: Policy Considerations." *Milbank Quarterly* 70 (1992): 629–659.

Wilkie, Tom. *Perilous Knowledge: The Human Genome Project and Its Implications.* London: Faber, 1993.

Wills, Christopher. *Exons, Introns, and Talking Genes: The Science behind the Human Genome Project.* New York: Basic Books, 1991.

Wright, Robert. "Achilles' Helix." *New Republic*, July 9, 1990.

Yesley, Michael S., ed. *ELSI Bibliography.* Springfield, Va.: NTIS, 1993.

Yoxen, Edward J. "Constructing Genetic Diseases." In Troy Duster and K. Garrett, eds., *Cultural Perspectives on Biological Knowledge.* Norwood, N.J.: Ablex, 1984, 41–62.

———. *Unnatural Selection: Coming to Terms with the New Genetics.* London: Heinemann, 1986.

Yoxen, E., and V. Di Martino, eds. *Biotechnology in Future Society: Scenarios and Options for Europe.* Brookfield, Vt.: Gower Publishing Co., 1989.

About the Authors

CARL F. CRANOR, Professor of Philosophy and Interim Dean of the College of Humanities and Social Sciences, University of California, Riverside. Professor Cranor's principal research interests are in legal and moral philosophy, with a current emphasis on the philosophy of environmental science and policy. These interests have been pursued in a number of articles and in *Regulating Toxic Substances: A Philosophy of Science and the Law.*

LARRY L. DEAVEN, Deputy Director, Center for Human Genome Studies, Los Alamos National Laboratory. Dr. Deaven has published numerous articles in cell biology, genetics, and cytogenetics.

RICHARD DOYLE, Lecturer in the Department of Rhetoric, University of California, Berkeley, and former Mellon Fellow, Program in Science, Technology, and Society at the Massachusetts Institute of Technology. He writes widely in the cultural studies of science.

JAMES R. GRIESEMER, Associate Professor of Philosophy and Director, Program in History and Philosophy of Science, University of California, Davis. Professor Griesemer has published articles in philosophy of biology, including some in the history and philosophy of genetics, the philosophy of ecology, and the philosophy of evolutionary theory.

GREGORY S. KAVKA, Professor of Philosophy, University of California, Irvine. Professor Kavka's major research interests in political philosophy and applied ethics are explored in numerous articles and in his books, *Hobbesian Moral and Political Theory* and *Moral Paradoxes of Deterrence.* He is currently working on *Governing Angels: Human Imperfections and the Need for Government* and a book on using new technologies to treat patients.

EVELYN FOX KELLER, Professor of History and Philosophy of Science in the Program in Science, Technology, and Society at the Massachusetts Institute of Technology. Professor Keller received her Ph.D. in theoretical physics at Harvard University and worked for a number of years at the interface of physics and biology. She is perhaps best known as the author of *A Feeling for the Organism: The Life and Work of Barbara McClintock; Reflections on Gender and Science;* and, most recently, *Secrets of Life, Secrets of Death: Essays on Language, Gender and Science.* Her current research is on the history of developmental biology.

CAMILLE LIMOGES, Professor at Centre de Recherche en Evaluation Sociale des Technologies and Director of the Program on Science, Technology, and Society, Université du Québec, Montréal, Canada. He is the founding director of the Institut d'Histoire et de Sociopolitique des Sciences at the Université de Montréal and former Deputy Minister for Higher Education and for Science and Technology. Professor Limoges has published extensively on diverse aspects of biotechnology and has coedited (with William Coleman) *Studies in the History of Biology.*

ELISABETH A. LLOYD, Professor of Philosophy, University of California, Berkeley. Professor Lloyd works primarily in philosophy of science but is also interested in philosophy of mind, history of philosophy, and history of science. Her published articles and books, *The Structure and Confirmation of Evolutionary Theory* and *Keywords in Evolutionary Biology* (edited with Evelyn Fox Keller), focus on theory structure, evolutionary genetics, theory confirmation, and scientific controversy and development.

DIANE B. PAUL, Professor of Political Science at the University of Massachusetts, Boston, where she teaches courses in political theory, the history of biology, and science and public policy. She is also Research Associate at the Museum of Comparative Zoology, Harvard University. Her essays, which are to be published by SUNY Press as *Evolutionary Biology, Social History, and Political Power,* explore the histories of Marxism and biology, genetics and agriculture, eugenics and the nature–nurture controversy, as well as practices in college textbook publishing.

WILLIAM C. THOMPSON, Associate Professor of Social Ecology, University of California, Irvine. He has published numerous articles on the use of genetic fingerprinting in the law and on the use of science in the law.

CHARLES WEINER, Professor of History of Science and Technology in the Program in Science, Technology, and Society at the Massachusetts Institute of Technology. His research, writing, and teaching focus on the political, social, and ethical dimensions of contemporary science and the responses of scientists to public controversies arising from their work. Among his books are *Robert Oppenheimer: Letters and Recollections* (with Alice Kimball Smith) and three edited volumes on the history of physics. Professor Weiner is currently completing a book on

ABOUT THE AUTHORS

the responses of scientists to ethical issues arising from their work since World War II.

MICHAEL S. YESLEY, Attorney, Los Alamos National Laboratory, and Coordinator of the U.S. Department of Energy's Program on Ethical, Legal, and Social Implications of the Human Genome Project. His areas of responsibility at Los Alamos include bioethics, health and safety, and research and development contracting. Mr. Yesley has written articles on the work of the National Committee for the Protection of Human Subjects, the use of moral experts in the courtroom, risk perception, medical malpractice screening, and the law of product liability. His current research interests are in the area of genetic privacy.

Index

abnormality. *See* normality
aboriginal populations, genomes of, 29
adenine, 13
albinism, as inborn metabolic error, 117
alchemy, and fifth essence, 65
alcoholism: as genetic disease, 97, 110; as polygenic disease, 133
alkaptonuria, as inborn metabolic error, 117
Alzheimer's disease, as genetic disease, 101
Annas, George, on ethical concerns, 49
Aristotle, on definition of metaphor, 53
arteriosclerosis, as genetic disease, 110–112
Asilomar Conference of February 1975, and hazards of recombinant DNA research, 42–43, 49
Atomic Energy Commission, 32
attention deficit disorder, as genetic disease, 97
autocatalysis, as mode of biological causation, 78
autorad, use of in DNA typing, 184
autosomes: in DNA libraries, 19; in human genome, 14

Baird, P. A., on genetic disease, 109, 135
bacteria: DNA in, 28; genome size of, 28; as model organisms, 28
bacteriophages. *See* cloning vectors

Baltimore, David, on hazards of recombinant-DNA research, 42
banding technology, and physical maps, 22
base pairs, in physical maps, 22. *See also* nucleotides, base pairs of
Beadle, George: credited Garrod with founding of biochemical genetics, 113–114, 116; his and Edward Tatum's foundational construction of Garrod, 118–119; "one gene, one enzyme" hypothesis of, 93–94
Belmont Commission, on medical ethics, 122
Berg, Paul, on conceptual re-examination of "gene," 120
biologists: and conflicts of interest, 45; motivations of, 38; transformed by genetic engineering, 44
biology, transformed by genetic engineering, 44
biotechnology, benefits of: "downside" benefits, 157; genetic screening for employment, 177–178; genetic screening of mates, 178–179; information, 157; medical experiments, 157
biotechnology, risks of: collective consciousness, 157; collective imbalance, 156–163; competitive goods, 156, 163–168; "Frankenstein factor," 171; gender imbalance resulting from sex selection, 158–161; longevity, 162; personality imbalance, 161–163; social

biotechnology, risks of (cont.)
inequality, 157, 168–171; "upside" risks, 156–157
body cells. *See* somata
"book of life," as metaphor for
human genome, 31, 52, 57–58,
60, 66, 68
Buck v. Bell, 150–151

cancer, as genetic disease, 100–
101, 109–111
Carlson, Elof, on definition of eugenics, 145
Caskey, Thomas, on DNA typing, 199
Caspari, Ernst, 34
causation: ascription of for engineering purposes, 133; autocatalysis in, 78; and blame, 127,
133; cavalier ascriptions of, 136;
distortion of, 126, 133, 138; genetic, 125–141; Griesemer on,
138; heterocatalysis in, 78; in-
adequacy of in describing biological research, 77; and nor-
mativity, 134; ordinary notions
of, 127, 131, 136; simplistic,
139; as sufficient set of conditions, 127, 131; tools for talking
about, 77; and Weismannian
diagrams, 77–78
causation, explanatory: 127–129;
of contingency, 128; dependent
on context, 128; dependent on
interests, 128; "lantern criterion" in, 129
causation, nonexplanatory: 127,
129–130; blaming in, 130;
"handle criterion" in, 129, 133;
manipulation, 129; "stain criterion" in, 130; suspect human
behavior in, 130
cDNA clones. *See* complementary
DNA clones
centimorgan, defined, 20
Chakraborty, Ranajit, on DNA
typing, 200
chemical individuality: Garrod as
discoverer of, 117–118; metabolic error as metaphor for, 118

Childs, Barton. *See* Scriver,
Charles, and Barton Childs
chromosomes: banding patterns
in, 22; called karyotype in humans, 22; DNA in, 13; in DNA
libraries, 19; number in humans, 13; separation of (*see*
flow sorting); set of in humans
(*see* karyotype); sex (*see* sex
chromosomes); sorting of (*see*
flow sorting)
chromosome walking: defined,
23; in physical map construction, 23; too slow, 23
cistrons, as subunits of DNA, 119
class II restriction endonucleases.
See restriction enzymes
Clapperton, Jane, on eugenics,
150
clones: 14, 15, 27; and chromosomal location of genes, 20;
and chromosome walking, 23;
cosmid vectors, 27; contigs, 22,
23; of entire genomes, 18; in
high-resolution physical mapping, 22; host cells for, 17, 18;
ingredients required for, 15;
number required for physical
mapping, 23, 27; process described, 17; recombinant, 17;
for sequence analysis, 27
cloning vectors: 17; bacteriophages as, 18; cosmids as, 18;
design of, 18; plasmids as, 18;
strengths and weaknesses of
for DNA libraries, 18; types of,
18; yeast artificial chromosomes
as, 18
cM. *See* centimorgan
code, as metaphor for human
genome, 53–54, 58–59, 68,
114
code-script, as metaphor for human genome, 55–58, 62, 114
Cohen, Seymour, 34
Commission of the European
Communities, proposal on human genome analysis, 143–144
compartmentalized thinking, as
obstacle to understanding, 71

complementary DNA clones, sequencing of, 28
comprehension gap, between technical advances and consequences, 76–77
Comte, Auguste, on meaning of "normal," 97
Congressional Office of Technology Assessment, 40; and "eugenics of normalcy," 97
contigs: defined as overlapping clones, 22; gaps between, 23; simultaneous identification of, 23
cosmids. See cloning vectors
cost-benefit analysis, of genetic research and therapy, 140; 143
Cranor, Carl, on genetic causation, 105, 109
Crick, Francis, 58–60, 62; central dogma of molecular biology, 79, 114; on double-helical structure of DNA, 59; on flow of genetic information, 79; inspired by Schrödinger, 54, 57
cystic fibrosis: caused by mutations, 110; as genetic disease, 47, 96, 110; as misleading model of disease, 96
cytosine, 13

Darwin, Charles, 74
Dausset, Jean, on genetic disease, 101
Davidson, Eric H.: on control of genes by organisms, 95; on "smart genes," 95
Davis, Bernard, as critic of the Human Genome Project, 111
DeMan, Paul, on theories of discourse, 55–56, 62
deoxyribonucleic acid. See DNA
Department of Energy, and the Human Genome Project, 12, 141
Derrida, Jacques, on the "book of nature," 52
Descartes, René, on metaphors in nature, 61

developmental biology: as biological model, 108; rapprochement with genetics, 94. See also embryology
diabetes, 47
diathesis, as inborn metabolic predisposition, 118
discourse, theories of, 55
disease. See genetic disease
DNA: in bacteria, 28; cistrons, 119; "fingerprinting" (see DNA typing); as "master molecule," 89, 94; and non-protein coding, 28; 28; and protein coding, 28; polymorphisms of, 21, 118, 124, 181; repair of, 115, 133; repeated sequences in, 13, 23; structure of, 13, 58, 60, 92, 113
DNA libraries, 27; analogous to conventional reference libraries, 18; autosomes in, 19; chromosomes in, 19; cloning vectors in, 18; construction of, 15–19; differences among, 18; insert sizes in, 18, 23; number necessary to include all human DNA, 19; and sequencing, 29; size of, 19; in somatic-cell hybridization, 15
DNA markers: distances between in genetic maps, 13; distances between in physical maps, 13; number needed for human genetic map, 22
DNA probes: and restriction fragment-length polymorphisms, 21; in somatic-cell hybridization, 15, 22, 23
DNA typing: 72; access to data in, 191, 193; access to funding for, 190; admissibility of, 188–190, 194; autorad in, 184; Caskey on, 199; cellmark DNA test, 192; Chakraborty on, 200; commercial development of, 195; confidentiality of discovery in, 192–193; corruption of peer review process, 199; electrophoresis in, 182; evolution of courtroom debate, 194–200;

DNA typing (continued)
FBI and, 186, 192, 199–200; financial motivations of expert witnesses, 197; *Frye v. United States*, 189, 196; Geisser on, 200; *Genetics* and, 200; harassment of critics, 199–200; Hartl on, 199; lack of information about, 195; Lewontin on, 199; Lifecodes forensic laboratory, 196; misinterpretation of tests in, 185; Mueller on, 198–200; and National Research Council of the National Academy of Sciences, 180, 186–188, 193, 197; *Nature* (journal) and, 199; *People v. Castro*, 184, 195; procedural legal issues in, 188, 190–194; proliferation of admissibility hearings, 194; questions about reliability of, 184–185; relevancy rule, 189; "relevant scientific community" and, 198; restriction enzymes in, 181–182; restriction fragment-length polymorphisms in, 181–182, 189, 194–195, 200; *Science* and, 199; scientific controversy over, 180–202; scientific critics of, 195–196; "slop" in, 184; southern transfer in, 182; substantive legal issues in, 188–190; use of expert witnesses in, 190–191; variable-number tandem repeats in, 182, 184
Down's syndrome: and eugenics, 146, 150, 152; as genetic disease, 110
Dounce, A. L., on template model of protein synthesis, 59
Dulbecco, Renato, on cancer research, 100–101

Eisenstadt v. Baird, 151
electrophoresis, 58; in DNA typing, 182
Eleventh International Congress of Genetics, 33
Ellis, Havelock, on compulsion in eugenics, 145

embryologists: resistance of to genetics, 90, 93; strategies of accommodation of genetics, 93
embryology: as biological model, 108; renamed "developmental biology," 93. *See also* developmental biology
environment, role of in genetic disease, 96, 110, 112, 118, 121, 137
epigenesis: as biological model, 108; meaning of "normal" in, 108
essence: "fifth," 65; as metaphor, 65–66
ethical concerns: Annas on, 49; Asilomar Conference and, 42; Baltimore on, 42; Belmont Commission and, 122; compartmentalization of, 48; Congressional Office of Technology Assessment and, 40; embedded in technology, 123; "genetic error" and, 123; Gordon Conference on Nucleic Acids and, 42; Hastings Center and, 41; ignored, 43; Kass on, 36; Kennedy on, 43; Kornberg on, 38, 49; Lander on, 46; Lederberg on, 36; Herman on, 41; London conference of 1970, 37; Luria on, 34; moratorium on hazardous research, 42; "normality," 123; National Academy of Sciences and, 40; National Endowment for the Humanities and, 41; National Research Council and, 41; National Science Foundation and, 41; Nirenberg on, 36; obstacles to, 32; Oppenheimer on, 32; paternalism, 35; postponement of, 42; public "overreaction," 33, 43; Rockefeller University meeting of 1966 and, 34–36; and Salk Institute, 41; scientific cultures and, 32; separated from technical concerns, 32, 34; unpredictability of problems, 40; U.S. Congress and, 37–41;

uses of genetic information and, 174–179; Watson on, 47
eugenics, 35, 72, 84, 142–154; abortion and, 146; as "approved" anxiety of Human Genome Project, 143; artificial insemination as, 146; autonomy as dominant value, 150, 152; "back door," 145; in Britain, 145; *Buck v. Bell* case, 150; Clapperton on, 150; "client-centered counseling" and, 151–152; coercion and, 145–147; Commission of the European Communities and, 143; consequences of, 144–145; Down's syndrome and, 146, 150, 152; *Eisenstadt v. Baird* case, 151; Ellis on, 145; ethical concerns of medical geneticists, 150; free-market approach to, 152; Galton on, 144, 149; genetic engineering as, 131; *Grady* case, 150–151; Grant on, 149; Hogben on, 149; Holmes on, 150; "homemade," 145, 152; indeterminate meaning of, 143–144; Kevles on, 147–148; naiveté of, 83; of "normalcy," 97; Nozick on, 152; "positive," 145–146; privacy and, 151; Russell on, 149; as science, 144; as secular religion, 149; as social policy, 144, 147–152; sex selection and, 150–151, 158–161; "sordid history" of, 151; Wright on, 142, 145
evolutionary biology: "genetic errors" and, 124; genome studies and, 29; role of in the Human Genome Project, 70; scientific image of, 75

fibrocystic breast disease, as normal condition, 105
Fletcher, John, study of attitudes of medical geneticists, 150–151
flow sorting: as genome analysis technique, 15; hybrid cell lines in, 15; and recombinant-DNA techniques, 19; and sequencing, 29
Fortun, Michael, on "genomics," 52
Foucault, Michel, 67
Fox-Genovese, Elizabeth, on contemporary feminist theory, 151
Freese, Ernst, on mutations, 114
Freud, Sigmund, on "verbal foolishness," 56
Friedmann, Theodore, on genetic disease, 101, 109, 136
fruit flies, as model organisms, 28
Frye v. United States, 189, 196
function: as biological model, 105; as medical model, 105, 112; organismic basis of, 106; and population genetics, 108; relationship of to environment, 108; socially negotiated standards of, 106

Gajdusek, Daniel Carleton, on human metabolic adaptation, 108
Galileo, on metaphors in nature, 61
Galton, Francis: coined the term "eugenics," 144; on science as religion, 149
Gamow, George: diamond code of, 60; on DNA-protein relation, 54, 59–60
Garrod, Archibald: as discoverer of chemical individuality, 117–118; as founder of biochemical genetics, 113; *Inborn Factors in Disease*, 117, 137; as non-founder of biochemical genetics, 116–117; as patron of "one gene, one enzyme" hypothesis, 116; "rediscovered," 116
Geisser, Seymour, on DNA typing, 200
genotype, metaphors of, 54, 55
genes: as causal agents, 58, 78, 87, 90–91, 94, 102, 116, 125–141; as components of complex networks, 94; conceptual reexamination of, 120; controlled by

genes (continued)
  organisms, 94; determining
  fate, 31; localization of on
  physical maps, 22; as locus of
  disease, 97; as "master molecules," 75, 86, 89, 94–95; as
  noncausal agents, 130, 131,
  134; number in humans, 13; relationship of to pathology, 116;
  relationship of to therapy, 116;
  size of, 13; theoretical robustness of, 75; transcription of,
  120
genetic causation, 125–141
genetic determinism, 134; as "act
  of faith," 93; influence of, 95;
  opponents of, 120; principle of,
  90; as simplistic, 122; as too
  rigid, 118
genetic disease: as abnormality,
  100, 105; alcoholism as, 97, 110,
  133; Alzheimer's disease as,
  101; arteriosclerosis as, 110–
  112; attention deficit disorder
  as, 97; Baird on, 109, 135; biochemical–causal model of, 103;
  biological complexity of, 132;
  cancer as, 100–101, 109–111;
  causes of, 29; Cranor on, 109;
  cure or prevention by genetic
  technology, 72; cystic fibrosis
  as, 47, 110; Dausset on, 101;
  determination of "normality"
  under, 109, 111–112; diabetes
  as, 47; Down's syndrome as,
  110, 152; emotional impact of,
  47; evidentiary standards for,
  134; fails to account for variation, 104; Friedmann on, 101,
  109, 136; and genetic counseling, 84; "genetic error" as
  ontological notion of, 118; and
  grant proposals, 31; Hartnup
  disorder as, 137; heart disease
  as, 47; homelessness as, 97;
  Huntington's disease as, 27,
  110, 141, 174; hypercholesterolemia as, 137; in humans, 12;
  and "individualized medicine,"

125; Jukes on, 102; and labeling
  of persons, 101; limits of genetic components of, 29; Lynch
  on, 111; McKusick on, 109;
  mental illness as, 47, 96, 101;
  misperceptions of, 111; number
  of, 96; oversimplification of,
  101; phenylketonuria as, 137;
  polygenic, 125–126, 133, 140;
  premenstrual syndrome as, 97;
  prevention of, 135; reading disability as, 97; and relation to
  health, 95–98; research objectives, 132, 140–141; restriction
  fragment-length polymorphism
  approach, 21; role of environment in, 96, 118, 121, 137; role
  of mutant gene in, 109, 125;
  Rotter on, 101; search for, 27;
  selection against carriers of, 84,
  135; sickle-cell anemia as, 102,
  131, 133, 141; single gene-
  caused, 125–126, 131, 133–135,
  140; and standards of "normality," 108–109; susceptibility to,
  111; Temkin on, 104; treatment
  of, 101, 131, 133, 136–138, 140;
  use of sequencing in diagnosis,
  96; usually recessive, 83; value
  judgments in, 102; Watson on,
  101
genetic engineering: commercialization of, 45; compared to
  atomic bomb, 36–38, 41; compared to Nazi Germany, 142;
  competitive goods and, 163–
  168; effects of on biology and
  biologists, 44; as eugenics, 131;
  existential dread and, 173; fears
  about, 76, 171; as "God-like
  power," 34; inevitability of, 35;
  Lockwood on dangers of, 142;
  patents and, 44; as social engineering, 87; social inequality
  and 170–171
genetic error: DNA replication
  and, 114; in ethical context,
  123; in informational context,
  115; in medical context, 113,

116; mutations as, 114–115, 124; as ontological notion of disease, 118; Schrödinger on, 114, 124; as source of evolution, 124

genetic information: as code, 13; effects of on employment, 174, 176–177; effects of on insurability, 174–176; flow of, 82; psychological effects of, 174–175; uses of, 174–179

genetic maps. *See* maps, genetic

genetics: physiological distinct from biochemical, 118; as proximate science, 71; rapprochement of with developmental biology, 94; social problems and, 72

Genetics, and DNA typing, 200

genetic screening, gray areas in, 110

genetic variation, 29, 107; role of in medicine, 30

genome: defined, 13; evolution of size of, 28; molecular cloning of, 18; no standard, 124; percentage of comprised of genes, 120; size of, 13

genome analysis technique: chromosome separation in, 14–15; DNA library construction in, 15–19; genetic map construction as, 19–22

germ cells: as causal agents, 78; continuity of, 76, 78; distinguished from soma cells, 69

germ plasm: continuity of, 80; defined, 80; distinct from germ cells, 80

Gilbert, Walter, on gene-body relation, 83

Gilbert's disease, as "nonfunctional disease," 104

Glover Commission, on gender imbalance resulting from sex selection, 159–161

Gordon Conference on Nucleic Acids, 41; and ethical concerns, 42

Gould, Steven Jay, on apocalyptic fears of biotechnology, 121

Grant, Madison, as advocate of coercive eugenics, 149

Green, T. H., on coercive eugenics, 146

Griesemer, James, on distortion of causation in biological research, 138

guanine, 13

Hacking, Ian: on meaning of "normal," 97; on narrow paths of research, 132, 138–139

Haller, Mark, on definition of eugenics, 144

Hartl, Daniel, on DNA typing, 199

Hartnup mutation, 122, 137

Harvard Medical School, 43, 111

Hastings Center, and ethical concerns, 41

health: and genetic technology, 30, 78; as "normality," 100; Senate subcommittee on, 39

heart disease, as genetic disease, 47

heterocatalysis, as mode of biological causation, 78

Hobbes, Thomas, on competition, 163

Hogben, Lancelot, on reproductive rights, 149

Holmes, Oliver Wendell, on compulsory sterilization, 150

Holtzman, Neil, on definition of eugenics, 145

homelessness, as genetic disease, 97

homosexuality: as "abnormality," 106–107; as "disease," 106

Hood, Leroy, on gene-society relation, 83

Hotchkiss, Robert, 34

human genome: of aboriginal populations, 29; autosomes in, 14; as "book of life," 31, 52, 54, 57–58, 60, 66, 68; as "book of nature," 52, 86; as "code," 53–

human genome (continued) 54, 58–59, 68; as "code-script," 55–58, 62; comparative studies of, 29; diversity of, 28–29; metaphors for, 31, 52–68, 86, 114; as "pattern," 56–57, 59; as "recipe to construct human beings," 112; sequencing of, 25; sex chromosomes in, 14; as "software," 55; subdivision of, 14; universal markers in, 19; variation among, 70, 107

Human Genome Initiative. See Human Genome Project

Human Genome Organization, 109

Human Genome Project: applications of for human health, 70, 84, 100, 112–113, 116, 143; conflicts between molecular and evolutionary biologists in, 70; consequences of, 83; costs of, 140, 143; criticisms of, 28, 31, 107, 111, 143; Department of Energy and, 12; descriptions of, 25, 27, 31; diversity of theories and models in, 99; ethical implications of, 31, 125; Ethical, Legal, and Social Implications (ELSI) program component of, 45, 48; evaluation of, 83; fears about, 82, 122; goals of, 22–23, 25, 29, 70, 81; implications of, 69–71, 73, 75, 81; ironies of, 94; launching of, 12; misconceptions about, 30; National Institutes of Health and, 12; philosophical interest of, 71, 75; problems raised by, 73; products and benefits of, 27–30; reference genome, 29; rhetoric of, 95; scope of, 12, 29; technology required to complete, 77; unintended consequences of, 71

human growth hormone, sequencing of, 25

human nature, biological differences in, 70; biological similarity in, 70; proximate explanations of, 69–71, 73–74, 81–82; ultimate explanations of, 69–71, 73–74, 82; ways of interpreting, 69

human subjects, rights of, 39

Huntington's disease: as genetic disease, 27, 96, 110, 141; as misleading model of disease, 96; test for, 174

hybrid cells. See somatic-cell hybridization

hypercholesteriolemia, as genetic disease, 137

Ingram, Vernon, on genetic error in sickle-cell hemoglobin, 114–115

Institute of Society, Ethics, and the Life Sciences (Hastings Center), 41

Jacob, François and Jacques Monod, on regulatory processes in organisms, 92–94, 115

Jukes, T. H., on description of genetic disease, 102

karyotype, arrangement standardized, 22

Kass, Leon, 36; and National Research Council, 41

Kennedy, Edward, on ethical concerns, 43

Kevles, Daniel, on "new eugenics," 147–148

kilobases. See maps, physical

Kornberg, Arthur, on ethical concerns, 38, 49

Lamarckism, decline of, 78

Lander, Eric, on ethical concerns, 46

Lederberg, Joshua, 36; on "one gene, one enzyme" hypothesis, 117

Lewis, Herman, 41

Lewontin, Richard, on DNA typing, 199

Lockwood, Michael, on dangers of genetic engineering, 142

Los Alamos: atomic bomb development at, 32; Human Genome Center at, 23

Luria, Salvador, on ethical concerns, 34

Lynch, Henry, on genetic disease, 111

McKusick, Victor, on genetic disease, 109

maps, genetic, 13; construction of, 19–22; desired resolution of, 21; DNA markers in, 13; DNA probes in, 15; insert size in, 23; meiosis in, 20; recombinant-DNA technology in, 20; restriction enzymes in, 21; somatic-cell hybridization in, 20

maps, physical, 13, 27; banding technology in, 22; chromosome walking in, 23; construction of, 22–25; cosmid contig assembly and, 27; DNA libraries in, 15, 29; DNA markers in, 13; flow cytometry in, 15; gaps in, 23; high resolution, 14, 22; insert size in, 23; kilobases in, 13, 14, 18; localization of genes on, 22; low resolution, 14, 22; megabases in, 13, 14; number of clones required for, 23; relationship to sequencing, 27; restriction enzymes in, 22; single base pairs in, 13; and yeast artificial chromosome contig assembly, 27

master molecule, as metaphor for genes, 75, 86, 89, 94

Mayr, Ernst: on "beanbag genetics," 91; on human nature, 69

megabases. See maps, physical

meiosis: definition of, 19; in genetic map construction, 20

Mendel, Gregor: and use of metaphors, 53; laws of, 74

mental illness, as genetic disease, 47, 96–97, 101

Metabolic Basis of Inherited Disease, as "bible" of medical genetics, 121

metabolic error: albinism as, 117; alkaptonuria as, 117; as metaphor for chemical individuality, 118

metaphor: Aristotle's definition of, 53; beanbag as, 91, 94–96; blame as, 130, 133; code as, 53–54, 58–59, 68, 114; code-script as, 55–58, 62, 114; Descartes on, 61; essence as, 65–66; factory as, 114; Galileo on, 61; of genotype, 54, 55; "God-like power" as, 34; hole as, 63, 66; holy grail as, 120; for human genome, 31, 52–68, 86, 114; lock as, 63; lock and key as, 63, 64; master molecule as, 75, 86, 89, 94; metabolic error as, 118; nose as, 53; pattern as, 54–57, 59, 114; of phenotype, 54; recipe as, 112; shift from phenotype to genotype, 54, 55; sloppy computer as, 95; tape recording as, 115; Weismannism as, 76

mice, as model organisms, 28

Mill, John Stuart, on reproductive liberty, 153

molecular biology, connection to medicine, 113, 115, 120–121; rate of progress in since 1940s, 77; role of in the Human Genome Project, 70; scientific image of, 75; success of, 92–93

Mondale, Walter, 37, 39–40

Monod, Jacques and François Jacob, on regulatory processes in organisms, 92–94, 115

Morgan, Thomas Hunt, on physical theory of genes, 72

Mueller, Laurence, as expert witness on DNA typing, 198–200

Muller, H. J., on artificial insemination, 146

Mulvihill, John, study on attitudes of medical geneticists, 150

mutations: as affecting vital functions, 91; causing cystic fibrosis, 110; as damage, 115; effect

mutations (continued)
of on phenotype, 119; as genetic errors, 114–115, 124; "Hartnup," 122, 137; influencing chemical reactions, 119; as maps for misreading, 90; as mistakes in base pairing, 114; as modifications of functional forms, 91; as non-dysfunctional, 119; as non-errors, 114; in relation to normal allele, 96; role of in biochemical-causal model of disease, 109

National Academy of Sciences, ethical concerns and, 40
National Advisory Commission on Health, Science, and Society, ethical concerns and, 39
National Commission for the Protection of Human Subjects of Biomedical and Behavioral Research, 39
National Endowment for the Humanities, ethical concerns and, 41
National Institutes of Health, and the Human Genome Project, 12, 50, 101, 141
National Research Council: DNA typing and, 180, 186–188, 193, 197; ethical concerns and, 41; National Science Foundation, ethical concerns and, 41
Nature, 59; and DNA typing, 199; as metaphor, 60
nature, as text, 61–64
Needham, Joseph, on doubts about genetic mechanisms, 92–93
nematode worms, as model organisms, 28
neo-Darwinism, Weismannian core of, 78
New York Times, 33, 38
Nirenberg, Marshall, 36
nitrogen, in DNA, 13
normality, allelic variation and, 121; biochemical-causal model

of disease and, 103, 111; competitive goods and, 166–167; definition of, 104; in epigenetic models, 108; as ethical issue, 99, 123; genetic analysis insufficient for understanding of, 91; "genetic error" and, 113; as including genetic diversity, 123; meaning of, 97, 124; need for revised definition of, 123; population genetics and, 107; significance of, 100; slippage between meanings of, 111; standards of, 102, 107, 118; value decisions concerning, 107
Nozick, Robert, on "genetic supermarket," 152
nucleic acids, 79; as causal agents, 80; Gordon Conference on, 41
nucleotides: adenine, 13; as building blocks of DNA, 13; combinations of, 31; cytosine, 13; guanine, 13; hydrogen bonds between, 13; number differing between individuals, 29, 107; number in human genome, 181; sequencing of, 25; as sites of polymorphisms, 181; thymine, 13
nucleotides, base pairs of: in DNA typing, 182; as metaphorical "letters," 46; as metaphorical "words," 31; number in humans, 13; on physical maps, 13; variable-number tandem repeats and, 182

"one gene, one enzyme" hypothesis: attributed to Garrod, 113, 116–117; of Beadle and Tatum, 93–94, 119; as obsolete model, 120
Oppenheimer, J. Robert, on ethical concerns about atomic weapons, 32
organism: as "beanbag," 91, 94, 96; as controller of genes, 94

OTA (Congressional Office of Technology Assessment), 40, 97
outbreeding, as mating pattern, 85

pattern: as metaphor for human genome, 56–57, 59, 114; as metaphor of genotype, 55; as metaphor of phenotype, 54
Pauling, Linus, identified sickle-cell anemia as "molecular disease," 113
Pencarinha, Deborah, study on attitudes of genetic counselors, 150
People v. Castro, 184, 195
phenotype: effect of mutation on, 119; metaphors of, 54; "pattern" as metaphor for, 54
phenylketonuria, as genetic disease, 137
philosophers, role of in Human Genome Project, 75
phosphate, in DNA, 13
polypeptides, as protein components, 119
physical maps. *See* maps, physical
plasmids, 18
population genetics, 107–108, 111; "normal" and "abnormal" in, 107
premenstrual syndrome, as genetic disease, 97
protein, 79; mechanics of synthesis of, 92; percentage of DNA used in coding of, 28; -protein interactions as gene transcription factors, 120; regulatory, 119

reading disability, as genetic disease, 97
recombinant-DNA technology, 33; in cloning, 17; development of, 94; flow sorting and, 19; as genome analysis technique, 15, 18; invention of, 41; patent on, 42; safety standards in, 43

reductionism, 89; consequences of, 82; as moral or political position, 71; problems with, 89–98; "reverse genetics" and, 122
restriction enzymes, 27; definition of, 21; as DNA polymorphisms, 21, 181; DNA typing and, 182; function of, 21; in genetic map construction, 21; in physical map construction, 22
restriction fragment-length polymorphisms, 21; DNA typing and, 181–182, 189, 194–195, 200; and genetic disease, 21; in genetic map construction, 21; restriction enzymes and, 21, 182
rhetoric: as basis of heredity, 53; of phenotype, 53; of science, 58
risk assessment: and genetic research and therapy, 140; "upside risks," 156. *See also* biotechnology, risks of
rodents, DNA of, 14, 15
Rogers, Carl, and "client-centered counseling," 151–152
Rotter, Jerome, on genetic disease, 101
Russell, Bertrand, on science as religion, 149

safety regulations, resistance to by scientists, 44
Salk Institute, Council for Biology in Human Affairs, 41
Sapp, Jan, on myth of Garrod as founder of biochemical genetics, 116–117
Schelling, Thomas, on sex selection, 158–160
Schrödinger, Erwin: as dilettante, 54; on genetic metaphors, 54–58, 65; on "genetic error," 114, 124; rhetoric of, 54–58; *What is Life?*, 54
science: as rhetoric, 58; visual representations in, 77
Science, 36; and DNA typing, 199

Scientific American, 94
scientists: culture of, 39, 140; re-
    sistance of to safety regula-
    tions, 44; sensitization of to
    public concerns, 42
Scriver, Charles, on genetic error,
    124
Scriver, Charles, and Barton
    Childs: on Garrod and the "one
    gene, one enzyme" hypothesis,
    117–124; on causes and treat-
    ment of genetic disease, 136–
    137
Sedgwick, Peter, on homosexual-
    ity as "disease," 106
Senate Subcommittee on Health, 39
sequence-tagged sites: on the hu-
    man genetic map, 21; in refer-
    ence genome, 29; as universal
    DNA markers, 19
sequencing: chromosome sorting
    and, 29; of complementary
    DNA clones, 28; cost per nu-
    cleotide, 25; defined, 25; in
    disease diagnosis, 96; DNA li-
    brary construction and, 29; of
    human growth hormone, 25; as
    method of genome analysis,
    25–27; not possible for single
    individual, 29; somatic-cell hy-
    brids and, 29; yeast artificial
    chromosomes and, 27
sex chromosomes, in human ge-
    nome, 14
sex selection: and gender imbal-
    ance, 158–161; Glover Commis-
    sion on, 160–161; prenatal di-
    agnosis for, 150–151, 158;
    Schelling on, 158
Shaw, George Bernard, on sci-
    ence as religion, 149
sickle-cell anemia: as genetic dis-
    ease, 102–103, 131, 133, 141;
    treatment of, 133
Shockley, William, and artificial
    insemination, 146
single base pairs, 13. *See also* nu-
    cleotides, base pairs of

Smith, Maynard, on Weismann-
    ism, 79
social problems, genetic technol-
    ogy and, 72
somata, discontinuity of, 76, 78,
    80
somatic-cell hybridization: chro-
    mosomal location of genes and,
    20; flow cytometry and, 15; ge-
    netic map construction and, 20;
    as genome analysis technique,
    14; rodent/human, 14; sequenc-
    ing and, 29
STS. *See* sequence-tagged sites
sugar, in DNA, 13

Tatum, Edward Laurie, 34, 113,
    117; his and George Beadle's
    foundational construction of
    Garrod, 118–119; on "one
    gene, one enzyme hypothesis,"
    119
Temkin, Owsei, on genetic dis-
    ease, 104
template, as metaphor for protein
    synthesis, 59–60
thymine, 13

U.S. Congress, and recombinant-
    DNA safety standards, 43

variable-number tandem repeats,
    in DNA typing, 182

Washington Post, 36
Watson, James, 34, 58–60, 62; on
    biochemical-causal model of
    disease, 103; on double-helical
    structure of DNA, 58–59; on
    ethical concerns, 47; on eugen-
    ics, 143; on gene-population re-
    lation, 83; on genetic disease,
    101; on Erwin Schrödinger's in-
    spiration of Crick, 57
Wertz, Dorothy, study of atti-
    tudes of medical geneticists,
    150–151

Weismann, August, on unified
   theory of heredity, 76–83
Weismannian diagrams, 77, 78;
   dual role of genes in, 87; influence of on biologists, 80
Weismannism, as guiding metaphor of biological causation,
   76, 78; implications of, 81; re-
   invention of, 81
Wilson, E. B.: influence on biologists, 80; and Weismannian
   diagram, 78, 87
Wright, Robert: on danger of
   "homemade eugenics," 145,
152; on dangers of free-market
   approach to eugenics, 152; on
   effects of genetic screening on
   insurability, 175; on fear of
   "new eugenics," 142

yeast, as model organism, 28
yeast artificial chromosomes: as
   cloning vectors, 18; too large
   for sequencing, 27

Zinder, Norman, 34, 44